Robinson's Locomotive Liveries
on the
Great Central Railway

Portrait of J.G. Robinson
John George Robinson was appointed locomotive superintendent of the GCR with effect from 2nd July 1900. He quickly impressed the board and within two years became chief mechanical engineer, a position that he held until the company was grouped into the L&NER.
Great Central Railway Journal

City of London, No. 427, has just departed London Marylebone with an express which is probably bound for Manchester. The locomotive is in green and crimson which dates this picture to after 22nd April 1921, when it left Gorton in that condition. The stock is interesting as it is the last 60-foot corridor stock built for the company's services. The first five vehicles are fitted with armoured ends – an idea of Robinson's which was designed to prevent telescoping in the event of an accident but, fortunately, was never put to the test in a serious collision.

F. Moore

ROBINSON'S LOCOMOTIVE LIVERIES
ON THE
GREAT CENTRAL RAILWAY

JOHN QUICK

LIGHTMOOR PRESS

GCR Class 11E, No. 437

A lovely study of a spotless engine. *Charles Stuart-Wortley* is standing at platform 11 at Nottingham Victoria with an Up stopping train. The lining and borders are worth a study and note the covered carriage truck, No. 1520, in the background, which appears to have been recently repainted at Dukinfield works. This picture probably dates from about 1914.   *R.K. Blencowe, F.H. Gillford*

CONTENTS

Published by LIGHTMOOR PRESS
© John Quick and Lightmoor Press 2013
Designed by Nigel Nicholson

British Library Cataloguing-in-Publication Data. A catalogue record for this book is available from the British Library

ISBN 9781 899889 75 4

LIGHTMOOR PRESS
Unit 144B, Lydney Trading Estate, Harbour Road, Lydney, Gloucestershire GL15 5EJ
www.lightmoor.co.uk

Lightmoor Press is an imprint of Black Dwarf Lightmoor Publications Ltd.
Printed by Berforts Information Press, Eynsham, Oxford

GCR Class 1B, No. 339
No. 339 is on Neasden shed on 1st July 1922. The condition of the locomotive is typical of many goods engines on the GCR at that time.   *J. Quick collection*

INTRODUCTION

The Great Central Railway Society was formed during the spring of 1974. The constitution was set out to encourage those with an interest in any activity of the company and a society journal was quickly produced. This was appropriately named 'Forward', as this was the company's motto. *Forward* has been published regularly since those early days and many valuable contributions towards the history of the GCR have been recorded within its pages.

David Jackson was a champion of the company, particularly of J.G. Robinson and his locomotives. He was an inveterate author, often as part of a joint effort with his long-standing friend and fellow enthusiast, Owen Russell. It was David who made the first suggestion in *Forward*, that members with an interest in locomotive liveries should meet on a semi-regular basis, with a view to the location of information and the publication of a register. Seven society members either attended the first meeting or indicated a desire for inclusion in the discussion. Those members were K. Grainger, D. Green, M. Hartley, D. Jackson, B. Longbone, B. Wainwright and myself. I offered to serve as secretary and some progress was made. In order to share the work it was decided that each member should study two or three classes of engine. Another decision was that only those classes built before the introduction of the 'Sir Sam Fay' Class 1 4-6-0s were to be included.

Further meetings showed that significant quantities of data were being found. However, Bryan Longbone soon informed the group that he was unable to devote the necessary time to research his subjects. A little later, Ken Grainger's health deteriorated to the extent that he was obliged to withdraw. D. Green was the next to leave, but the very serious blow was the death of David Jackson, which occurred towards the end of 1999. This had a grave effect on the project, but at least the foundations had been laid. I remained keen to continue the work, albeit single-handed. There were, however, many changes in my career at that time and this brought the research to a virtual standstill. One important change of direction was made and that was to include the remaining classes of locomotives and this would complete the liveries of all Robinson designed engines on the GCR. Retirement has allowed the work to recommence and to be completed using, wherever possible, the researches of former members of the original group. This work, therefore, is mainly mine, but with significant sections from Ken Grainger and Brian Wainwright.

I have received help from many fellow enthusiasts and this is acknowledged with grateful thanks. Messrs. W.A. Brown, J. Braithwaite, the late Malcolm Crawley, A. Dow, M. Fish, the chairman of the Bassett-Lowke Society M. Green, and K. Plant. A special mention must be made of Jack Braithwaite's contribution. Jack's library has been a fund of information, but his infectious enthusiasm for the steam locomotive generally has, at times, acted as a great motivation. My thanks must also be recorded for the assistance of the committee of the G.C.R.S., The Barrow Hill Roundhouse, Andy Croxton and the staff at the National Railway Museum, the staff at the University of Glasgow Archive Services and at the Museum of Science and Industry at Manchester.

Two colleagues in the G.C.R.S., J. Richard Morton and Keith Parkin, have been of enormous help. They have carefully checked through the pages of this work. They have not only proof read my writings but have made very many constructive suggestions.

On a personal note I must mention certain members of my family. My dear wife Diane has been a treasure, making helpful comments but also supporting me over the many years that it has taken to complete this study. When an earlier form of information technology crashed, our younger son, Edward, offered to ease me into the latest methods and, despite the inevitable early problems, he has been successful. Neither Diane nor Edward share my passion for railways but both have toiled beyond the boundaries of family duty to help me.

John Quick

Anyone wishing to join the membership of the G.C.R.S. should contact
Mr E. Latusek, 41 Spire Hollin, Glossop, Derbyshire, SK13 7BJ.

ABOVE: Plate 1.1   Waterford, Limerick & Western Railway 0-6-0, No. 2, *Shannon*
Robinson's last engines for the WL&WR were three goods tender 0-6-0s. No. 2, *Shannon*, which is illustrated here, shows some features of their future cousins, the 'Pom-Poms' of GCR Class 9J. The livery is more complicated than that on the 9J, but the black lined red and white scheme was adopted for Robinson's goods and mixed traffic locomotives.   *B. Longbone collection*

Plate 1.2   GCR Class 13, No. 972
No. 972 was photographed at Gorton about 1901. This engine was not of Robinson's design, being the last of Harry Pollitt's singles of Class 13. Robinson had been in office for only five months when No. 972 was delivered. Nevertheless, it carries his chimney, his first version of a number plate and an early experimental livery of darker green, possibly Brunswick, with a broad crimson border lined white. The white line appears to have a black stripe on its outside, with a vermilion line separating the black from the crimson. As all the elements of the future painting style are present in this picture, perhaps it was the combination of green and crimson that provided the inspiration to adopt these colours.   *E. Pouteau GC 168*

CHAPTER 1

JOHN GEORGE ROBINSON AND THE GREAT CENTRAL RAILWAY

J.G. Robinson was born in Newcastle during July 1856 into a railway family. His father, Matthew Robinson, was employed by the Newcastle & Carlisle Railway before he married J.G.'s mother. The Robinson family moved south to advance Matthew's career prospects when J.G. was a very small child. Matthew found a position on the Great Western Railway and in time so did James, J.G.'s elder brother. J.G. Robinson began work for the GWR in 1872 and it appears that initially he was quite unambitious. However, when Henry Appleby of the Waterford, Limerick & Western Railway of Ireland required an assistant, Robinson was successful with his application. Later, as Appleby's health began to fail, Robinson was taking additional responsibility, until in April 1889 he was appointed locomotive superintendent.

At the time of Robinson's promotion, Thomas Parker held the equivalent post on the Manchester, Sheffield & Lincolnshire Railway. He retired towards the end of 1893 and was replaced by the erstwhile works manager at Gorton, Harry Pollitt. Harry – the younger son of William Pollitt, the general manager of the MS&LR – was enjoying a meteoric rise in his professional life. All was not well, however, as Pollitt had inherited an unsatisfactory situation at Gorton. There were problems with the workforce, some of which may have been of Pollitt's own making; also, because the company was not a prosperous concern, the necessary finance for modern tooling was not forthcoming and this must have exacerbated the difficulties. Before long the MS&LR changed its name to Great Central Railway, completed its extension to London and thereby became a trunk line. The works at Gorton were rapidly becoming unsuitable for the needs of a major railway and when circumstances there did not improve, one suspects that the GCR board accepted Pollitt's resignation with some relief in the spring of 1900. A new locomotive engineer was required and with some urgency.

Robinson, who had received significant recommendation from various quarters, notably from S.W. Johnson of the Midland Railway, was appointed locomotive superintendent of the GCR, with effect from 2nd July 1900. He faced a totally different state of affairs from what he had left at Limerick. Fortunately his skills in organisation, management and engineering were more than adequate to meet the challenge. Within a short period the troubles at Gorton were over, modern locomotives were at work, traffic was increasing and he had been promoted to chief mechanical engineer.

There was a lot of public interest in the latest railway to enter London, with much speculation regarding locomotives and rolling stock, services and so on. The journals of the day answered questions on these and other matters. Liveries were, and remain, one of the most popular subjects for discussion and the March 1901 issue of *Locomotives and Railways* on page 70 contained a reply to '*Railway Lover*', who had noticed some GCR engines painted grey:

All the G.C.R. engines will in future be painted black, the same colour as the engines you saw. The reason why several of their engines are painted grey is because they are short of engines and cannot wait to have them painted properly at present.

The Railway Magazine, January 1902, under 'The why and the wherefore' on page 89, published a question and their answer to '*Driver G.C.R.*':

Q. Is the G.C.R. going to change the colour of their locomotives from green to black?

A. If you refer to p. 428 of Railway Magazine *for November [1901], you will see that black is to be the standard colour for goods and shunting engines.*

The first-named journal, in the reply to a certain '*H.Y.E.*', stated in its November 1902 copy, page 112:

All the G.C.R. goods engines are, or will be, painted black and some of the older passenger engines [mainly Sacré types] are similarly treated, but the standard passenger engine colour is green.

The same magazine carried a particularly interesting, but probably incorrect, report, about the new 9K 4-4-2T passenger types in its May 1903 issue. A good broadside view of No. 1055 was included but the article contained the following statement: '*the painting is black with red lining, a serviceable and economical colour*'.

Even as late as 1922 a correspondent '*Belmont*' was expressing an opinion regarding liveries in *The Locomotive News and Railway Contractor* – but to return to the turn of the twentieth century, there is evidence that black was being considered as the future finish for GCR engines. What may not be generally known is that the company specified black for the first two 'Atlantics'. This will be enlarged upon later but if this news had leaked from Gorton and Beyer, Peacock & Co., then it would have spread amongst enthusiasts relatively quickly. Black would always be more economical to apply but someone at Gorton, possibly Robinson himself, had rather different ideas.

Alexander Henderson was by now the chairman of the GCR. His skills as a financier were about to be exercised. The last member of the group of three that made the GCR great, Sam Fay, became the general manager of the company in 1902. He joined Henderson and Robinson in guiding the GCR through the remaining years of independence, until it became part of the London & North Eastern Railway. Sam Fay proved to be a brilliant manager and provided a constant flow of schemes in an attempt to improve the company's profitability. It has been said that when Fay had an idea accepted, Henderson financed it and Robinson supplied the hardware. Robinson, then, led a very busy locomotive department. From 1900 until the time of his retirement, he produced no less than twenty-eight classes of locomotive. There were engines for heavy goods and mixed traffic, for suburban, excursion and express passenger trains and for shunting marshalling yards. Robinson had effectively given the GCR a stock of modern engines, many of which used the latest ideas in steam locomotive technology, and some of the ideas were his own. Nearly 700 engines were built by Robinson but there were only two basic liveries. Quite simply, goods and mixed traffic types received black and were normally lined, and locomotives which usually worked passenger traffic were finished with green paint and lined.

When the London extension was approaching completion, Robinson was still at Limerick but the GCR board was deliberating upon the use of a new livery to mark the company's entry to London. The new corridor carriages were painted in a quite distinctive two-tone style, but the last MS&LR livery for passenger engines was continued. Harry Pollitt's only original design of express locomotive, the Class 13 'Single', was in the process of being built when Robinson took charge at Gorton. The first two examples, Nos 967 and 968, were painted in the final MS&LR scheme, whereas the other four were the subject of some livery trials, carrying a darker shade of green with some changes in lining. Robinson was already making his presence felt! His first design for fast passenger traffic was a 4-4-0, Class 11B. The first batch also carried a version of the last livery used by the MS&LR, but the introduction of the Vulcan Foundry-built engines of Class 11B settled the matter, for passenger engines at least. Robinson decided upon the darker shade of green with claret frames, which had found favour with C.R. Sacré on the MS&LR over thirty years earlier.

The goods engine livery was probably a much easier decision to make. One of his last Irish engines to be built was an 0-6-0 goods tender type which, not surprisingly, was very similar to his later 9J GCR design. The Irish engine was painted black and was lined red and white and it was this painting style that Robinson used, with some modification, on his GCR mixed traffic and goods locomotives.

The choice of a painting specification for a railway's rolling stock would have been an important decision, with several conditions requiring careful consideration. The paints and pigments must be readily available, be economic, both in application and price, and be durable. Another essential property was that the finished product should enhance the company's public image. The colours carried by locomotives and carriages at this time would give an almost instant identification of the owning company. Robinson was on safe ground

with his choice of green, however, as not only did Charles Sacré use the same basic livery on the MS&LR, but several other British railway companies also used something that was very similar.

One question does come to mind: did the board influence Robinson at all in his choice of liveries? There is no evidence to suggest that this happened. The problems then facing the GCR were serious, far more important than how the company's stock should be painted. Notwithstanding, Robinson was paid to make such decisions as it was all part of his job. Many years ago Mr E.B. Woodruffe-Peacock, who was at that time the president of the G.C.R.S., was asked the above question. Mr Woodruffe-Peacock's reply is contained in a letter to the author dated 20th August 1981:

In the case of the paintwork on locomotives there is no doubt that the directors permitted the locomotive superintendent and later chief mechanical engineer to use his own judgement in the matter of embellishments.

Mr Woodruffe-Peacock's comments regarding the GCR are important. He was taken to see the celebrations at Immingham when the first sod of the new dock was being cut and, later, he became a serious student of the company's history. The early copies of *Forward* contain many of his excellent articles.

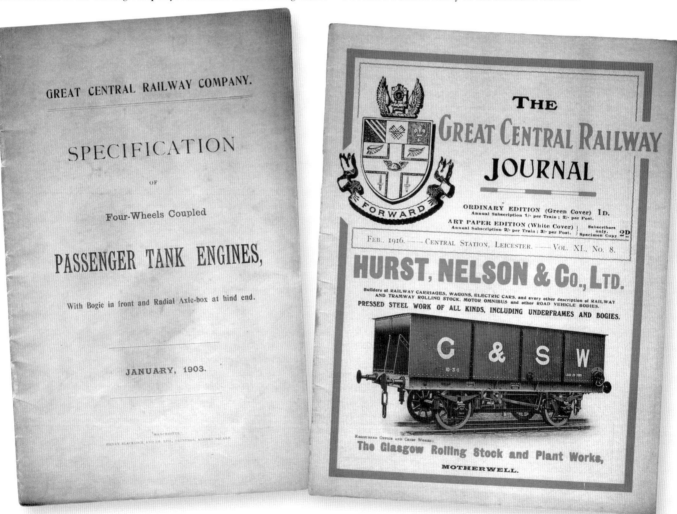

ABOVE LEFT: Plate 2.1   Cover of building specification
This is the front cover of a building specification for the 9K 4-4-2 passenger tank locomotives. Painting details occupy the last few pages – 23, 24 and 25 – and are reproduced in chapter 10.   *J. Quick collection*

ABOVE RIGHT: Plate 2.2   *Great Central Railway Journal*
The GCR house magazine was published for the majority of the company's existence. This copy is the better quality version, being printed on superior paper. 'Locomotive Notes' was a regular feature and this provided much invaluable information.   *J. Quick collection*

CHAPTER 2

SOURCES OF INFORMATION

There are several sources of data which may be profitably examined. Some of these must be looked at with care but, by taking all the evidence into account, a reasonably accurate statement of liveries may be made.

LOCOMOTIVE BUILDING SPECIFICATIONS

The documents which Gorton issued from time to time in respect of building locomotives contain much invaluable information. They set out the strict instructions regarding the materials to be used, their quality and their provenance. The GCR reserved the right to inspect the work and only approved suppliers were allowed. It should be remembered that board members also had business interests elsewhere, hence Gorton stipulated the suppliers of the iron, steel and other matters. The specification was sometimes sent out in the form of a booklet, which contained a 'Form of Tender' and this was to be completed by the prospective builder. Other specifications were handwritten but, unfortunately, not all are known for contractor-built engines, and none of those for Gorton-built locomotives have survived. Gorton had been building engines since 1858 and the drawings, papers, etc., were presumably always close to hand – but any historic documents may have been destroyed years ago or lost when the works closed. It is plausible, however, that Gorton did not issue documents concerning livery; the foreman painter and his staff must have been very familiar with the essentials of painting and lining, sufficient to make such documents unnecessary.

The painting instructions for contractor-built locomotives were usually at the end of the specification. They contained the directions for the preparation and finishing of the work but, in the case of a tender engine, the painting of engine and tender were specified separately. Unfortunately, not all the information that one would wish for is given, for example, the lining colours are not normally noted. Nevertheless, these official records are the primary source of data for the painting of a GCR locomotive.

CONTEMPORARY JOURNALS

There were many railway journals being published in or about the turn of the twentieth century. Periodicals such as *The Railway Magazine* regularly featured articles of general appeal. This was a period of continuous development in all railway matters and, because of the almost insatiable desire for information, new classes or types of engine often received a lot of attention. Photographs, drawings, technical data and, possibly, a mention of livery, were brought to the public's notice. At times coloured illustrations were included and these are extremely helpful.

The GCR produced a house magazine, *The Great Central Railway Journal*. The copy in green covers cost one old penny, but the one within white covers was printed on rather better quality paper – this was probably meant to be bound and cost two pence. The journal was a monthly publication and comprised all the activities of the staff and the company. Although the duration of its publication did not extend to the whole of the existence of the GCR, it contains many references to liveries. For example, it helped explain the green and black livery periods of Class 8F, as well as important notes concerning the 'Atlantics' and other classes.

The late Guy Hemingway began recording details of the pre-grouping railway scene about 1910. He measured and photographed rolling stock and much more, later preparing drawings and models. He also examined many of the early magazines, such as *Locomotives and Railways*, *The Locomotive Magazine* and others. From these he made lists of livery references, later donating these to the G.C.R.S. archives. These have been another fund of data.

Readers' letters to magazines often contain items of useful information and are worth a study.

Mention has already been made of the coloured illustrations which have appeared in journals at various times. These are often extremely informative, but some contain quite serious errors. Similar comment may be made of the coloured postcards which have been offered for sale by certain publishing houses. These views are sometimes based on photographs which have been tinted by hand, but the use of artists' licence often results in inaccuracies; one coloured card of an 8K 2-8-0 heavy mineral engine painted in the passenger green and claret is a good example (see page 17). The 8K locomotives were finished in lined black when new, which is when the card was first published. Apart from the above caveat, coloured pictures are a very valuable source of knowledge.

The list which follows records coloured views which were published during the pre-grouping years by *The Railway Magazine* and *The Railway and Travel Monthly*.

Plate 2.3   GCR Class 9J, No. 976
No. 976 finished in photographic grey livery at Neilson's works, about September 1901. Notice the offset company name with the coat-of-arms placed over the centre axle box of the 3,250 gallon tender.

J. Quick collection

The Railway Magazine

November	1899	11A	4-4-0	No. 881
April	1902	11B	4-4-0	No. 1017
October	1904	8B	4-4-2	No. 192
September	1906	8D	4-4-2	No. 258
July	1908	8G	4-6-0	No. 1113
June	1909	8J	4-4-2	No. 1090
August	1909	8B	4-4-2	No. 1085
October	1911	8B	4-4-2	No. 26?
July	1914	11E	4-4-0	

The Railway and Travel Monthly

May	1910	8E	4-4-2	No. 364
May	1911	9N	4-6-2T	No. 165
March	1912	11C	4-4-0	No. 110
February	1913	1	4-6-0	No. 423
February	1914	11E	4-4-0	No. 429
March	1915	1B	2-6-4T	No. 272
December	1916	13	4-2-2	No. 969
December	1917	1	4-6-0	No. 427
June	1919	8N	4-6-0	No. 416

Two illustrations are not of Robinson's engines, viz., the Pollitt express locomotives, classes 11A and 13. These are included here for interest and because the livery carried by the 11A would have been very similar to that applied to the early 11B 4-4-0s. The last example, that of 4-6-0 No. 416, is a little unusual. The engine and tender are illustrated in dark grey but the lining, which appears to have been rather crudely added, is red. Polished brasswork is represented by yellow but the whole seems to be an afterthought.

RAILWAYMEN'S MEMORIES, DIARIES, ETC.

Nearly ninety years after the demise of the old pre-grouping railway companies, those who are able to remember them must be very few indeed. If the clock could be turned back, who could recall the precise shade of a colour? The memory can be notoriously erroneous on such matters. Some railwaymen recorded details of their working day and occasionally livery information. One such man was P.H.V. Banyard. Percy, born in 1903, began work as a cleaner on the GCR at Leicester in 1916 and retired as a locomotive inspector for British Railways. He died on 7th May 1984 but the author, and others, conducted a long period of correspondence with him. Percy's letters are the basis of a fascinating study of his work, and although in later years some of his information has proved to be inaccurate, his observations of the GCR in its later years have been very helpful. Percy's notes helped greatly with the special livery of Driver Arthur King's 'Atlantic', No. 264, the Tuxford-painted 9J 0-6-0s and very much more.

LOCOMOTIVE RECORD CARDS

Although it is an incomplete collection, many of the company's locomotive record cards have survived and W.A. Brown kindly gave permission for an inspection of these. The cards record when an engine entered works, when it left and the date of entry into traffic. Other data is often included but not all information is available, particularly towards the end of the company's existence. At times some locomotives' liveries changed, for example from green to black, or possibly *vice versa*. Two classes were subject to these changes, Class 1 and 8F, both 4-6-0s. Dated photographs used in conjunction with the cards help to date the change. The records also allow other information to be deduced, such as the period spent by a locomotive under repair or in the paintshop.

PHOTOGRAPHS, OFFICIAL VIEWS

One of the requirements of the building specification was that a locomotive should be weighed and photographed. The maker was asked to supply copies of photographs, which could be as large as 42 inches by 26 inches. They had to be suitably framed and were of the 'platinotype' in some specifications. A platinotype was a photographic print of superior quality, which had been developed in the presence of a platinum salt. The pictures were often of a broadside view and showed the subject in grey livery. The grey paint was applied in order to show better detail, particularly below footplate level. This livery is often referred to as 'photographic' or 'works' grey, and black, white and various shades of grey were used to apply the lining. The position and style of lining was accurately applied in some cases but on a later batch of the same class it could change. The subject of the official photograph may have been the only class member so recorded, the remaining examples receiving grey but only as an undercoat. The author owns a large framed photograph of 8C 4-6-0, No. 195, which is painted in photographic grey. It appears to be the work of G. Grundy of Manchester who may have been commissioned by Beyer, Peacock & Co.

Photographs and notes indicate that engines painted grey were used in traffic and an example of this is noted in chapter 1. There is no doubt that, at times, the GCR was short of locomotives and that before the final livery was applied engines were 'run in' whilst painted grey. *The Railway Magazine*, February 1919, p 126, included an interesting reply to a letter from a G.H. Wallis. Under the title *'The why and the wherefore'*, the editor commented:

> *As a temporary measure a shade of French grey (not blue as you state) has been adopted as a livery for new G.C.R. locomotives, whilst they are making their trial runs.*

French grey is an extremely light shade of grey and it was used, presumably, because of some post-war shortage.

PHOTOGRAPH COLLECTIONS AND PUBLISHED VIEWS

Several well-known enthusiasts' collections have been examined. Those of Jack Braithwaite, M. Hartley, J. Minnis and J.R. Morton have been very helpful. The author's collection consists of many views and these have probably provided more information than others.

Very many photographs have been published over the years. They may be found in what may seem an endless list of books and journals. *Trains Illustrated*, *Locomotives Illustrated*, *The Railway Magazine*, and the works of George Dow and David Jackson are only a few examples, some of which contain coloured pictures. Modern printing methods do not help with the study of some of these, as detail under a magnifying glass becomes a series of dots. The best sources of data are without question the really good photographs as offered for sale by The Real Photograph Co., Locomotive Publishing Co. and others but viewed with some optical assistance. Only one further problem remains and lies in the nature of the photographic emulsions that were in use by early railway photographers.

The earliest photographic materials were only sensitive to blue light. This meant that they were only capable of recording light in the blue half of the spectrum and, thus, a red object would record at best as very dark grey or, more likely, black. Early photographers did not find this a problem for much of their work but a search was begun to improve the nature of films. In 1873, H.W. Vogel made a significant advance when he added certain dyes to the emulsion and this increased the sensitivity to light in the centre of the spectrum. This type of film became the basis of orthochromatic material, but it was still insensitive to red light. It was not until 1904 that film was made which would record all colours. The first panchromatic

Plate 2.4 L&NER Class B2, No. 426C
This photograph is of a 'Sir Sam Fay' 4-6-0, No. 426C *City of Chester*, and was taken at Gorton shed. The tender has received a 'C' suffix and this dates the view after April 1923. However, the main interest in this picture is that it was recorded on panchromatic film. Note the red buffer beam of 426C's tender which appears light grey. The black tender on the left belongs to 9Q 4-6-0, No. 470; the buffer beam appears light grey and the red lining bands which differ in width are clearly visible.

R.K. Blencowe 10649

film was on the market by about 1906 but it was some time before photographers used it in quantity. Many of the cameras at that time were unsuitable due to them having a 'red window'. Very few pictures taken during the period of this study were recorded on panchromatic film, as orthochromatic materials seem to have been used almost universally.

In order to explain the problems with early emulsions, we must assume that our camera is loaded with orthochromatic film. The subject is a black mixed traffic engine. It has vermilion (bright red) buffer beams and some vermilion lining. The photograph is taken, the focussing, the exposure and initial processing are all satisfactory. The image is now at the negative stage. When a print is made from the negative the buffer beam is a very dark tone and the red lining cannot be seen. The red areas of the subject have not affected the film, because there is insufficient energy in the red light to initiate the break-up of the photo-sensitive portion of the emulsion. When the film is being developed those parts which were affected by light are amplified and metallic silver is left on the plate, but where red light fell, those areas remain unchanged. The fixer solution is added, which combines with the unaffected silver compounds, which are then removed by washing. The negative is printed and where parts of it have no silver deposit maximum light transmission will occur and this gives corresponding black areas on the final print. Thus red painted parts of the locomotive are not recorded.

In 1912/13, the GCR built six engines of Class 1. When new, three were painted in passenger green and the remaining three were finished in lined black. Many years ago a problem arose when a model of a black locomotive required painting: what were the lining colours? The white lines were obvious from photographs but much time was spent studying views of these engines. Eventually, after a lot of deliberation, it was realised that on a perfectly exposed, focussed and processed print, which was recorded in excellent lighting conditions, the red band on the outside of the outer white line on the cab and tender sides was just discernible. It was also possible to see the much narrower red line alongside the white one on valance frames, but a magnifying glass was more or less essential. The red lines appeared as a very slightly lighter shade of dark grey, against the darker image of the engine. It is not easy to explain why the red has recorded, because the film which was used was not panchromatic, but the circumstances under which the view was taken must have been a major factor.

The photograph which most assisted in this matter has been published, in *Locomotives of the G.C.R.* by E. Johnson, vol. 1, p. 124. Unfortunately, a glass will only reveal dots, but the single red line which was applied around the frames beneath the smoke-box is visible with some optical aid. The essence of all the above is that the study of old locomotive photographs becomes a little easier when the student knows what to look for and where to look for it.

Coloured Photographs

E. Becquerel carried out experiments in colour photography in 1848. Thirteen years later, Clerk Maxwell produced the first three-colour photograph. 'Autochrome' plates became available during 1907 and Eastman Kodak offered the first 'Kodachrome' process in 1914. Despite these developments not many early colour photographs of steam locomotives are known and none have been found of GCR subjects. Some modern colour prints tend to be unstable in terms of their colour fidelity; consequently, if original views existed, it is unlikely that they would offer much assistance. Percy Banyard was an occasional visitor at the home of S.W.A. Newton, the Leicester photographer who recorded much of the construction of the Great Central main line to London. Whilst Sidney Newton claimed to be one of the first colour photographers and possessed a number of colour negatives and prints, it is unknown if any were of railway interest.

Contemporary Models

Several manufacturers produced models of GCR locomotives during and after the period of the company's independent existence. The gauges, scales and forms of propulsion varied but at least seven classes were represented, mainly by passenger types. Nowadays some of these models, though highly collectable and therefore valuable, would not be classed as 'scale' models. However, from the point of view of their livery these are notable references. It has not been possible to check the majority but two models have proved to be extremely helpful in this study. A model of a Class 11B 4-4-0 was instrumental in deducing the early livery of that class. Similarly, a photograph of a large scale live steam model of 8F 4-6-0, No. 1097 assisted with some details of the 'Immingham' class.

GCR Express Locomotive No. 506 *Butler-Henderson*

Two former GCR locomotives are preserved. As part of the national collection, two of Robinson's best designs were saved, an 8K 2-8-0, No. 102 and an 11F 4-4-0, No. 506. The 2-8-0 has never been restored to lined black livery, but the 4-4-0 was returned to its original green and it later worked some passenger trains on the present-day GCR at Loughborough. Before its retirement at Loughborough it was repainted black to run in its last British Railways livery and numbered 62660. Shortly afterwards it was again repainted in GCR green before moving to the National Railway Museum at York. In this state the engine and tender were carefully inspected and much useful information was obtained.

CHAPTER 3

PIGMENTS, PAINTS, VARNISHES AND OTHER MATERIALS

The GCR nominated Docker Brothers as their preferred supplier of paints and varnishes which were to be used for the finishing of locomotives. Previously mentioned is that some railway board members had other business interests and it was for this reason that Dockers was chosen, because Ludford Charles Docker, who was a partner in the company, was also a director of the East & West Junction Railway, a small concern with which the GCR exchanged some traffic at Woodford. An alternative manufacturer was usually allowed, but this must have been with the written agreement of the GCR. *'High class varnishes, paints and fine colours for all climates'* and *'Hermator paints for structural and every description of railway engineering works'* – these were advertisements placed by Docker Brothers during the pre-grouping period. With their head office at Saltley, Birmingham, by 1912 the company was part of the Metropolitan Amalgamated Railway, Carriage & Wagon Company.

It may be helpful at this point to discuss the wide variety of substances that were employed during the painting processes. They fall into two categories, the first for the initial preparation and the other for the final stages. In the former class are all the undercoat and primer paints, with white lead, staining and fillers. The second category consists of all the gloss paints, varnishes, pumice and horsehair, gold size, etc. The following materials are described in the approximate order of their use, as stipulated in the painting instructions.

Primer and undercoat paints were of great importance, as it was, and always has been, an essential requisite that a sound base must be prepared for the final coats of paint. Ideal properties were good bonding qualities and corrosion resistance. In the example of 'oxide of iron', which was used on the boiler, this must have possessed some degree of flexibility, as a steam locomotive boiler spent long periods producing steam, then, later, it would be at an ambient temperature. Oxide of iron, or ferric oxide, was commonly used in the manufacture of red pigments. Apart from its use in primer paints, it was extensively employed in the making of paints used as a final covering. The pigment was miscible with others, also with oil, water or other vehicle used in paint or varnish formulation. The physical state of the pigment was of paramount importance. Many colours, such as 'Indian red', 'Turkey red' and 'Venetian red' contained ferric oxide.

Two lead-bearing pigments were also used in large quantities. One of them, red lead, a double oxide of the metal, was the pigment which was employed to formulate the paint of the same name. Red lead is a fiery red colour and it formed about 80 per cent of the solid content of the paint. White lead, which is a basic carbonate of lead, was particularly important, the best grades being made by the 'stack' process. It possessed every property which made the perfect pigment. By mixing a paste of it with linseed oil, the basis of white lead paint resulted. It has good covering powers, mixes with oil easily and flows well from a brush. It is permanent when exposed to light and air, but it darkens in the presence of sulphur-bearing compounds. It could be mixed with barytes, which is natural barium sulphate, the mixture then enabling further pigments to be manufactured. 'Lead colour' and 'dark lead' were used as undercoat paints, the basis of both being white lead with an addition of black.

'Staining' was a combination of vegetable black, turpentine and gold size. Whereas turpentine was obtained by tapping larch and pine trees, vegetable black was prepared by burning various oils in conditions of incomplete combustion. The residue was, to all intents and purposes, pure carbon and was a lighter variety of lamp black. 'Stopping' was made by adding white lead to putty in about equal proportions. It sets quickly and has elasticity. 'Fillers' was manufactured by the addition of japanners' gold size to turpentine and an extender. Horsehair and pumice were used in the rubbing down process; the latter is a form of larva, being a double silicate of potassium and aluminium.

We pass now to the paints, varnishes and other materials which were used in the finishing processes. 'Ivory black' paint was manufactured using the pigment of the same name. This was obtained in a similar way to that used for vegetable black, except ivory waste or chippings were burned. The product was of a very high quality, worked well and was much prized by artists. The 'stone colour' which finished the cab interior was probably prepared by adding a little chrome yellow to white lead. Mainframes' interiors received a coat of 'flesh' coloured paint. This was probably composed of white

Above: Plates 2.6 and 2.7   Models of 11B 4-4-0, No. 1021, and a Parker dining car
One of Fay's publicity stunts was to offer working models of the company's stock to the winners of a competition. Models such as these were exhibited at GCR offices and agencies up and down the country. A set of rails was also included which permitted the fortunate winners to operate them. The information required by the model maker was supplied by Gorton.   *By permission*, The Railway Magazine, *vol. XIV, p. 244*

FACING PAGE: **Plate 2.5   GCR Class 5, No. 890**
The main subject of this photograph was not a Robinson locomotive but the Pollitt Class 5 0-6-0ST on the right. This is another taken on panchromatic film and reveals the outer red band on 'Fish engine' No. 1071, the cab of which is on the left. The power classification of these 4-6-0s was 3 and a stencilled serif '3' is below the running number. The location is Gorton works and the date is July 1923.   *J. Quick collection*

Plate 3.1   Docker Brothers works
Docker Bros of Saltley were named in building specifications as the GCR's preferred paint and varnish maker. Their cochineal process for the manufacture of crimson lake pigment was guaranteed light-permanent.   *By permission*, The Railway Magazine, *vol. III, p. 551*

lead and a little vermilion. 'Vermilion' was applied to complete the frames and also on buffer beams. The pigment for this bright red paint was made from a mineral known as cinnabar, a naturally occurring form of mercuric sulphide.

'Brunswick green' pigment was made from barytes, chrome yellow and Prussian blue. Chrome yellow is a form of lead chromate; Prussian blue is a compound of either potassium ferri or ferrocyanide and a ferrous or ferric salt respectively. The paint was produced in at least four standard shades, ranging from 'pale' to 'extra deep'. Similarly, chrome yellow was made in a variety of tints. As a consequence of these diversities, one maker's shade of pigment or paint would not necessarily correspond with that of another manufacturer. The pigment which was used to make 'crimson lake' was of a dark crimson colour and was sold in small conical-shaped masses. It was made by adding alum and soda to a solution of cochineal, which was obtained from the dried female bodies of the cochineal insect. 'Gold size' is an adhesive, one use of which was for applying gold leaf to a surface. It dries quickly, initially to a tacky state for several hours before finally hardening. It was made by plasticising a soft resin with drying oil, then dissolving the product in a large proportion of a volatile solvent.

What was the precise shade of Brunswick green? This is a question which has been asked many times. After a hundred years it is not possible to describe it with accuracy and there are few written references which help. It was described by Martin Evans in his book *Atlantic Era* as 'a rich medium green' and David Jackson used the words 'rich and deep'. In volume 3 of *Great Central* by George Dow, the author stated that the green 'approximated in shade to the Brunswick green used by Sacré' and readers were advised to study the colour view on page 109 of Dow's second volume; this picture is one of Sacré's 2-4-0 passenger engines painted in the colours to which the author referred. Robin Orchard said of the green: 'A rich dark green was chosen by the G.C.R. for its passenger engines. It was a lovely colour, with just the merest trace of olive in it'. Perhaps

the most informative statement was made by C. Langley Aldrich in his booklet, *The Robinson Locomotives of the G.C.R. 1900–23*. On page 41 appears the following:

During Mr. J.G. Robinson's time, the passenger livery was green, of a shade that the writer would describe as something between the G.W.R. dark green and the G.N.R. light green.

There are some references to variations in the shade of green in Percy Banyard's letters. In one of 10th April 1978, he comments:

Strange though it may seem to a layman, no two engines looked the same in sheds where they stood together. Admittedly some had been out of shops longer than others.

In another of 10th September 1980, Percy said that old MS&LR enginemen had told him that in earlier days locomotive greens seemed to vary. He continued:

One could walk between the roads in such sheds as Leicester, Woodford, Neasden and Neepsend on which stood reasonably clean 4-4-0s, 4-4-2s, 4-4-2Ts and 4-6-2Ts all painted green. Strangely enough, noticeable differences could be detected.

Finally, a letter of 19th September 1981 contained a further observation: 'I have actually seen four passenger engines newly painted green, all different shades'! Some of these differences were obviously due to the weather and working conditions but he remembered and recorded them on individual engines and these are noted in the appropriate chapters.

The frames' colour of crimson lake has also been variously described. George Dow referred to it as 'reddish brown', whereas Robin Orchard said of it: 'chocolate brown'. Langley Aldrich described it as 'red-brown', J.N. Maskelyne used the words 'a nice

ABOVE: Plate C.1   GCR Class 8K, No. 966
This postcard is based on an official photograph of No. 966, but is an ideal example of the maximum use of the so-called 'artist's licence' as these locomotives were not painted green.   *Valentine's series*

RIGHT: Plate C.2   Green and crimson colour panels
These panels are the closest approximation found to the shades of Brunswick green and crimson lake employed by the GCR.

BELOW: Plate C.3   GCR Class 8B, No. 192
This illustration was published in *The Railway Magazine*. Nos 192 and 194 were the first 'Atlantics' and were to be painted black until someone decided otherwise. The livery of Brunswick green and crimson as depicted in this picture is accurate, but the shades of those colours may be doubtful. The green sides to splashers are noteworthy.
By permission, The Railway Magazine, *vol. XV*

Plate 3.2   GCR Class 9J, No. 198
Henry Salmon was probably the photographer of this 'Pom-Pom' No. 198
at Leicester shed, about 1920. The engine is very shabby and typical of
goods types during and after the First World War. It seems devoid of lining
with only the number plate as identity.   *L.G.R.P. 16293*

deep maroon' and Martin Evans *'purple brown'*. The last comment,
which has been made more than once, appeared in the *Model
Engineer* of 7th February 1963, p. 181. It generated a response from
GCR enthusiast, Mr C.A. Reddy, which was published in the 28th
March issue. Mr Reddy wrote:

*It is always difficult to describe colours by the written word
alone, but I would say that Robinson's colour for the frames
is better described as dark red than as purple brown. Last
July I had the pleasure of seeing the restored Director Butler
Henderson at Gorton, Manchester. The shade of red almost
defies description. It is a deep rich colour. I have seen it
described as claret, which I would say is correct: certainly
there is no trace of brown.*

In a letter to the author dated 20th August 1981, Mr E.B.
Woodruffe-Peacock gave his opinion of GCR crimson:

*The external paintwork on the frames of the engines finished in
green was maroon, i.e., a brownish-crimson colour resembling
claret.*

In a response to Maskelyne's description as maroon, David
Jackson was of the opinion that the maroon would indicate an
alteration in shade due to atmosphere and weather conditions,
as the official specification stated crimson lake and this may, to
some extent, be correct. However, it was well known that the
cochineal process for the manufacture of the pigment guaranteed
permanency.

It is not known if the GCR purchased their paints ready to use,
or as pigments along with the other ingredients. The fact that
the company would save money buying the constituents would
be a sufficient incentive. The paintshop foreman was probably
responsible for the correct mixing and preparation of paints but,
unfortunately, no detailed information is available on this matter.

Varnish was applied at certain stages during the painting process
and many types were in use. Generally, they were made by combining
resins and drying oils with a volatile solvent. 'Under varnish' dried
quickly, was hard and could be rubbed down within a few hours. It
usually contained a high proportion of hard resins such as congo.
The best varnishes were always made to the highest standards using
hard resins and a minimum of driers. 'Japans' are black varnishes
and made in the same way, but the natural resins were replaced
by bitumen. Japans were also made from asphalts and pitch. The
cheapest, which was known as 'Brunswick black', consisted of
a solution of pitch in a white spirit. 'Rubber varnish' was used
to protect brake pipes and possessed two important properties,
flexibility and durability.

The GCR insisted on an interval of two days between each
application of the last three coats of varnish. It is obvious, therefore,
that to apply so many layers of paint and varnish, in addition to the
attendant preparatory work, must have taken considerable time.
Another question arises from this; how long did it take to paint an
engine? The locomotive record cards, which have been mentioned
earlier, help to answer this interesting query.

When Robinson arrived at Gorton the company was in urgent
need of motive power. In order to provide locomotives relatively
quickly, further examples of Pollitt's Class 9H 0-6-0 tender engines
were ordered. During 1901, twenty-two of these useful machines
were delivered, with another eighteen in the following year. The
record cards for many from these batches have survived and some
give details of how long an engine spent in the paintshop. Out of
the total of forty, thirteen spent between eleven and thirty-one days
being painted, the average period being twenty days. It should be
noted that these figures represent the time required to paint a new
locomotive, but it is not easy after the passage of 100 years or more,
to explain the significant divergences from the mean figure. Several
possible reasons come to mind. The South African war may have
been responsible for a shortfall in staff. The domestic locomotive
building industry was working at capacity at that time and this may

Plate 3.3 GCR Class 9H, No. 90

This 9H 0-6-0 was a Pollitt design. Robinson ordered forty examples in addition to those built for work on the new main line and No. 90 was one of them. Note the WL&WR style of number plate, the lined black livery and the shapely Robinson chimney. The location is the sidings at Barnsley Junction, Penistone. This locomotive spent all its GCR service allocated to Liverpool Brunswick shed.

Biltcliffe collection

ABOVE: Plate C.4   Boiler bands on Brunswick green engines
These bands were applied to all classes of green locomotives, except
Class 11B engines built by Sharp, Stewart and when they were
new. Those locomotives carried the same style of
lining, but the white was replaced by yellow.
This illustration is about full size.

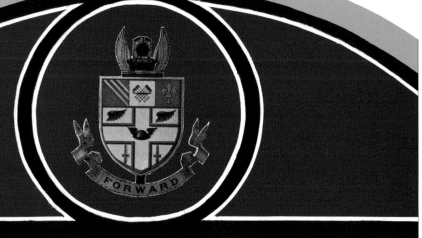

**ABOVE: Plate C.5   Green
locomotives, green splasher
sides**
This represents the lining
arrangements on the splashers
of Class 8B locomotives. It is
believed that this is applicable
only to the following locomotives when they were new:
Nos 192, 194 and 263–267.
This illustration is about one
eighth full size.

**Plate C.6   Green locomotive and tender valance
framing**
 This represents the lining arrangements on green locomotives.
The wide, horizontal black areas are the steps. On certain classes,
11E and 11F, the valance frames and crank-pin splashers were
lined separately. This illustration is about one eighth full size.

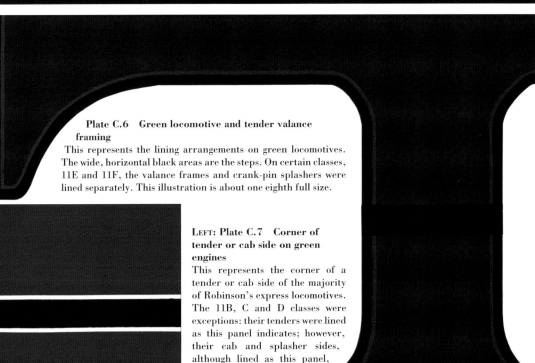

**LEFT: Plate C.7   Corner of
tender or cab side on green
engines**
This represents the corner of a
tender or cab side of the majority
of Robinson's express locomotives.
The 11B, C and D classes were
exceptions: their tenders were lined
as this panel indicates; however,
their cab and splasher sides,
although lined as this panel,
carried white lines in place
of red. This illustration is
about one eighth full size.

ABOVE: Plate C.8   Boiler bands on black engines
These bands were applied to the majority of black locomotives. In many cases where photographs were taken using orthochromatic film the red lines will not be visible. This illustration is about full size.

RIGHT: Plate C.9   Upper right-hand corner of tender, black engines
This represents the top rear right-hand corner of a black tender. The upper portion is the curved flare which curves towards the viewer, rendering the top stripe of red/white invisible. Note that the widths of the red bands varied. This illustration is about one eighth full size.

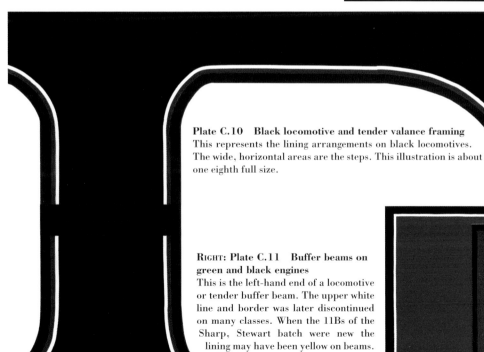

Plate C.10   Black locomotive and tender valance framing
This represents the lining arrangements on black locomotives. The wide, horizontal areas are the steps. This illustration is about one eighth full size.

RIGHT: Plate C.11   Buffer beams on green and black engines
This is the left-hand end of a locomotive or tender buffer beam. The upper white line and border was later discontinued on many classes. When the 11Bs of the Sharp, Stewart batch were new the lining may have been yellow on beams. The large square area represents the buffer base. This illustration is about one eighth full size.

Plate 3.4   GCR Class 8B, No. 264

8B 4-4-2, No. 264, is standing at platform 5 at Manchester Central. Percy Banyard remembered this engine when it was at Leicester shed from November 1919, as it had received an extra-special paint finish. In this view No. 264 is in an exceptional state. The engine spent periods both at Neasden and Gorton sheds before moving to Leicester.

Real Photographs W7127

have created a temporary shortage of paint. The fact that some engines were being finished over the Christmas and New Year may also have delayed matters.

When an older locomotive entered works for repair it was not always necessary to carry out a full repaint. Many would receive only some degree of 'touching up' with, perhaps, a final coat of varnish – but the First World War was responsible for some profound changes. Although passenger engines were normally kept in good condition, the state of goods locomotives deteriorated. Due to a severe shortage of motive power, men and materials, many were not painted at all or, at best, received minimal attention. Generally, however, passenger locomotives were repainted on each works visit.

Percy Banyard, always a keen observer of the GCR scene, made some revealing notes on the state of the company's engines. His letter to the author of 3rd January 1977 contains a particularly interesting note regarding the 8K and 8M 2-8-0s, which were heavy mineral haulers. Percy wrote '*2-8-0s in many instances still retained builder's colours showing for years almost to grouping*' and in another note of 10th September 1980, he made further comments:

The G.C.R. did not spend much money painting 2-8-0, 0-8-0, 0-6-0 and 0-6-2T engines. Never once did I see 2-8-0s, 0-8-0s, 0-6-0s repainted when they went into shops. They came out patchy, linings could still be seen. During economy drives many engines received a coat of unvarnished flat black colour. The 2-6-4Ts 'Crabs' [Class 1B] had only the one coat received when built. Drab black ever after.

It is important to point out that Percy's observations were all made during the First World War and in the following few years.

Percy's first job with the GCR was as a cleaner at Leicester

locomotive shed. He worked with other young men and, presumably, women as the country was at war. His letters, written in the summer of 1975, shed light upon the cleaning routine and the materials that were used. He wrote:

Cylinder covers were usually unpainted steel and had to be scoured with emery cloth. The reversing rod was usually unpainted, this meant more 'spit and polish' to keep it bright, also greasing so that rust did not set in. Smokebox door hinge and band, also hand rails were kept bright and polished too. Buffer heads had to be filed to rid them of paint and/or rust. Guard irons received no paint until, many years later, they were coloured black.

Later, he added:

For brasswork we made a paste consisting of rape oil mixed with crushed bath brick, emery cloth being used on steelwork, usually grades 1 and 2. The regular engine in my and another chap's care was 4-4-2 no. 264. This had a better quality of paint.

The application of paint to a steam locomotive provided two important benefits. The first has already been mentioned and that is the public's perception of the company through the livery. The other is that because engines are mainly made from iron, a metal that will rust with ease, the paint furnishes some degree of protection. Polished metal surfaces always contrast well with paintwork of any colour and many of the earliest locomotives were adorned with bright metal. It is a fact, however, that due to the problems during and after the First World War, bright metal surfaces on many engines were not maintained or simply painted over.

CHAPTER 4
LININGS AND BORDERS

The arrival of Britain's railways coincided with an historical period when craftsmanship was supreme. The Victorians abhorred plain surfaces and, as a consequence, decorative additions were made to relieve what was considered to be a visual monotony. These could take the form of mouldings, panels or coloured lines, and this obsession was found in all aspects of life during this time. It is not surprising, then, that when the early steam locomotives began work they were usually finished quite elaborately, with lots of richly painted parts, all relieved with lines or panels of suitably contrasting colours. Early railway passenger carriages were really horse-drawn road vehicles that had been adapted for rail use. It followed, therefore, that they were painted in a similarly flamboyant manner, but often in a style which complemented that of the locomotive.

As the years passed things began to change. Slowly, but certainly, the often highly complicated livery styles were simplified. The main reason for this was, of course, economic. A locomotive engineer of the time, in charge of perhaps 1,000 engines, could save his employer a significant amount of money over a few years. A simplification of the livery, of the lining possibly, would be all that was required. Nevertheless, at the time Robinson began his career with the GCR, locomotives were kept in very fine condition. Footplatemen were usually immensely proud of their engines. Cleaners were employed but many drivers, particularly of express trains, went to great lengths to ensure that their steeds were in a superlative state. A good example of this is Driver Arthur King who was based at York with 'Atlantic' No. 264. The enhanced livery carried by this engine is noted in the chapter which deals with these locomotives. The application of lining to a locomotive was a time-consuming affair, and yet that feature alone did so much to improve the large painted areas of a tender or tank side.

Unfortunately, the paint specifications for GCR engines that have been found give few details of the lining. The usual reference is *'sample panels will be provided'*. It is most unlikely that any of these have survived, certainly none have been located. Presumably a sample panel was a coloured board with the required lining thereon. There is only one mention in the specifications which gives a value for the width of a line, this being for the ⅛-inch white line which formed an ellipse around the running number on the number plate.

An attempt has been made to reproduce some sample panels. To do this it was necessary to make a thorough examination of the preserved GCR passenger locomotive, Class 11F *Butler-Henderson*. Permission from the authorities at Barrow Hill, near Chesterfield, was obtained and much useful data recorded. Despite some fairly serious errors in the repainting of the engine, it is believed that the basic layout of the lining, borders etc., are sufficiently accurate to enable sample panels to be made.

The following notes will help to explain the accompanying coloured illustrations. It is important to remember that they do not necessarily refer to all classes of locomotive. Where divergences occurred these are covered in the relevant chapters.

BOILER BANDS

These were about 2 inches wide. On green engines they were painted black, but each edge, to a width of about ¼ inch, was white. On black locomotives they were also black, but each edge, to a width of about ½ inch, was equally divided into two strips. The outer strips were red, the inner white.

BUFFER BEAMS

On locomotive and tender buffer beams, for green and black engines, the finish was vermilion. A black border, about ¾ inch wide, was painted all around. A single white line, about ¼ inch wide, was painted alongside the border which formed a separation from the main vermilion area. Later, on some classes, the lining along the top of the beam was discontinued.

LOCOMOTIVE CAB SIDE, TENDER SIDE AND END

Green engines had a black border, about 2½ inches wide, painted around the outline. Alongside this was a single red line, which was about ¼ inch wide. Then a green border, about 3 inches wide, was made before the white/black/white panel completed the lining. The white lines were about ¼ inch wide and the black band between them about 2¼ inches wide. This scheme was repeated on the tender sides and end, also on the cab and tank sides and rear of the bunker on tank locomotives, except for one variation: on tank engines, the single red line was replaced by a white line.

Black engines were lined differently. Approximately 4½ inches inside the outline was a red band, about 1 inch wide. Inside that, but alongside its inner edge, were two white lines, which were about ¼ inch wide. The black between them was about 1¼ inches wide. This arrangement was repeated on tender sides and end.

LOCOMOTIVE AND TENDER VALANCE FRAMING

These notes refer to the shallow frames immediately below the footplate of engine and tender and including the footstep plates.

Green tender engines had crimson valance frames on both locomotive and tender. A black border, about ¾ inch wide, was applied around the outline of the framings but not along the upper edge. A red line, about ¼ inch wide, was painted alongside the border, thus separating that from the main crimson area. The tops of footsteps, and all of what may be described as 'walking surfaces', were black. Tank locomotives normally used on passenger work were finished in a similar manner, but the red line was replaced by a white one of the same width. The framing on the 9N 4-6-2T engines was also crimson but the lining was red, that is, as on green tender locomotives.

Black engines had black valances and the lining was different. Inside a black border, of about ¾ inch in width, were two lines, one was white, the other red. Each line was about ¼ inch wide, painted alongside each other, but the red was always on the outside and on some classes it was a little wider than the white.

LOCOMOTIVE SPLASHER SIDES

The decoration on locomotives' splasher sides was quite complex.

GREEN SPLASHERS
The following notes refer to the 8B 4-4-2 engines, Nos 192, 194 and 263–267 inclusive, and only during the locomotives' early service. This is because when those engines were repainted the splashers received crimson lake and, consequently, different lining. Around the curved edge was a flat brass beading which was about 2 inches wide. Inside this was a black border, about 1 inch wide. This border continued along the bottom of the splasher, but it was a little wider

Plate C.12 Green locomotives, crimson splasher sides
In conjunction with Plate C.13, this represents the lining arrangement on the splashers of 'Atlantic' locomotives. The leading splashers of locomotives of classes 8D and 8E were lined in this style. The polished brass beadings completely surround the coat-of-arms. Both leading and driving splashers on Class 8B engines were finished in this manner, although the bottom brass beading was replaced by a wider black border. The solitary member of Class 8J, No. 1090, was similarly finished. The ten engines of Class 8F were also finished in this scheme when they were new.

Plate C.13   Green locomotives, crimson splasher sides
The company monogram was placed in the centre of the splasher carrying the nameplate of classes 8D and 8E. The nameplate is represented by the wider area of brass at the top of the splasher. These illustrations are about one eighth full size.

Plate C.14   Class 1 4-6-0 locomotives' splasher side, green livery
This represents the lining arrangements applied to Class 1 engines. The narrow gold represents the brass beading, the rectangular section the nameplate. This illustration is about one eighth full size.

Plate C.15   Class 8C 4-6-0 locomotives' splasher side
This represents the lining arrangements on engines Nos 195 and 196 when the monogram was applied. This illustration is about one eighth full size.

Plate C.16   Class 8F 4-6-0 locomotives' splasher side
This represents the lining arrangements on engines nos 1095–1104 when they were painted black. This illustration is about one eighth full size.

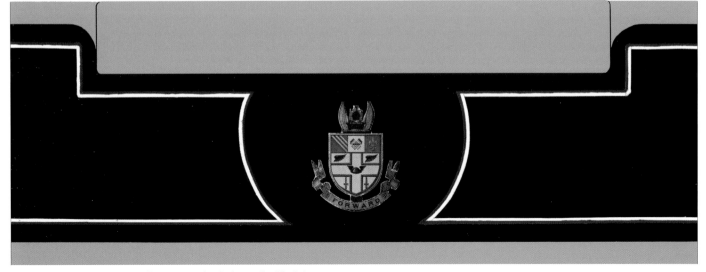

Plate C.17   Class 1 4-6-0 locomotives' splasher side, black livery
This represents the lining arrangements applied to black Class 1 engines, but only after they were named. This illustration is about one eighth full size.

at about 1¾ inches. A white line, about ¼ inch in width, separated the border from the green. This line ended on each side of the centre of the splasher, both at the top and the bottom. Arcs of a circle, formed by ¼ inch wide white lines and about 1 foot 9 inches in diameter, joined the white lining at the top and at the bottom. Thus was completed a continuous white line on both the left and right sides of the splasher. Inside the incomplete white circle, and separated by a black annulus, was a complete white circle, which was about 1 foot 6 inches in diameter. In the centre of the central circle, and set on a green ground, was the company's coat-of-arms, which was about 1 foot 3 inches tall.

CRIMSON SPLASHERS

These notes apply mainly to the compound 'Atlantics' of classes 8D and 8E, engine Nos 258, 259, 364 and 365. Around the curved edge and along the bottom was a flat brass beading about 2 inches wide. On the leading splasher the lining and border were identical to those on green splashers, except the lining was red, or probably vermilion. The coat-of-arms was applied in the centre on the crimson ground. On the trailing splasher the width of the nameplate required some changes. The black border was set inside the beading, but it was altered in shape to accommodate the nameplate. A red or vermilion line, about ¼ inch wide, was applied to the inner edge of the border. This formed a continuous panel of black border and red set immediately inside the beading. In the centre of the remaining crimson area was the company's monogram, which was about 9 inches tall.

The following notes refer to engines of Class 8F, Nos 1095–1104, but only when they were painted green. The notes may also be used to study members of Class 8B built after 1904. They were Nos 1083–1094, 260, 261, 262, 358 and 360–363. These locomotives, and all those of Class 8F, had crimson splashers when new. The flat brass beading was fitted to the curved part of the splasher, but this did not continue along the bottom edge. The 8F engines carried the monogram on the leading and trailing splashers, and the coat-of-arms on the centre splasher. On all three splashers red lining was applied as described for the leading splashers of classes 8D and 8E. The 8B locomotives enumerated above received the identical style of red lining on all splasher sides, with the coat-of-arms set in the splasher centre. The solitary example of Class 8J, No. 1090, which was created by a rebuild, had identical decoration. This engine was the subject of a retrogressive rebuild in September 1922, when it became an 8B, but the linings were the same. The smaller coats-of-arms were applied, however, a minor change which became a common practice on other classes towards the end of the GCR as an independent concern.

Three of the Class 1 4-6-0s, the 'Sam Fays', were finished green when new, but by grouping all six examples were green and, in this state, their splasher sides were painted crimson. A flat brass beading, about 2 inches wide, was attached around the edge of the splasher and this formed a continuous band of brass. A black border, about 1½ inches wide, was painted inside the beading and followed the under-edge of the nameplate. A red line separated the border from the crimson. This was about ¼ inch wide and formed an incomplete circle, another red line making a complete circle, all as described. The larger circle was about 1 foot 2 inches in diameter, the smaller about 11 inches across and a black border separated them. Placed in the centre of the inner circle, on a crimson ground, was a coat-of-arms, which was about 9½ inches tall.

BLACK SPLASHER SIDES

These notes refer to the two engines, Nos 195 and 196, which comprised Class 8C. The 8Cs and classes 8D, 8E and 8F all carried the company's monogram at some stage, although it was not applied to Nos 195 and 196 when they were new. A flat brass beading was fitted to the curved edge of the splasher and inside this was a black border about 1¼ inches wide. Then two lines were painted, the outer was red and the inner white. They were about ¼ inch wide, were applied alongside each other and made a continuous line. When new only the leading and trailing splashers were so finished. Later, the monogram was placed on these splashers. The intermediate splashers carried the coat-of-arms, which had the red and white lining surrounding it, formed by the incomplete and complete circles, as outlined above.

The 8F 4-6-0s were almost identical to the 8Cs. They were green when new, but, before long, they were to be seen painted black. In that livery the monogram was applied to the leading and trailing splashers, with a coat-of-arms on the centre splasher. The lining details were as mentioned, but the named member of the class, No. 1097 *Immingham*, was unique. The situation was reversed because of the nameplate: the monogram was placed below it, the other splashers carrying the coats-of-arms.

When the Class 1 engines, Nos 424, 426 and 427, were new they were painted black. Before naming, the splashers were finished with the usual red and white lines, with a coat-of-arms placed in line with the centre driving axle. Later, the nameplate required a change in the lining's position and this was described earlier for the green members of the class. A rather smaller coat-of-arms was used at this time.

The notes regarding black locomotives may be used to study other classes that were painted black. Examples are: 1A, 1B, 5A, 8, 8A, 8G, 8H, 8K, 8M, 8N, 9J and 9Q. Similarly, other green painted classes may be examined using the appropriate notes. These classes are: 9K, 9L, 9N, 9P, 11B, 11E and 11F. Where variations occur they will be found in the relevant chapters.

The other components of locomotives and tenders not illustrated here were lined as described in the notes which follow. They have been compiled with the assistance of very many photographs. It is important to understand that not all engines carried the decorations that are noted. Where different finishes are known to have been employed, details will be found in the appropriate pages.

FRAMES BENEATH SMOKE-BOX

GREEN ENGINES

These framings were finished in crimson lake. A black border was painted around the outline of the frames, the width of which varied between one class and another. A red line, about ¼ inch wide, separated the border from the remaining crimson area.

BLACK ENGINES

Frames on these engines were painted black, but not all classes received lining thereon. When lining was applied it normally consisted of one red line which passed around the shape of the frames set inside a black border, but the width of the border varied at times. It is wise to remember the difficulties encountered when trying to interpret old photographs of locomotives which may have carried red lining. Unfortunately, really useful views which show this detail are very scarce. Classes which received this lining are as follows: classes 1 (when black), 1B, 8, 8C, 8F (when black) and 8N. Photographs showing the lining on classes 8A, 8G, 8K, 8M and 9J have not been found.

LINING AROUND DOME

GREEN ENGINES

Many photographs do not show this feature clearly. Those that are helpful indicate that the bottom edge of the dome received a continuous band of white/black/white, that is, the lining that adorned boiler bands. There were slight variations on this arrangement.

BLACK ENGINES

There are few views which show the lining and therefore it is difficult to be sure if it was applied to certain classes. Generally, it consisted of one red line above, but alongside, a white line, both of which were on the base of the dome. A few classes exhibited a slightly enhanced form of decoration when a pair of red/white lines were applied. This was the same lining that was painted on the boiler bands of black locomotives.

SPECTACLE PLATE

GREEN ENGINES

On green locomotives this plate was always painted green, with a black border of about ¾ inch width. A white line, about ¼ inch wide, separated the border from the green but this varied somewhat. Often the white line and border ended by the side of the splasher. On some engines the lining continued over the top of the firebox. On others it ended just below the lower, square spectacle.

BLACK ENGINES

On most classes the plate was lined with red and white stripes, the red always on the outside. On Class 8 and the other similar classes, 8C, 8F (when black) and 8G, the lining continued on to the splasher tops forming a nearly continuous double line, over the firebox and the other side of the engine.

BUFFER BODIES

GREEN ENGINES

The buffer bodies were painted crimson on green engines. The mouth of the body had a black band about ¾ inch wide, with a red line, ¼ inch wide, alongside it. The square section which held the retaining bolts carried one red line on the facing edge and this passed around the section. The four flat surfaces beyond the red were black. A handful of early views of classes 8B and 8F show that a white line was painted in place of the red just mentioned. On some passenger tank engines white lining was also used on buffer bodies.

BLACK ENGINES

Buffer bodies on black engines were also black, but photographs which show the lining are hard to find. However, the mouth of the body was usually lined with the red and white stripes, the red always being nearer the opening. The leading edges of the square section were finished in the same manner but not all black locomotives had lined buffer guides.

TOPS OF SPLASHERS

GREEN ENGINES

The tops of splashers were normally green. A black border was applied with a white line next to it. Certain express types, which were built later, had black tops to splashers and were devoid of lining.

BLACK ENGINES

These had black tops to splashers. When the tops were lined it was the red/white style that was applied but the red was always on the outside.

CYLINDERS

GREEN ENGINES

On classes 8B, 8D, 8E and 8F (when green) the cylinders were painted crimson but only on the central section. A black band was added around both outer edges of the crimson and each band had a red line separating the two colours. The front and rear ends of the cylinders and the steel bands were polished metal. The other green painted class with outside cylinders was 9P and these engines exhibited a slightly modified scheme. The whole of the cylinder was crimson, but the steel bands and ends were black. A red line separated the black from the crimson. The large circular end covers were polished and all remaining parts were probably black. The massive fabrication which supported the slide bars, crosshead etc., was also crimson. It carried a black border with one red line. This included the tubular section through which the piston rod moved.

BLACK ENGINES

The central portion of the outside cylinders was also black. Not all classes received lining on cylinders but, where it was added, the usual red and white stripes were applied, the red line always being on the outside. The metal bands that were prominent near the ends were sometimes included in the lining. The large support through which the piston rods moved on Class 9Q was black and lined with a red and white stripe.

CAB INTERIOR

During the early period of the GCR both green and black locomotives' cab interiors were finished in a very pale yellow colour. Although the specifications state *'stone colour'*, Percy Banyard remembered it as cream. A black edge, about 1½ inches wide, was painted around the outline of the cab. A red line, which was about ¼ inch wide, separated the border from the stone.

A change in this policy may be detected in the specification for the 8K 2-8-0, which required a green finished cab interior. Unfortunately, a complete lack of specifications for later classes precludes a conclusive statement on this matter.

WHEELS

GREEN ENGINES

The bogie and driving wheels were lined with white. The axle ends were black and a ¼ inch wide white line surrounded the end. The annulus around it was green, then another white line completed the lining around the centre. There were variations on this style. On certain classes, for example 1 and 9L, the tyres were polished. On others, the tyres were black and a white line formed a separation from the centre. There were various schemes used on Class 9K, but on classes 9P, 11E and 11F they were remarkably consistent.

BLACK ENGINES

On these engines all the wheels were black. Several classes appear not to have had any lining on the wheels, but it varied on those that did. The red and white scheme was applied to some, but others only received a red line. It was added, either around the hub and cranks, or around the axle ends only. On other classes it was added to both cranks and axle ends. Some black engines had polished tyres.

TENDERS

GREEN ENGINES

Tenders were lined in the same style as used on engines. The lined parts included the sides and end, buffer beams and buffer bodies, valance framing and steps. The curved flares were green, had a black border about 2 inches wide and this had a red line about ¼ inch wide alongside. The rear flare was similarly finished. The top coal plate was also green. The beading and about ½ inch inside the flat area of the plate was black. A red line, about ¼ inch wide, provided a separation from the green section. The tender top was black and this included the coal rails if they were fitted. Some of Robinson's later passenger engines carried additional linings on their tenders. Classes 11E, 11F and 9P received this enhanced decoration and the Class 1 4-6-0s may also have. Tender fronts, cupboards and lockers were crimson. A black border was added, then a red line painted alongside. The outsides of mainframes, axle boxes and springs were also crimson. A black border was applied around cut-outs, axle boxes and the like, then a red line divided the border from the crimson. The wheels were green but they were unlined. Tyres normally matched those on the engine, that is, either black or polished metal. When certain locomotives were fitted with oil-burning equipment, the tank fitted on the top of the tender was probably plain black.

BLACK ENGINES

Tenders were lined in the same manner as the engine. The sides and end, buffer beam and buffer bodies, valance frames and steps were all lined. Mainframes were also black and, when they were lined, it consisted of one red line around cut-outs, axle boxes, springs and dampers. The curved flares on the sides and end were lined with red and white stripes but the upper coal plate received only one red line. Not all black tenders carried this lining and good photographs are essential for further study. Some engines were adapted to burn experimental fuels. The additional fuel tanks were probably painted unrelieved black.

Plate C.18   Buffer beam numerals
Some of Robinson's early engines were numbered using 6 inches tall, black-shaded, numerals, although blue shading quickly replaced the black. The 4½ inches tall characters with blue shading were introduced quite early and these were employed on the majority of Robinson's locomotives.

J. Quick collection

ABOVE: Plate C.19 Tender and tank side lettering

Although the height of the letters of GREAT CENTRAL varied, the character face and the shading both appear to have been consistent. Some early Parker and Pollitt locomotives were finished with lettering that was about 7½ inches tall. Robinson's engines, however, usually received 6 inches tall characters. The 4½-inch variety began to be used later but, generally, on smaller locomotives.

J. Quick collection

LEFT: Plate C.20 Number plate numerals

The character of both the alphabet and numerals adopted by Robinson, and used on his locomotives, was almost identical to that in use on the GWR. These numerals are quarter full size.

J. Quick collection

Plate 5.1 *Immingham* **nameplate**
This plate is from Class 8F 4-6-0 locomotive, No. 1097 *Immingham*.   *Private collection*

Plate 5.2   Class 11B No. 1040
This 11B 4-4-0, No. 1040, is in original condition and is waiting at London Marylebone's platform 4. Of interest in the enlargement below are the 6 inches tall buffer beam characters. They appear to be shaded with blue of three shades and highlighted with white lines. This is also a particularly good view of the headlamp.   *J. Quick collection*

CHAPTER 5

COATS-OF-ARMS, MONOGRAMS AND OTHER DECORATIONS

The company's title, 'Great Central', was placed on the side of the tender or on the tank side of a locomotive. Unfortunately, the centre of the lined panel on a tender in which the title was placed did not quite coincide with the centre of the central axle box. Another complication was that the words Great Central did not consist of the same number of letters. The policy with regard to early classes 9J and 8 was to place the coat-of-arms over the central axle box. This was satisfactory when viewing the left side of the tender, but on the opposite side, the tender lettering had a semblance of imbalance. Photographs show this clearly and it is possible that two other classes built in the early period, 8A and 11B, may also have been so lettered. One or two pictures of North British Locomotive Company-built 'Atlantics' of Class 8B show this feature but all subsequently built classes appear to have been finished with the lettering being placed in the centre of the panel, irrespective of the axle box, on both sides of the tender. The earlier engines which had the 'out of balance' lettering were probably relettered to conform with later types.

The letters which formed 'GREAT CENTRAL' were plain block in style. A few pre-Robinson classes received characters that were about 7½ inches tall, but 6 inches high letters were adopted very early and were used on the majority of engines. A smaller version was also in use: the letters were about 4½ inches tall and were applied to the smaller engines. Their appearance suited the older MS&LR and Pollitt designs rather well and a good example of this is Class 12AT. Robinson rebuilt some of these elderly 2-4-0Ts of Sacré origin as Class 12AM and the smaller characters were applied to their tank sides. The 4½ inches tall letters began to replace the 6-inch variety, but, generally, not on the larger engines of Robinson's design.

Despite the variations in their height, the character face of the letters was consistent. They were gold, shaded to the right and below and this contrasted the gold with the green or black of the engine. The shading was about ½ inch wide and consisted of two shades of red, the darker being used on the underside and the lower part of the character. Highlights were picked out with fine white lines, which divided the shades of red. The effect was, of course, to make the lettering 'stand out' in a three dimensional manner. After a prolonged photographic study, a set of the letters has been made

Plate 5.3 Display of nameplates
This very impressive exhibition of GCR railwayana was assembled for the weekend of 2nd/3rd June 2001. This was in connection with an event at the Ruddington Heritage Centre and jointly organised by the Great Central Railway Society and the Great Central Railway Rolling Stock Trust. No less than nine classes of locomotive are represented here. Ruddington is the centre of operations for the Nottingham Transport Heritage Centre, which includes the Great Central Railway (Nottingham) Limited.
M. Crawley

ABOVE: Plate C.21   GCR Class 1, No. 423
This coloured postcard of the prototype engine, No. 423 *Sir Sam Fay*, is a very good representation of the green livery as applied to this locomotive when it was new. The lined top edge of the buffer beam is not correct and the guard irons should be polished steel but, nevertheless, a very good effort.
Locomotive Publishing Co.

Plate C.22   GCR Class 11F, No. 506
Butler-Henderson is standing by the Down-side water column on the present-day GCR at Loughborough, Leicestershire, around 1988. The condition of the locomotive is as restored and repainted in 1961. At the time of writing the engine is in the custody of the Barrow Hill roundhouse near Chesterfield.   *J. Quick*

Plate 5.4 *Lady Faringdon* and *Lord Faringdon* **nameplates**
The curved plate was fitted to the driving splasher of compound 'Atlantic', No. 364 of Class 8E. The small oval plate was the L&NER builder/maker's plate which was fixed to the cab side of this engine. The other, straight, plate was carried by Class 9P 4-6-0, No. 1169. *Private collection*

and they are illustrated here. The late Guy Hemingway recorded vital information regarding the lettering. He measured the spacing of 6 inches tall characters and found that over the G of GREAT and the L of CENTRAL was 9 feet 2 inches. The word GREAT was 3 feet 6 inches over the G and T, and there was 4 feet 4 inches over the C and L of CENTRAL. If the letters prepared for this volume are set out to form the company's name, the values for distances over the letters, as mentioned above, are very close to Guy's measurements.

The running number of a GCR locomotive usually appeared in four positions. These were: on each cab side and both buffer beams of tender engines, and on each bunker side, bunker rear and the front buffer beam of a tank locomotive. The numbers carried on buffer beams varied in height. During the early period 6 inches tall characters were applied but, later, another smaller version of about 4½ inches height was employed. Apart from their dimensions the characters appear to have been identical. They were gold and shaded to the right and below. Three of Robinson's early classes, that is, 9J, 8A and 8, received numerals that were plain black shaded. However, specifications for classes 8B, 8F and 8K all state blue shading and this was added in three sections. The lightest blue appeared on the upper right area of the numeral. The intermediate shade of blue was added to the lower part and a very dark shade, which may have been black, was used on the underside of the numbers. White lines highlighted the division of the shades, and an abbreviated form of number, Nº, which had a very short line underneath the 'o', was placed to the left of the draw hook, the running number being in the opposite position. A set of these numerals has been made and these are illustrated on page 28.

Older engines of MS&LR origin, and those designed by Harry Pollitt, carried running numbers in the form of transfers when Robinson joined the company. A cast number plate soon appeared on some engines of Class 13 and on the last batches of 9H 0-6-0s but it was nearly rectangular in shape, a reminder of his Irish engines. A new type of plate was introduced with Robinson's first class, the 9J 0-6-0. It was cast in brass and elliptical in shape. One of these is illustrated in Eddie Johnson's, *Locomotives of the G.C.R.*, vol. 2, p. 159. A set of the numerals which appeared on plates has been prepared and these are also reproduced. The character face on these was dissimilar from that on the WL&WR locomotives, but was remarkably similar to the type in use on the GWR, being marginally taller.

Number plates usually had a black ground to the numerals, but early examples of classes, 9J, 8A and 9K had a vermilion ground. J.N. Maskelyne in an article which was published in the *Model Railway News* of May 1952, p. 100, referred to the background colour on the plates of 'Atlantic' No. 267 as maroon, and that '*the plate was surrounded by a narrow black border and a white line;*

inside the raised brass border there was a vermilion line'. The reasoning behind this statement is unknown, but it may be as a result of the publication of the coloured illustrations that were noted in chapter 2. It may be correct, but many photographs of all the 8B 4-4-2s have been checked, including No. 267, and none indicate that the ground colour was anything other than black with a thin white line around the numerals, although the white line was later discontinued.

A handful of photographs have been found which show a small number immediately below the running number on the plate. They seem to be about 1½ inches tall, are of the serif type and painted a light colour: white or possibly yellow. The December 1908 issue of volume 4 of the *G.C.R.J.* explains the significance of the numbers. On page 113 in 'Locomotive News', it commented '*It will have been noticed that our goods engines have now a small number under the engine number on the cab side. This has reference to the class of load the engine is classified to take*'. The classification was from 1–5 and a good view of 8K No. 353 shows that it was placed in class 1, whereas the 4-6-0s of classes 8 and 8F occupied class 3. An interesting variation is of 9C 0-6-2T, No. 517 – although not of Robinson design, it had a transferred '3' under the running number, which itself is composed of transfers.

When Robinson's 11B 4-4-0 No. 1014 was named *Sir Alexander*, the company restored the practice of naming certain engines. Well over forty years had passed since a named locomotive had been seen on the line, C.R. Sacré having abolished the custom. A typical nameplate and the alphabet adopted by the GCR are reproduced in Eddie Johnson's work, which has already been cited. The GCR letters are more or less identical to those in use on GWR nameplates, only a few were different. The very similar nature of the numerals and letters on GCR plates suggests that GWR practices did not go unnoticed by Robinson during his employment with that company. The ground colour on GCR nameplates was probably always black and many have survived, mainly in enthusiasts' collections. Unfortunately, the same cannot be said of number plates. Like as not they were melted down and the residue reused or sold when the newly-formed L&NER issued the order to replace them with transfers.

The company's heraldic symbol, or coat-of-arms, was the first to be authorised for a railway by the College of Arms. It was illustrated in colour and comprehensively described by George Dow in volume 2 of his trilogy, *Great Central*. It must have created quite a stir when it first appeared and the GCR made full public use of it. Anywhere where Sam Fay's energetic publicity department considered it appropriate, it was to be seen: timetables, crockery, ash trays – even chamber pots were adorned with one or more. Some of Robinson's locomotives carried as many as six, whilst passenger carriages built for the opening of the London line also had that number, in addition to those etched into the glass of lavatory lights. The trams that plied their way along the Grimsby to Immingham electric railway usually had one at each end. When later designs of passenger carriages were introduced, the coat-of-arms was etched into lavatory lights. The usual version was about 1 foot 3 inches tall, but a smaller type was also in use. Indeed, the small symbol was used increasingly in the later years of the company.

The words 'Great Central', the buffer beam numerals, the coat-of-arms and the monograms were all supplied as transfers. Around the turn of the twentieth century many transfers for British railways were made in Germany but those used by the GCR were usually obtained from Tearne & Co. of All Saints Road, Birmingham. When the L&NER became owners of the east coast group of railways most of the embellishments noted above passed into railway history. The motto 'Forward', however, survived rather longer as it was used by the new company on its own heraldic device. Some of the original GCR coats-of-arms have survived, as David Jackson owned at least two of them.

The monogram was applied to only four classes of locomotive – viz., 8C, 8D, 8E and 8F – and it was reproduced in George Dow's work. It was about 9 inches tall and consisted of the company's initials overlapping each other. The G was emphasised as wider than normal, the C and R being set inside the G, with various parts of the characters intertwined. The letters were gold and of a very ornamental style, with detail added in black. They were shaded, to the right and below, with red.

Engines normally carried other cast metal plates, apart from number and possibly nameplates. Two maker's plates were fitted, but their positions varied according to the locomotive type. Often they were on the framing below the smoke-box or on a splasher

side, but the diminutive dock shunters of Class 5A had plates which were fixed to the upper part of the cab. The massive 0-8-4Ts of Class 8H had them attached to their sandboxes and the memorial locomotive, *Valour*, had plates fastened to the cylinder sides. Some private locomotive builders used their own often quite distinctively shaped plates, but if an engine was a product of Gorton works then, in the majority of cases, it carried elliptical-shaped cast brass maker's plates, which were about 10 inches by 6 inches.

One batch, or certain members of that batch, of 9J 0-6-0s broke the rules regarding maker's plates. They were made at Gorton in 1903–04 and were provided with a type of combined number and maker's plate. The running number appeared in the normal position, but above and around it were the words 'Great Central' in small characters. Below the number was 'Gorton Works' but, strangely, the building date was omitted. It is likely that all the members of this group of 9Js had this type of plate fitted. Three other, older classes also had combined plates. These were 18, 18A and 18T and, although not of Robinson's design, some were rebuilt under his direction with new plates being fitted at the time. Many former GCR locomotives worked well into the era of British Railways and, as a consequence, their maker's plates have survived. They are highly collectable and generally fetch a handsome price. A Gorton plate is shown in George Dow's *Great Central*, vol. 3, p. 348. Black was probably the standard background colour but all raised surfaces would have been polished brass.

Tenders carried a number plate, which was often fitted at the top centre of the tank rear. They were rather smaller than a maker's plate and were cast metal – iron or possibly brass. The plates attached to the tenders of the 9J 0-6-0s built by Vulcan Foundry were cast iron, measuring 9¾ inches by 6¼ inches and elliptical in

Top: Plate 5.5   Gorton maker's plate
This plate is from an engine of classes 8A 0-8-0, 9N 4-6-2T or 8K 2-8-0.   *Private collection*

Above: Plate 5.6   Maker's plates
Amongst a very fine collection of locomotive maker's plates are these from three builders. Top left is from a 9Q 4-6-0 or an 11F 4-4-0 and top right is one from an 11F 4-4-0. Bottom left is a Neilson, Reid example from a 9J 0-6-0. In the centre is a North British Locomotive Company plate which was carried by a 'Jersey Lily', No. 1089, and on the right is a plate which was fitted to a Pollitt 9H 0-6-0, one of Robinson's batch of forty.   *Private collection*

outline. The numerals were 2 inches tall and were of the *sans-serif* style. Some of the tenders coupled to the 8B engines also had cast iron plates. Iron plates were most likely painted black with white-painted numbers and raised edges. Brass examples may also have been black with polished raised areas, but in later years received an overall coat of paint.

The London area locomotive sheds on the GCR were at Neasden. This depot was visited at fairly regular intervals by members of the Stephenson Locomotive Society, the earliest recorded occasion being on 10th November 1903. Nearly sixteen years later, on another visit, a useful list of engines that were present was published in *The Locomotive News and Railway Notes*. In the list were three locomotives which had letters painted inside their cabs. The engines were: 0-6-2T No. 772 which had an 'A' on the inner cab side, 4-6-0 No. 444 which had an 'N', and 0-6-0 No. 954 which had an 'S' inside the cab. The visit took place on 10th May 1919 and it appears to have been the first time that the letters had been noted. It was suggested that the letters might indicate the sheds to which the engines were allocated.

The same journal, in the issue of 10th June 1920, reported 'G.C.R. engines are now having the sheds painted inside the cab, after the G.W. idea. Neasden engines have "NEASDEN" in full, but *for other sheds, contractions are used'*. A list of sheds then followed, with their abbreviations, but unfortunately, this was incomplete. A full list was published in the edition for 10th May 1921 and was as follows:

A	Annesley	NH	New Holland
B	Barnsley	NR	Northwich
BD	Bidston	R	Retford
C	Chester	S	Sheffield
G	Gorton	SK	Stockport
I	Immingham	ST	Staveley
K	Keadby	T	Tuxford
L	Lincoln	TP	Trafford Park
LG	Langwith	W	Woodford
LP	Brunswick	WK	Wakefield
LR	Leicester	WL	Walton
M	Mexborough	WR	Wrexham
N	Neasden		

The Locomotive News and Railway Contractor, no. 8 of 25th April 1922, p. 251, added that the letters were usually on the right-hand side of the cab. Percy Banyard wrote a letter on this subject, which was included in *Forward*, no. 43 of January 1984. In a notebook for 1919/20, he recorded the following abbreviations in use:

NSD	Neasden	RTD	Retford
WD	Woodford	LIN	Lincoln
LR	Leicester	GY	Grimsby
AY	Annesley	IMM	Immingham
STAV	Staveley	LANG	Langwith
NPSD	Neepsend (Sheffield)	TUX	Tuxford
MEX	Mexborough	BARN	Barnsley
GTN	Gorton		

But he failed to record anything for several other very important depots. Some of the above codes do not agree for the same shed, but this may be because the shed staff applied the letters. Percy also noted that the letters were white and painted on the driver's, or right-hand, side of the cab. He believed that the custom began soon after the end of the First World War. White letters would not have contrasted well against the light-coloured cab interior, but they may have been shaded with red or black, or applied on a black background. The height of the characters is not known but something in the order of 3 inches seems reasonable.

Some locomotives carried various decorative symbols, usually on the smoke-box door. It is believed that they were unofficial and probably the work of the shed staff. The classes involved in the practice were numerous, but it is unlikely that every example of a class was so decorated. Photographs of engines of the following classes showing these are: 1, 1A, 8B, 8D, 8F, 8G, 8N, 11A, 11B and 11E. The marks varied considerably: an arrow, sword or perhaps a scimitar-shaped symbol; others were of a diamond shape or a star, some with five points and others with six. A view of 8F No. 1103 exhibits no less than three decorations and all are different. The March 1916 edition of *The Railway and Travel Monthly* contained an interesting comment from a Manchester reader. He wrote that he had seen, on the smoke box door of 11A No. 853, two dogs painted silver and that the handle of the screw in the centre had silver bands around it. In his reply the editor commented: '*Decorations like this, though not uncommon, are generally unauthorised. It is caused by emery paper removing black paint*'. Pictures of Robinson's later engines do not show any marks. This may indicate that the practice had been declared contrary to the locomotive department's wishes.

Plate 5.7   Locomotive headlamp
This is an example of the square-bodied variety of locomotive headlamp. This type of lamp always seems to have been painted black with polished brass fittings.   *Private collection*

ABOVE: Plate 6.1   GCR Class 9J, No. 980
No. 980 is on Neasden shed and is having ash removed by a member of staff. This is an early view, c. 1902. Note that the company name is slightly offset to the right as the coat-of-arms lies over the centre axle box. The buffer beam numerals are probably shaded black.   *J. Quick collection*

Plate 6.2   GCR Class 9J, No. 204
No. 204, a Gorton-built engine of January 1904, is standing on the south side of Leicester shed. The absence of a maker's plate should be noted. The cab side number plate gives details of its provenance.
J. Quick collection

CHAPTER 6
CLASS 9J 0-6-0

We begin the study of the liveries of individual classes with the 9J tender engines, which were generally known as 'Pom-Poms' and were Robinson's first design for the GCR.

During the spring of 1899 the company was desperately short of engines and traffic was increasing. In order to alleviate the situation, William Pollitt arranged to hire locomotives from the Great Eastern, Great Northern and North Eastern railways. The GER increased its share by four engines six months later, in October 1899. The total at that time was forty-six but, eventually, at least fifty-four engines were on loan and the Lancashire & Yorkshire Railway was also supplying motive power.

Robinson arrived at Gorton in early July 1900 and, clearly, he had inherited an unenviable state of affairs. He was, however, more than equal to the task. He knew a tried and tested design and expediently ordered forty further examples of Harry Pollitt's Class 9H 0-6-0. The first of these appeared in February 1901, the last in July 1902, and they were all built at Gorton. As the 9H engines entered service, those locomotives that were on loan were gradually returned, until by February 1902 only six remained on hire.

As useful as the Pollitt engines were, what was really required was a modern, larger, six-coupled type to haul the heavy coal and goods traffic, and the GCR board was asked to finance the construction of suitable engines. At the same time that Gorton was preparing to build the 9H locomotives, the first order for the larger 0-6-0s was placed with Neilson, Reid & Co. of Glasgow. The 9Js were an immediate success and, over the following ten years, 174 were built in total. They could be described as the company's standard goods engines and were so highly regarded that the last examples were not removed from service until the final few years of steam locomotive operation on British Railways.

The 9J locomotives were built as follows:

- Neilson, Reid & Company built Nos 973–1012 and 1043–1051 between early September 1901 and November 1902.
- Beyer, Peacock & Company made Nos 198, 201, 203, 205, 206, 209, 210, 211, 214–216, 218, 219, 221–231 and 234 between the end of September 1903 and the end of April 1904.
- Vulcan Foundry Limited supplied fifteen engines, Nos 235–239, 242–250 and 252 during June and August of 1904.

- Yorkshire Engine Company built fifteen examples between March 1904 and August 1906. They were Nos 253–257, 1078–1082 and 1115–1119.
- Gorton works made four batches, which were completed over the period from late November 1903 to May 1910. They were Nos 177, 197, 202, 204, 207, 208, 217, 220, 232, 233, 240 and 241 in 1903–1904; Nos 281–309, 311–320 and 322–330 were finished during 1906–1908; engine No. 16 was built in 1909, and finally Nos 947–955 in 1910.

The National Railway Museum at York holds rolls of original drawings of these locomotives. They appear to have survived because prospective builders were supplied with a set as part of the tendering process. Each roll consists of approximately 170 drawings to various scales, the drawings being executed in what was probably Indian ink on linen. In the belief that the drawings may include some livery notes they were studied, but to no avail.

At least two painting specifications have survived. The earlier, which is dated October 1900, probably applies to the Neilson, Reid batch; unfortunately, the section which deals with tender painting is missing. The other document of October 1905 concerns the Yorkshire Engine-built locomotives and is quoted verbatim here. The first section applied to the locomotive.

The specifications of 1900 and 1905 are almost identical, but there are some interesting differences. In the sixth paragraph, the 1900 version asks for: *'Company's Coat of Arms (Transfers of which will be supplied) on each Driving Splasher, and Brass Number-Plate fixed on Trailing Splashers, to be painted red between numbers'*. It is unlikely that the last members of Class 9J, notably engine Nos 16 and 947–955, ever carried the coat-of-arms. However, the majority of the other members probably did, particularly when new. Photographs of one with the heraldic symbol on the splasher side are unknown, as it was always applied to the tender tank sides, and the Neilson, Reid locomotives had their maker's plates fitted to the driving splashers. The earlier painting instructions of 1900 did not require a white line to be painted around the numerals on the number plate. This was probably because the specified ground colour was red, but a few early views of members of the first batch show that a white line was added around the numbers. A final point of interest is that these locomotives did not have external trailing

---

Plate 6.3   GCR Class 9J, No. 984

No. 984 is also on Neasden shed, about 1902 as the engine is in original condition. Notice that the ground colour to the number plate appears darker than the black of the cab. This is an indication that the numerals had a vermilion ground.   *F. Moore 0735*

PAINTING.

Boiler to receive two coats of oxide of iron before being lagged, one whilst hot.

Clothing Plates, two coats lead colour, inside.

Splashers, Cab, Clothing [external boiler or lagging plates], Wheels, Outside Frames, Sand Boxes, Footsteps, and Buffers to receive two coats lead colour, filled up with white lead mixed with gold size, then coat of staining (vegetable black, turpentine, and gold size), rubbed down, followed by another dark lead colour, sand-papered, after which one coat ivory black paint, then coat of ivory black and varnish mixed. Lining to be done same as sample panels, afterwards to receive one coat under varnish, and two coats best finishing body varnish. To be flatted down with pumice powder and horse hair between each coat.

To be Numbered on Buffer Beam, to sample, after first coat of varnish.

A Brass Number-plate fixed on Trailing Splashers, to be painted black between numbers, and with 1/8in. white line 1/2in. within the raised edge.

Inside of Main Frames, Frame Stay, and Slide-bar Brackets to have two coats lead colour, filled up with white lead mixed with gold size, rubbed down, one coat flesh colour, sand-papered, one coat of quick-drying vermillion [sic], then two coats vermillion, mixed with varnish.

Outside of Main Frames and Guard Bars to receive two coats lead colour, filled up, rubbed down, one coat ivory black, and one coat ivory black mixed with varnish, and one coat hard-drying body varnish.

Webs of Crank Axle and Body of Straight Axles, one coat white lead and one coat varnish.

Ends of Axles to be lined, otherwise same as Wheels, and varnished.

Smoke-box, back of Fire-box, Platforms, Brake-hangers, &c., one coat black, and one coat japan.

Chimney to have two coats lead colour, filled up with white lead mixed with gold size, rubbed down, and one coat black and one japan.

Inside Cab, one coat lead colour, filled up, rubbed down, sand-papered, two coats stone colour (to sample), one coat under varnish, and one coat finishing body varnish. To be lined as per sample panel.

Two days to intervene between each of the last three coats of varnish.

Buffer Beams same as Inside Frames, with the addition of being lined to sample panel, and varnished same as clothing.

Brake Pipes to have two coats of approved rubber varnish.

The Paint and Varnish to be obtained from Messrs. Docker Bros.

Sample Panels will be provided, and the greatest care must be taken that all the Engines are painted strictly in accordance therewith, and of the same shades throughout.

[Tender]

Tank Sides, End and Protector Plate, Main Frames, Outside Frames, Axle-box Lids, Footsteps, and Buffers to receive two coats lead colour, filled up with white lead mixed with gold size, then coat of staining (vegetable black, turpentine, and gold size), rubbed down, followed by another coat dark lead colour, sand-papered, after which one coat ivory black, then coat of ivory black and varnish mixed. Transfers of coat of arms to be fixed, which will be supplied, and lining to be done same as sample panels, afterwards to receive one coat under varnish and two coats best finishing body varnish.

Company's name, with letters in gold leaf, to be placed on each side of tank, to sample.

Buffer Beam, similar to Engine.

Inside Tanks, Outside top of Tank, and Coal Space to have two coats red lead, finished with black.

Tool Box and Sand Boxes, two coats lead colour, finished black, and varnished.

Axles and Tyres, same as Engine.

Inside of Frames, two coats lead colour, finished in oil black.

Brake Work and Intermediate Buffers to receive one coat lead colour, one coat oil black, and varnished.

Brake Pipes to have two coats of approved rubber varnish.

The Paint and Varnish to be obtained from Messrs. Docker Bros.

JNO. G. ROBINSON,
Chief Mechanical Engineer.

GORTON,
    October, 1905.

Plate 6.4   GCR Class 9J, No. 1050
This 'Pom-Pom' is little more than eighteen months old in this view
which was taken on 4th June 1904, at Neasden.   *J. Quick collection*

splashers, as they were behind the cab sides. The number plates were positioned a foot or more above the bottom of the sides.

Certain parts of the engine and tender were to be left as bright metal. These included: *'Smoke-box Door Centre Washer, Ring and Handle, Wheel, Hinges, and Brackets to be finished bright and polished'*, safety valves *'Pillars to be polished'*, coupling rods *'finished bright'*, buffer rams *'turned all over outside'* and handrails and pillars *'Of polished Steel Tubing … by polished Wrought-iron Pillars'*. To this list may be added all brass beadings and raised surfaces on number and maker's plates.

GREY LIVERY

The photographic grey livery has already been noted in chapter 2. Several photographs exist of 9J engines wearing this special painting scheme. Locomotives which are known to have been so finished are Nos 16, 198, 228, 234, 247, 252 and 976, but it is more than likely that there were others. The livery consisted of grey with white and darker shades of grey lining. A first class job was made of this, even to the coat-of-arms being applied. An interesting feature regarding the lining was that at least four different arrangements were used. A photograph of a 9J painted grey and actually working a train has not been found but it is known that No. 16 did run in grey paint. *The Great Central Railway Journal* of June 1909, p. 269, reported that No. 16 *'is now running in slate colour'*. This locomotive was probably repainted black during the autumn of 1909.

BLACK LIVERY

The service livery of the 9Js throughout their working lives was always black. Whilst in Ireland Robinson had three very similar engines built for the Limerick company. The black livery that was applied to those goods locomotives was, to all intents and purposes, that used on his GCR 0-6-0s. There is more than one reference in the contemporary journals but that in *The Locomotive Magazine*, vol. 6, November 1901, p. 182, is typical. In referring to the new 0-6-0s, Nos 973–1012, they were *'painted black, picked out with red panel bands and white lines'*.

Photographs of examples of all batches of these 0-6-0s indicate that, although there were minor differences they all received the same basic black lined livery. Chapter 4 should be consulted for details of this, but the following will assist.

The boiler and firebox were finished with the double red/white stripes as illustrated in chapter 4, although at the point where the smoke-box met the boiler a single red/white line was applied. Some locomotives also had the same lining added to the base of the dome but there are few photographs which show this feature. The cab sides, tender sides and end were lined with the double white and a broad red band arrangement, which is also shown in chapter 4. Other parts of the engine and tender carried only a single red/white stripe. The lines were painted alongside each other but the red was always on the outside. Areas that were decorated thus were the spectacle plate, valance framing and step plates on engine and tender, splasher sides, buffer guides and curved flare to the tender top. Buffer beams were finished as the example in chapter 4, but, later, the top under-edge line was omitted. The cab interior was painted as earlier described. Driving wheels on the early examples were lined around the cranks with a single red/white stripe. The tender main frames probably carried a single red line around the outline, axle boxes, etc.

As a consequence of being built over a period of about ten years, and in several batches, not all the locomotives of the class received the lining described. Indeed, as time passed the lining style was either simplified or discontinued. Examples of this are on driving wheels, dome or buffer guides. Photographs taken soon after the end of the First World War show that many engines were running with little, or no, decoration, with no buffer beam identification and generally looking rather unkempt.

The 9Js all carried brass number plates but some of the locomotives built at Gorton in 1903–1904 were not fitted with the standard one. Nos 177, 204, 217 and 233 all had a combined maker's/number plate. The transfers of the company's name always appear to have been formed of 6 inches tall characters. The coat-of-arms was not applied to tenders of some of the later examples and it is likely that during the last years of the GCR other engines of the class were not so adorned. The early engines built by Neilson,

Reid had the heraldic device placed over the central axle box. On the right-hand side of the tender this arrangement looked a little unsatisfactory, a situation that was probably remedied at their first repaint.

During the later years of the company some 9Js were repaired and repainted at the former works of the Lancashire, Derbyshire & East Coast Railway. Tuxford had at least seven engines for overhaul at this time, with others in the L&NER period. Locomotive record cards list the following locomotives visiting the Nottinghamshire works: Nos 1008, 289, 301, 305, 311, 313 and 316. Percy Banyard's letters disclose a little additional information. In one dated 9th November 1974, he noted:

The 0-6-2Ts that went to Tuxford L.D.E.C. works for overhaul came out painted and lined in L.D.E.C. style and so did the goods Pom-Poms. Incidentally, some series of these 0-6-0s had red side rods when new, numbers of the class still sported them when I started in 1916, and Pollitts too.

In another communication of 16th June 1975, he referred to the subject again:

When engines went into Tuxford works they emerged sporting the L.D.E.C. colour scheme and smart they looked, red side

rods, backs of number plates a brilliant red. I well remember being on no. 1008 and 0-6-2Ts in this livery.

It is unfortunate that no photograph of any GCR engine finished in this style has been located. As a consequence of this, details of the scheme are unknown, although the various views of former LD&ECR locomotives so painted are very helpful. Tuxford may have applied the non-standard '3' to the locomotive buffer beam of No. 311. The numeral had a rounded top and is clearly shown in W. Bradshaw's photograph, which is reproduced in *William Bradshaw Leicester Railway Cameraman*. Another engine which exhibited an unusual livery feature was No. 16. This locomotive was unique in having a Schmidt superheater which necessitated the provision of extended frames at the front. A view of the locomotive shows that the cab side lining avoided the bottom corner of the cab and formed a 90° change in direction. Normally the lining followed the short curve which led to the footplate.

The last 9J to work was British Railways No. 64354, by then classified as a J11. It was originally GCR No. 177 and worked a rail tour on 13th October 1962. Although the engine had been greatly altered, it was specially prepared for the day. The brass beadings had been painted over but this was scraped off at Retford shed and the coupling rods painted red, all of which gave No. 64354 a splendid appearance.

ABOVE: Plate 6.5   GCR Class 9J, No. 214
No. 214 is on Leicester shed and in a rather unkempt state. The brand new 9Q 4-6-0 behind supplies a clue to the date, 1921/22. This is probably a Henry Salmon photograph.
L.G.R.P. 16292

Plate 6.6   GCR Class 9J, No. 983
This engine is ready for a comprehensive overhaul in this picture at Gorton. No. 983 entered works on 21st January 1922, and left on 15th April, being officially returned to traffic by 2nd June. The chimney is one of Robinson's later designs.
J. Quick collection

CHAPTER 7
CLASSES 11B, 11C AND 11D 4-4-0s

Having provided the company with a modern class of locomotive for coal and goods trains, Robinson now turned his attention to the passenger traffic of the Great Central Railway.

The express engines of Pollitt's design, classes 11A and 13, were perfectly capable of working the modestly loaded trains at that time. Indeed, some fine runs were recorded by the single drivers of Class 13. The original order for the singles was for ten examples, but only six were built. It is generally accepted that the balance of four was cancelled by Robinson after he had made some modifications to those built once he had joined the company. Obviously he had very different ideas from his predecessor and believed that the way forward was to employ larger, more modern locomotives. The 11B was his first GCR design for express passenger work and has been described as an engine which linked both Victorian and Edwardian eras of locomotive development, as features from both periods are noteworthy.

The new 4-4-0s were very elegant machines and characteristic of Robinson's early work. Soon after their introduction, the company's publicity department improved the public timetables by adding a side elevation of an 11B on the front cover. Also, at this time, the *G.C.R. ABC Railway Guide* offered prizes to the winners of a competition, the prize being a working model of No. 1014 and a Parker dining car. The models were made by Messrs Bassett-Lowke Ltd and these days would fetch a very high price at auction. Examples of them were on display in the museum at Immingham until recently; these were, at one time, the property of S.W.A. Newton, the noted Leicester photographer.

Shortly after the first 9J 'Pom-Poms' appeared, the first of the new 4-4-0s was delivered. This, and the fact that the two classes shared certain common parts, led to the 11Bs taking the *sobriquet* of 'Bogie Pom-Poms' or 'Passenger Pom-Poms'. The latter nickname appeared on the oil allowance notices at Leicester engine shed.

The 11B locomotives were built as follows:

- Sharp, Stewart & Company completed the first batch of five during October 1901. They were numbered 1013–1017. Nos 1018–1037 formed the second group, being built between February and April 1902. The last five were finished in March 1903 and carried Nos 1038–1042.
- Vulcan Foundry Limited made the final ten examples in the period, beginning in late March to late May 1904. They were numbered 104–113.

It should be noted that four engines were named. No. 1014 became *Sir Alexander* in 1902 and No. 1021 was named *Queen Mary* in 1913. During 1907 No. 104 was fitted with plates bearing the name *Queen Alexandra*, with No. 110 being named *King George V* in 1911. The bestowal of nameplates on No. 1014 was quite significant, as it was the first named locomotive to be seen on MS&LR or GCR lines for more than forty years.

GREY LIVERY

There are only a few photographs of 11B engines painted in grey. No. 1017 was recorded so finished, probably when it was new.

Plate 7.1   GCR Class 11B, No. 1020
An 11B, as supplied by Sharp, Stewart in February 1902, in original condition. No. 1020 is on Neasden shed, c. 1902. The yellow lining on frames, cab and tender sides is clearly visible. This locomotive spent all its GCR career working from the London line sheds of Neasden, Leicester and Nottingham Arkwright Street.

L.G.R.P. 8052

Another Sharp, Stewart locomotive, No. 1021, was also photographed in the grey livery; it is likely that it was taken when the engine was rebuilt to Class 11D in April 1913. The third example known to have been grey is No. 113, a Vulcan Foundry engine; a view of it is available in the E. Pouteau collection of GCR subjects, ref. no. 53. Illustrations of any of these 4-4-0s working a train in grey livery are unknown.

GREEN LIVERY

Although both Sharp, Stewart and Vulcan Foundry engines were painted green when new, photographic and written evidence indicate that two different liveries were used. All the Sharp locomotives were finished in the same scheme on delivery, but the last batch of ten built at the Vulcan works received a different style. The two schemes differ in many aspects, thus separate studies must be made of them.

SHARP, STEWART LOCOMOTIVES

There are many early photographs of examples of all three batches built at Sharp's works. They show that all thirty engines were painted in the same manner but it was not the later livery of Brunswick green and crimson lake frames. It was, more or less, the last painting style that was employed by Pollitt on the MS&LR. It should be remembered that at this point in Robinson's career he had not made a firm decision on all livery matters and, as a consequence, some experiments took place which were conducted with interesting results on the last four of Pollitt's Class 13 4-2-2 tender engines. The green paint which was applied to the new 4-4-0s was of a lighter shade than Brunswick and was probably the colour that was described by *Locomotives and Railways*, vol. 1, p. 45, as *middle chrome green*. The framings were finished with brown, which may have been dark in shade and referred to in MS&LR board minutes as *old oak brown*.

Before we examine the livery of the Sharp engines in detail, a most important feature regarding the lining colours requires discussion. Unfortunately, the evidence for this is contradictory. *The Railway Magazine*, vol. X, January 1902, p. 74 refers to the 11Bs: *'These engines (only 5 delivered so far, 20 more on order) are painted green and relieved with black panels and white lines. The outside frames, tender axle boxes, etc., are painted brown'*. Note well the white lines! On page 282 of the same volume, a coloured plate of No. 1017 was published as part of the April issue. The picture was the work of Alf Cooke, a colour painter of Leeds, and is based on an official photograph of the engine in grey livery, but it clearly shows white lines. These references form a fairly solid testimony for white lining.

Other evidence suggests that the lining colour was yellow. In George Dow's *Great Central*, vol. 3, p. 127, the author claims that black and yellow were the lining colours and in the same work opposite page 41 is what he describes as *'the contemporary F. Moore oil painting of no. 1022'*. This picture shows the locomotive lined with black and yellow. A very informative examination of the major railways' liveries was published in *The Railway Magazine*, vol. XV, October 1904, p. 282 and written by J.B. Baron Collins. The article included a comprehensive list of liveries used on locomotives and rolling stock, and even the colours of the various tickets are noted. The section devoted to the GCR states quite clearly that engines were green with black and yellow lining. The author's comments obviously refer to passenger locomotives, as all the accompanying sketches show passenger types. The next piece of information which is in favour of black and yellow concerns the model of No. 1014, to which reference has already been made. The idea of having models made for publicity purposes was promoted by Sam Fay, who had replaced Sir William Pollitt as the company's general manager at the beginning of 1902. In accordance with Fay's wishes, the locomotive

department at Gorton furnished all the necessary information to the model maker, Bassett-Lowke, and this included the painting details. The model of No. 1014 that, until recently, was admired at the Immingham museum is lined with black and yellow. Finally, as in so many other cases, the study of really good photographs provides much data. Indeed, these are without doubt the main reference source for these locomotives.

Some of the early views of Sharp, Stewart engines show excellent lining detail. The lining is certainly light in tone but it is of a darker shade than that of the shield on the coat-of-arms which was mainly white. In truth, the shade of the lining matches exactly that of the brass beading and this strongly suggests that the lining colour was yellow.

In conclusion, it does seem that black and yellow were the lining colours, but it is possible that some early engines were lined with white and later relined yellow, although this seems highly unlikely.

It is difficult to be precise in the absence of official documents, but the following is believed to be the livery applied to the first thirty 11B engines when they were new.

Painting: Locomotive Boiler, firebox, dome, splasher sides and tops, cab, spectacle plate, driving and bogie wheels were finished a middle shade of green paint. This colour was noted in a report on the completion of Pollitt single No. 967, which appeared in *Locomotives and Railways*, vol. 1, April 1900, p. 45, which commented: *'7' 9" single no. 967 has been painted a medium chrome green, much lighter than the standard tint, lined out as usual'*. Frames below smoke-box, valance frames and step plates and buffer guides were painted dark brown. Smoke-box, chimney, cab roof, tops of running plates and steps were black. The buffer beam was vermilion and the cab interior a very pale yellow. Insides of mainframes were vermilion, outsides probably the dark red/brown as portrayed on page 41 of *Great Central*, vol. 3. This may have been the *dark red, almost lake* colour, as mentioned in *Moore's Monthly Magazine*, August 1896, p. 82.

Painting: Tender Sides, end, curved plate above cupboards on tender front, curved flares and wheels were green. Valance frames and step plates, mainframes and buffer guides were dark brown. Tops of steps, running platform, tank top and the lower front of tender were black. The axle boxes also appear to have been painted black. Buffer beams were vermilion as on the engine; insides of mainframes were probably black.

The following components were usually polished metal: buffer heads, smoke-box handle, rim, wheel and hinge, couplings, all hand rails, all wheel tyres, coupling and reversing rods, all brass beadings, raised parts of number/maker's plates, whistles and safety valves.

Lining: Locomotive The lining details which follow have been established from photographs. The boiler and firebox received twin yellow lines which had a black band between them. At the union of the boiler and of the smoke-box only one yellow line was painted alongside the black stripe. The base of the dome also carried the two yellow lines and black centre decoration. The cab, splasher sides, tops and the lower curved openings and the spectacle plate, all had a black edge alongside which was a yellow line. The riveted strip which covered the joint of the firebox with the spectacle plate and splasher tops was black, each edge having a yellow line. The cab interior was probably lined around with red, or possibly yellow, against a black border. The buffer beam had a similar border and the lining which formed a separation from the vermilion appears to have been yellow, but this was not applied beneath the upper edge. The square section of the buffer guides was black and this had a yellow line on the edge which was furthest from the buffer beam. The mouths of the guides had the same lining as the boiler, i.e., double yellow and a black

Plate 7.2   GCR Class 11B, No. 1031

This is another example of an 11B in original condition, No. 1031 photographed at York south depot, NER, about 1903. The livery is the lighter shade of green, with black borders, brown framing and yellow lining. The 11Bs were Robinson's first essay into express passenger locomotive design, which produced a perfectly proportioned machine containing features of both Victorian and Edwardian eras.   *Real Photographs 65333*

Plate 7.3   GCR Class 11B, No. 106

Vulcan Foundry made ten examples of the class and here is No. 106 in original condition at Neasden shed. Brunswick green and crimson is now the livery of choice, which became the standard for express types. Unfortunately the orthochromatic film has not recorded the red lining, but what a handsome engine!

E. Pouteau GC 136

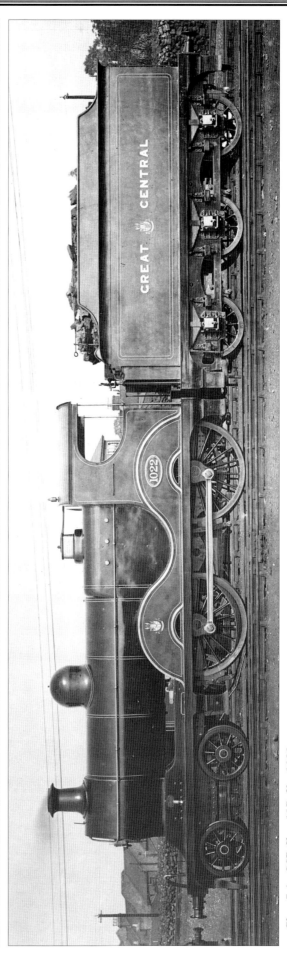

Plate 7.4   GCR Class 11B, No. 1022

Another Sharp, Stewart product of February 1902, No. 1022, is on Neasden shed. This was taken later in its GCR service when it was finished in the Brunswick green and crimson scheme. The locomotive buffers and safety valves are not original. The tender is not the one fitted when No. 1022 was new, being of 4,000 gallons capacity; it retains its MS&LR type tapered buffers but has had an upper coal plate fitted.

F. Moore 4180

centre. The framing below the smoke-box, valances and step plates all had a black border and a yellow line. The guard irons and the outsides of the mainframes may have been lined, but photographs are not clear on this matter. Driving and bogie wheels had black axle ends around which was a yellow line.

Lining: Tender   The end and sides had a black border with a yellow line. Inside the remaining green panel were two yellow lines which contained a broader black band and this formed a continuously lined stripe. The small, lower plate which supported the handrails appears to have been unlined green. The curved coal plate above the front was edged black and this had a yellow line against it. The curved flares above the sides and end received a slightly narrower version of the twin yellow and black lining and this formed another continuously lined band. The coal rails and the beading at the top of the flares were black but photographs suggest that the usual black border was not painted around the flares. The valances, step plates, mainframes and axle boxes etc., were lined yellow, which separated the black border from the brown. The buffer beams and guides were finished as the engine. The guard irons appear to have been painted brown, edged black and lined yellow. This is shown on a good picture of No. 1014 which is part of the author's collection. Strangely, the photograph does not show the same pattern of decoration on the locomotive irons.

Photographs indicate that the standard 6 inches tall letters formed the company name on the tender. The buffer beam numerals were also 6 inches tall and shaded. Chapter 5 gives more detail of both lettering and numbers. Some engines had a light coloured line painted around the running number on the number plate, being set just inside the raised edge and this was probably yellow. The usual size of coat-of-arms was applied to the tender and the leading

driving wheel splasher. Illustrations of these locomotives with the coat-of-arms placed over the central axle box on the right-hand side of the tender are not known.

As the Sharp engines were repaired and repainted, Brunswick green and crimson lake livery began to be applied. It is not easy to date when all had been so treated, but 1906/07 would be a reasonable estimate, by which time all the 11Bs would have presented a more or less uniform appearance.

Vulcan Foundry Locomotives

When new, these engines were finished in what was, by then, Robinson's standard passenger style of Brunswick green and crimson lake but unfortunately an official specification is unknown.

Painting: Locomotive   The boiler, firebox, dome, splasher sides and tops, cab, spectacle plate and all wheels were green. Frames below smoke-box, valance frames and step plates and buffer guides were painted crimson lake. Smoke-box, chimney, cab roof, tops of running plates and steps were black. Buffer beams were vermilion, the cab interior a pale yellow. Insides of mainframes were also vermilion, the outsides were probably black. The guard irons may have been finished crimson, in which case a black border and a red or vermilion line may have been applied.

Painting: Tender   The sides, curved flares, end and wheels were green. The valance framing and step plates, mainframes, axle boxes etc. and buffer guides were crimson. The tops of the tank and steps, coal rails and tender front were black. Buffer beam as on the engine. The insides of the mainframes were probably black, but the guard irons may have been crimson and lined as the locomotive.

The list of polished metal parts was as noted for the Sharp examples.

Plate 7.5   GCR Class 11C, No. 110
This has been published before, but it is a good photograph of an 11C 4-4-0. The livery is the usual green and crimson but the smoke-box door seems to have had a recent coat of black or japan. The vehicle behind, which is a covered carriage truck, may be doing duty as a newspaper van. The faded lettering may read 'Daily Mail War Express', a reminder of when the GCR ran newspaper expresses during the Boer War. No. 110 was photographed at Leicester Central in September 1910.
                                                   W. Bradshaw

Lining: Locomotive Again, the details of lining which follow have been assembled from a study of photographs. The boiler and firebox received two white lines which had a black band between them, as illustrated in chapter 4. At the point where the boiler joins the smoke-box only one white line was applied. The dome was lined with the twin white and black centre stripe. This arrangement was mainly on the base of the dome, but the lower white line was on the boiler and encircled the base. The cab, spectacle plate, splasher sides and tops all had a black border and this had a white line alongside. The curved openings at the bottom of the splasher sides also received this border and lining. The frames below the smoke-box, valances and step plates had a border of black with a red or vermilion line next to it. The buffer beam was edged black and lined white all round. Photographs do not record lines on buffer guides very well but they would have been lined. The square section was black with a red or vermilion line on the edge which was furthest from the beam. The openings also had a black stripe with another red line. The inside of the cab was probably edged black with a red line alongside. The outsides of the mainframes were more than likely unlined black but the wheels had black axle-ends with a white line around them.

Lining: Tender The tender sides, end, curved flares and upper coal plate (when fitted) all had black borders which had vermilion or red lines separating the border and green. On some engines the short plate to which the handrail was fixed was similarly finished. Inside the green panel of the sides and end was set twin white lines, one on each side of a black band, as illustrated in chapter 4. This formed a continuous stripe of decoration. The valance frames and step plates, mainframes, axle boxes, etc. all received a black border with a red or vermilion line but this does not record well on orthochromatic film. The buffer beam and guides and the guard irons were finished as the engine.

One or two additional comments are necessary regarding the Vulcan locomotives. On some examples, possibly all of them, the brass number plate was surrounded by a white line. This was a little unusual as the line was normally around the numerals. Another variation concerns the lined corner immediately where the cab handrail meets the cab side. On some engines it was square, on others it had a convex corner.

REBUILT LOCOMOTIVES

As the 11Bs were rebuilt as classes 11C and 11D they lacked the elegance that they originally possessed, but they became better locomotives. The livery that was applied changed very little. The lining on the dome was modified so that it was all on the base but there were variations. The top edge of lining on buffer beams was omitted and, also, that around the number plate. Some engines left Gorton with the company's title formed of the smaller characters about 4½ inches tall and similar size numerals were being applied to buffer beams. The coat-of-arms was not always placed on the tender side and the small heraldic device was probably used in the later GCR period. Percy Banyard noticed some livery variations c. 1918. He saw Nos 1021 and 1025 running with unvarnished paintwork and No. 1026 in a darker olive shade of green. These may have been as a result of shortages of materials but, generally, they were maintained to a high standard, as they worked some of the company's important passenger trains.

Some engines were photographed carrying decorative marks. No. 1022 had a five-pointed star at the base of the smoke-box very early in its career. William Bradshaw recorded No. 104 with eight small bright discs which formed a circle around the smoke-box door and, during 1920, No. 1014 carried an anchor symbol and light-coloured marks around it on the upper part of the smoke-box.

The 4-4-0s of classes 11B, 11C and 11D became L&NER property in 1923. That concern classified them as D9 and they continued to give excellent service until the last one, BR No. 62305, formerly GCR 1018, was withdrawn from traffic.

Plate 7.6   GCR Class 11D, No. 1038
No. 1038 has been rebuilt to Class 11D in this picture, which was taken during February 1923 at Leicester shed, probably by Henry Salmon. The livery remains green and crimson but, note that a coat-of-arms has not been applied to the tender which has received the smaller transfers of the company's name.

L.G.R.P. 16271

CHAPTER 8
CLASS 8A 0-8-0

The 9J 0-6-0s proved to be very satisfactory in traffic but there remained a requirement for a larger locomotive to haul heavy coal trains. Robinson's solution to the problem was to design a massive 8-coupled tender engine, the like of which had not been seen before by GCR men. The 8As took the nickname of 'Tinies', as they were the largest engines at that time to be built for the company. The first examples appeared in the autumn of 1902, but over the following eight years a total of eighty-nine entered service.

The majority of the class was built by two contractors, but Gorton also contributed by making large numbers. They were built as follows:

- Neilson, Reid & Company supplied Nos 1052–1054 in November 1902.
- Kitson & Company made three batches. Nos 56–59, 64, 65, 67, 68, 70, 71, 85–87, 91, 92, 135–140 and 142–153 were built between September 1903 and May 1904. Engines Nos 1073–1077 were completed during July and August 1905. Their final batch, Nos 1132–1144, was delivered in the spring of 1907.
- Gorton works was responsible for the following built in 1909: Nos 39, 44, 48, 49, 62, 63, 212, 213, 356 and 159–164. Nos 401, 956–965 and 1174–1182 left the works between June 1910 and February 1911.

GREY LIVERY

Some photographs exist of engines painted in the special photographic grey style. The first example, No. 1052, was recorded as such, lined out in white and grey. The wheels are lined and the coat-of-arms is carried on the tender, over the central axle box. The *G.C.R.J.*, vol. XI, no. 12, published a view of No. 57 painted in a similar scheme but without a coat-of-arms, and this probably dates from April 1914. A photograph of No. 1134 in *Great Central Album* is entirely different; engine and tender are plain grey, relieved only by the number plate, the company's name and some black areas. Finally, a picture of No. 1136 will be found in *Per Rail*, which was a GCR publication and included comprehensive details of the company's goods services. No. 1136 is lined, but the numerals on the number plate and the 'Great Central' lettering are very dark in tone, either black or dark grey. This view may have been enhanced or altered for publication purposes. At times of a temporary shortage of motive power it is possible that an engine may have worked trains whilst in grey, but evidence to support this notion is unknown.

BLACK LIVERY

As they were built to work heavy goods and coal trains they were painted in the lined black livery style when new, and there are several references to this. The *G.C.R.J.* published three references in volumes IV and V, but that which appeared on page 209 of volume V is the most helpful. Under the title 'New Engines', it was mentioned that: '*Nos. 159, 160, and 161, new 8-w.c. mineral engines are now in traffic painted the standard black with red and white lining and Nos. 162, 163, and 164 are now being painted*'.

A painting specification for the 8As has not be found. It is possible that, as Neilson, Reid had been building the 9J 0-6-0s, they were asked to finish the 0-8-0s in the same livery. The 9J painting

Plate 8.1   GCR Class 8A, No. 1074
No. 1074, probably photographed on Gorton shed c. 1906. The locomotive looks in very good condition, clean and well maintained. Note the early 6 inches tall buffer beam numerals, which are probably shaded black, and a coat-of-arms on the tender side.   *Real Photographs 65226*

Plate 8.2   GCR Class 8A, No. 957
This is a late-built example, No. 957, which on the date of the photograph, 14th July 1911, had been in service for less than a year. The black livery is more or less as applied to No. 1074 but one obvious change is the lack of a coat-of-arms. Notice also the use of the smaller buffer beam numbers and the absence of splasher beading. This engine is fitted with a single splasher in the place of two separate ones. It is taking a Down mineral empties through Nottingham Victoria station.

R.K. Blencowe collection, F.H. Gillford

Plate 8.3   GCR Class 8A, No. 212
An almost unidentifiable 8A, No. 212, is passing Charwelton Signal Box about 1920, with an Up goods train. It is running under what years earlier had been Class A express goods lights, but head codes seem to change. The rather shabby state of the engine is fairly typical of that time. Iron bridge No. 489 straddles all tracks and a Down goods recedes into the distance towards Catesby Tunnel.   *L.G.R.P. 16178*

instructions, therefore, may be studied in place of any other, as it is unlikely that there were many differences.

There are few photographs of the 8As which show lining details well. An early picture of No. 1074 indicates that the same decorations that were applied to the 9Js, though reduced in certain areas, were also employed on the 0-8-0s. The notes for the earlier class should, therefore, be consulted. The lining consisted of the following: the double red/white stripes, single red/white lines or the double white lines with an outer red band and all these have already been described. The buffer beam was lined, but not along the upper edge. Parts that appear not to have been decorated were the spectacle plate, dome, driving wheels, tops of splashers and the frames which support the smoke-box. The tender was finished as those fitted to the 9J locomotives, but it is uncertain if the mainframes or the curved flares carried lining.

Another early view of No. 91 is in accordance with the main details of No. 1074, but there are a few differences. The buffer beam is lined all around, the driving wheels have received a red/white stripe around each crank and the spectacle plate is similarly lined. The tender flare is also lined in this style but it is not possible to be sure if the mainframes had a red line applied.

The usual polished parts are all evident in both photographs. They also show that the standard size coat-of-arms was employed but only on the tender side and not on the splasher. On No. 1074, it was placed in the centre of the side and not over the central axle box. The 6 inches tall version of the company's name was used and, also, the larger buffer beam numbers. These were shaded with black on No. 1074 and, possibly, on No. 91. The former does not appear to have a white line around the inset edge of the number plate, but one is certainly to be seen on No. 91. The first three examples of Class 8A, Nos 1052–1054, probably had a vermilion ground to their number plates when they were new.

Another photograph, this one of No. 957, is also helpful. The engine is lined in much the same manner as has already been described but,

generally, it is a little simpler. The buffer beam is unlined along the top and 4½ inches tall numerals have been applied thereon. The driving wheels and number plates are unlined; the tender does not carry the heraldic symbol, but 6 inches tall letters form the company's title. Throughout their pre-grouping service it is as likely as not that the cab interior was painted in the customary manner, that is, stone colour and a black border with a red separating line.

Although these photographs are indicative of a slightly mixed record of how the 8As were painted, all of them show that these engines appear to have been kept in an excellent state of cleanliness and that, when they were new, all of them were probably lined in red and white. This situation was to change completely, however, during the First World War.

Rather more 8As were recorded photographically between c. 1918 and the end of the GCR as an independent concern. Many of them are of examples with little or no lining and the locomotives in rather poor external state. *The Railway and Travel Monthly* for August 1916, p. 136, included some relevant comments regarding the wartime period: *'Understood that war duration colour of goods engines will be black, no lining, "Great Central" on tender, no. 198 (a 9J 0-6-0) has so appeared'*. On page 84 of the issue is a good illustration of No. 1134, which although quite clean, exemplified the journal's comments perfectly. That there are no less than seven women cleaners present is an indication of the problems that were experienced by the locomotive departments of every railway at that time – gone were the days when male staff could easily be found.

These locomotives became Class Q4 in 1923. Their service with the L&NER continued much as before and mainly on heavy goods and coal trains. An interesting development occurred when the decision was made to rebuild them as 0-8-0 tank engines, but only thirteen were converted. Although thirty-four of the tender types survived to work for BR, the class was made extinct in late 1951 when No. 63243 was removed from traffic. This example was originally GCR No. 1180, one of the last engines to be built.

Plate 9.1   GCR Class 8, No. 1067
'Fish engine' No. 1067, the first of the class, is standing on no. 5 road at Neasden shed, c. 1903. The engine is in original condition, with the coat-of-arms placed over the central axle box of the tender, and the slightly narrower type of chimney. Note the polished components; the handrails, beadings, reversing rod, etc. The black lined livery suited these very attractive engines.
L.G.R.P. 8053

Plate 9.2   GCR Class 8, No. 1069
No. 1069 is waiting in Neasden sidings with a Class A express goods train. The engine is new and has the 6 inches tall characters on the buffer beam (*detail, right*) which are probably black-shaded, but are not highlighted with white. These locomotives earned a lot of money for the GCR, being highly successful in their haulage of the all-important fish traffic out of Grimsby docks.
J. Quick collection

CHAPTER 9
CLASS 8 4-6-0

The Class 8 4-6-0 was the first of that wheel arrangement to work on the GCR. They were handsome, superbly proportioned locomotives, which were always in demand to haul the company's fast perishable goods trains, or, at times, heavy excursion traffic. The carriage of fish out of Grimsby docks was a very important element of GCR income and it was the working of these trains that earned the class its nickname of 'Fish engines'. On page 62 of David Jackson's excellent biography of Robinson, *A Lifetime's Work*, is a publicity view of No. 1072 with a train of new 15-ton bogie fish vans. Robinson could have claimed this train to have been the most up-to-date fast goods train in the country and that the company's locomotive stock was beginning to look like one from the twentieth century.

Two batches of engines were built as follows:

– Neilson, Reid & Company supplied Nos 1067–1072 during the last two weeks of 1902.
– Beyer, Peacock & Company made Nos 180–187 in early 1904.

GREY LIVERY

The *Model Railway News* of January 1964 published drawings, some livery notes and a fine photograph of No. 1067. The engine is painted grey and is fully lined with a coat-of-arms on the driving splasher. The lining is white with various shades of grey and black. The picture was taken when No. 1067 was new, but the chimney appears to be of a different type from others fitted during the early period of the engines' service. The first of the second batch, No. 180, was also photographed in grey but this one is very different as the locomotive wheels are finished dark grey. Finally, No. 186 was

recorded painted in this special livery. This view and that of No. 180 appear to show the subjects in new condition.

GREEN LIVERY?

Before we discuss the black livery of these engines it is necessary to examine the evidence for them being painted green. The livery notes which appeared in the *Model Railway News* contained a suggestion that they may have been green. In the March issue a Mr Taylor responded to the article. Mr Taylor, senior, was a GCR driver and he was *'quite certain that these engines were never green – when they came out new they were painted black and nicely lined out in red and white'*. Mr Taylor also stated that they were known to the GCR men as *'Kangaroos'!* No. 1067 also featured on a postcard which was published in the Wrench Series and this clearly shows a green engine. Another green 4-6-0 is the subject of a coloured card published by the Locomotive Publishing Co.; it shows the locomotive on a Down express passing Rickmansworth goods shed. These cards are based on photographs and close study of the original of the L.P.C. copy indicates that the locomotive is a Class 8, No. 1069. The illustrations are, presumably, hand tinted, and are further examples of artists' licence to which reference was made in chapter 2.

BLACK LIVERY

The service livery applied to the Class 8 engines was always black. The class was the first truly mixed traffic type on the GCR and received the fully lined painting scheme. A paint specification for the first batch is not available but it is possible that Neilson, Reid were asked to work with the 9J instructions of only a few months

Plate 9.3   GCR Class 8, No. 181
No. 181, a Beyer, Peacock locomotive, is not quite in original condition in this view at Leicester Central, on 13th May 1910. Apart from the tender upper coal plate and a scorched smoke box door, a small coat-of-arms has been added to the driving wheel splasher, around which is modified red/white lining.   *W. Bradshaw*

Painting

Boiler to receive 2 coats of Oxide of Iron before being lagged, One whilst hot.

Clothing plates 2 coats Lead colour inside.

Splashers, Cab, Clothing, Wheels, Outside frames, Sandboxes, Footsteps, and *Buffers* to receive 2 coats Lead colour, filled up with White lead mixed with Gold size, then coat of staining (vegetable black, turpentine, & Gold size,) rubbed down, followed by another dark lead colour, sand papered, after which, one coat ivory black paint, then coat of ivory black and varnish mixed. Lining to be done same as sample panels, afterwards to receive one coat under varnish, & 2 coats of best finishing body varnish. To be flatted down with pumice powder & horse hair between each coat.

To be numbered on Buffer beam, to sample, after first coat of varnish. Company's coat of arms, transfers of which will be supplied, to be placed on each driving splasher.

A Brass number plate fixed on trailing splashers [trailing splashers is crossed out and replaced with cab side] to be painted Black between numbers and with ⅛" white line ½" within raised edge.

Inside of Mainframes, Frame stay, and *Slide bar brackets* to have 2 coats Lead colour, filled up with white lead mixed with Gold size, rubbed down, One coat Flesh colour, sand papered, One coat of quick drying vermillion [sic], then 2 coats vermillion mixed with varnish.

Outside of Mainframes, Bogie, and *Guard bars* to receive 2 coats of Lead colour, filled up, rubbed down, one coat ivory black, and one coat ivory black mixed with varnish, and one coat hard drying body varnish.

Bodies of Axles to receive one coat white lead and one coat varnish.

Ends of Axles to be lined, otherwise same as wheels, and varnished.

Smokebox, back of Firebox, Platforms, Brake hangers, &c.:-
One coat Black and One coat Japan.

Chimney to have 2 coats Lead colour, filled up with White lead mixed with Gold size, rubbed down, and one coat black, and one coat Japan.

Inside Cab. One coat lead colour, filled up, rubbed down, sand papered, 2 coats Stone colour (to sample), One coat under varnish, and one coat finishing body varnish. To be lined to sample panel.

Two days to intervene between each of the last 3 coats of varnish.

Buffer beams same as Inside frames, with the addition of being lined to sample panel, and varnished same as clothing.

Brake pipes to have 2 coats of approved rubber varnish.

The Paint and Varnish to be obtained from Messrs Docker *Bros.* or approved makers.

Sample Panels will be provided, and the greatest care must be taken that all the Engines are painted strictly in accordance therewith, and of the same shades throughout.

---

earlier. The document issued by Gorton to Beyer, Peacock & Co. in respect of painting requirements was handwritten and is reproduced in full. The original is deposited in the records of the Museum of Science and Industry in Manchester and the author acknowledges the assistance of the museum's staff in providing access to it.

It should be noted that there are no instructions for painting the tender. That section may have been lost, or it may not have been included, but it is also possible that the tenders were painted at Gorton. Beyer, Peacock's works and Gorton lay opposite each other across the main lines and the two did cooperate when it was considered necessary.

The document also specified that certain parts of the engine were to be bright, polished metal. These were the wheel tyres, smoke-box centre washer, ring, handle, wheel, hinges and bracket, draw hooks, shackles and buffer heads. Other components were all brass beadings, raised surfaces on number and maker's plates, lubricator cups, all handrails, whistles, safety valves, cylinder front, reversing rod etc.

Other notes of interest required one engine to be weighed and one engine and tender to be photographed. Robinson asked for four locomotives to be steamed during December 1903 and the other four in the following month but in the event the steaming conditions were not met.

The liveries that were applied to the two batches when new were not quite identical, as early photographs indicate. The tyres on driving and bogie wheels of the Neilson, Reid engines were painted black. The lining, which probably consisted of a single stripe of white and red, was added around the cranks and about halfway between the axle end and the bosses of the bogie wheels, with the

red always being on the outside. The red-insensitive nature of the film has, however, not helped to record that colour. On the Beyer, Peacock examples the wheels appear not to have received any decoration but all the tyres are polished. Another distinction was that the splasher tops of the first batch were unlined but were lined on the second group. Finally, the frames that supported the smoke-box received one red line on Nos 1067–1072 but it appears that the Beyer, Peacock engines were unlined on these parts.

Chapter 4 furnishes further lining details on these locomotives. The boiler and firebox carried the double red/white lines, but only one was added at the point where the boiler and smoke-box met. Similar lines were painted on the base of the dome. The cab, tender sides and end all received the double white lines which had a red band on the outside of the outer white line. The spectacle plate, valance frames and step plates on engine and tender, splasher sides and, on the Beyer, Peacock engines, the tops, buffer guides, curved flares on tender and the cylinders were all finished with the single red/white stripe. The buffer beams were edged with black and lined all around with white. The cab interior also had a black border but with a red line alongside it. The locomotive's mainframes were probably plain black, but some of the early ones had polished guard irons. Tender mainframes had a red line applied around the cut-outs, axle boxes etc. Later, when upper coal plates were added to tenders, they also had one red line painted just inside the beading.

As time passed the lining style changed a little. The splasher tops of engines Nos 1067–1072 were lined to match the others. The lines on the dome began to be applied half on the base and half on the boiler around it but the lining on the wheels was beginning to be

Plate 9.4 GCR Class 8, No. 186
This engine is standing at the Manchester end of platform 4 at Guide Bridge station, c. 1920. The tender has a coal plate which probably has a fine red line just inside the beading. A large coat-of-arms has been applied but the lettering is of the 4½ inches tall variety. The engine appears to have had the original MS&LR tapered buffers exchanged for the parallel type. A small coat-of-arms, surrounded by an incomplete circle of red/white lines, adorns the driving splasher (*above*). The double lines around the dome can also be seen (*left*).   *J. Quick collection*

omitted and it was not being painted along the upper edge of the buffer beams. Beyer, Peacock engine No. 181 was photographed by William Bradshaw on 13th May 1910; this view shows modified lining on the centre splasher, which now formed a complete stripe around a small coat-of-arms.

The usual 6 inches tall letters of 'Great Central' always appear to have been used, with a standard size of coat-of-arms on the tender. This was placed over the central axle box of tenders on engines Nos 1067–1072 when they were new. The smaller device adorned splasher sides later, but a view of No. 187, which was probably taken late in the locomotive's GCR service, shows the tender without one. Originally all engines appear to have carried the 6 inches tall buffer beam characters, which were shaded black, but in time they were replaced by the small version and these were shaded with blue. The cab side numerals were usually surrounded by a white line but the monogram was not used and a picture of a 'Fish engine' bearing a distinctive symbol has not been found. At the end of its GCR career, No. 1071 was carrying a number plate upon which was painted the power classification of '3'.

The Class 8 locomotives became Class B5 on the L&NER and worked out their last days on mundane duties. During the first year or so of British Railways, some of them were banking heavy trains in the South Yorkshire region but they had served the GCR and the L&NER well. Photographs of them taken whilst in GCR ownership show them to have been kept in first rate condition. This is only to be expected as, apart from their work on fast, perishable goods traffic, they were particularly useful machines on the numerous heavy passenger excursions that were operated by the company.

Plate 10.1   GCR Class 9K, No. 178
No. 178 is on Barnsley shed in this view taken between 1912 and grouping, when the locomotive was allocated to Mexborough. Despite the number of staff, the lining and livery is particularly clear.
R. Silverwood collection

CHAPTER 10
CLASSES 9K AND 9L 4-4-2TS

Brian Wainwright

Whilst in Ireland Robinson ordered a small batch of 4-4-2 tank locomotives for passenger traffic. His first GCR passenger tank design with the same wheel arrangement was larger but, otherwise, was very similar to the Limerick locomotives. The 9Ks first appeared in 1903 when suburban passenger receipts were increasing.

The twelve engines that comprised Class 9L and built by Beyer, Peacock & Company were a development of the 9K. They had wider tanks, bunker and running platform. The modified bunker arrangement, which had coal guard rails was, according to the *G.C.R.J.*, designed to prevent coal being stacked too high and, therefore, blocking the crew's forward view when running bunker first.

The 9K locomotives were built as follows:

– Vulcan Foundry Ltd built Nos 1055–1066 in the spring of 1903.
– Gorton works made Nos 171, 178, 179, 188, 190, 191, 193 and 199 between May and September of 1903. Production at Gorton resumed in 1904 when Nos 2, 9, 18, 20, 27, 28, 29, 47, 50 and 55 appeared between August and Christmas of that year. Gorton completed the class in early 1905 when Nos 114, 115, 310, 357, 359 and 453–457 entered traffic.

The 9L contract was placed with Beyer, Peacock & Company and they built Nos 1120–1131 during May and June of 1907.

The first 9Ks worked in the London area but some were soon based at a range of sheds, including Wrexham, from as early as 1905. The *G.C.R.J.* for November 1908 mentions them working from Chester, Bidston, Sheffield, Nottingham, Staveley and Leicester and goes on to state that they were frequently called upon to work express trains. The 9Ls at this time were all at Neasden, but were transferred to other sheds from 1912 when the 9N 4-6-2Ts became available to work the new, heavier London suburban trains. By 1922 most of the 9Ls were in the Nottinghamshire area, apart from one engine each at Woodford and Neasden and two at Stockport; the 9Ks were all in the north on the Cheshire Lines and former MS&LR systems.

GREY LIVERY: CLASS 9K

The prototype locomotive, No. 1055, was painted and photographed carrying that livery. The November 1903 issue of *Locomotives and Railways* published the picture in the article concerning these engines on pages 51 and 52. No. 188 was also recorded in grey paint but it was an unrelieved grey – only the number plate breaking the uniform finish. The only other example that has been noted so finished was No. 1060; this one is painted in a style very similar to that used on No. 1055.

GREY LIVERY: CLASS 9L

Two photographs of 9L engines in grey are known. *The Railway and Travel Monthly* of November 1915, p. 319, included a picture of No. 1129. *Great Central Steam*, plate 35, shows No. 1131 in a very light shade of grey, which is lined out in the usual manner.

Plate 10.2   GCR Class 9K, No. 47
This is a fairly early photograph of No. 47 which is standing at South Harrow's Up platform in about 1907 and is coupled to a clerestory brake vehicle. The locomotive is a little work-stained and note the small letters of 'Great Central'.
Real Photographs 65271

BLACK LIVERY?

According to the contemporary journal, *Locomotives and Railways*, in the issue to which reference has already been made, at least one 9K appeared in a variation of the lined black livery. Some technical data was given but the relevant notes on page 52 state *'the painting is black with red lines, a serviceable and economical colour'*. An illustration of the first engine, No. 1055, is included but this is painted grey. A photograph of a black 9K in the GCR period has not been located but it is possible that one was so finished. Perhaps some error had been made on the part of the magazine because the January 1903 specification, which follows, makes it quite clear that the class was to receive green livery.

GREEN LIVERY: CLASS 9K

This specification, reproduced below, is part of a booklet issued by the company and printed by Henry Blacklock of Manchester.

GREEN LIVERY: CLASS 9L

The painting specification for the later, Class 9L locomotives, is dated 18th September 1906 and may be consulted in the first issue of *Great Central Link*, April 1994. It is, however, more or less the same as that used to finish Class 9K engines.

The customary practice of leaving various parts of locomotives as polished metal was continued. *'Smoke-box, Door Centre Washer, Ring and Handle, Wheel, Hinges, and Brackets to be finished bright and polished'*. Safety valves were *'Pillars of Polished Brass'* and coupling rods were *'forged without weld and finished bright'*. Buffers had turned heads and hand rails were *'Of polished steel tubing … attached … by polished Wrought-iron Pillars'*. Raised sections of number and maker's plates were polished. Two final points of interest were that the maker must supply twelve large mounted platinotype photographs of the engines, in addition to three enlarged platinotype prints, not less than 29½ inches by 19 inches.

It is convenient at this point to study both classes' livery as one.

PAINTING

Tank, Cab, Clothing, and Wheels to receive two coats lead colour, filled up with white lead mixed with gold size, rubbed down, followed up with two other coats lead colour, sand-papered, after which two coats Brunswick Green in oil.

Outside Frames, Main Frame above platform near Smoke-box, Sand-boxes, Buffers, and Footstep Plates, same as Tank, &c., except two coats crimson lake in oil instead of green.

Outside Frames, Wheels, Sand-boxes, Buffers, Footstep Plates, Tank, Cab, and Clothing to receive one coat under varnish, picked out with black and lined with white, afterwards to receive one more coat under varnish, and two coats best finishing body varnish. To be flatted down with pumice stone and horse hair between each coat.

Company's name with letters in gold leaf to be placed on each side of Tank, to sample.

Numbers, in gold leaf, to be placed on Buffer Beam and back of Tank after first coat of varnish.

Company's Coat of Arms (Transfers of which will be supplied) to be placed on sides of Tank.

A Brass Number-plate to be fixed on each side of Coal Bunker, to be painted vermillion [sic] between the numbers.

Inside of Main Frames, Frame Stay, and Slide-bar Bracket to have two coats lead colour, filled up with white lead mixed with gold size, rubbed down, one coat flesh colour, sand-papered, two coats vermillion, and three coats hard-drying body varnish.

Outside of Main Frames, Bogie, and Guard Bars to receive two coats lead colour, filled up, rubbed down, one coat ivory black, and then one coat ivory black mixed with varnish, and one coat hard-drying body varnish.

Inside Tanks and Coal space to have two coats red lead, finished with black.

Webs of Crank Axle and Body of Straight Axles, one coat white lead and one coat varnish.

Ends of Axles black, lined with white, and varnished.

Smoke-box, Bogie, back of Fire-box, Platform, and Brake-hangers, &c., one coat black and one coat japan.

Chimney to have two coats lead colour, filled up with white lead, mixed with gold size, rubbed down, then one coat black and one japan.

Inside Cab, one coat lead colour, filled up, rubbed down, sand-papered, two coats stone colour (to sample), one coat under varnish, and one coat finishing body varnish. To be lined as per sample panel.

Two days to intervene between each of the last three coats of varnish.

Buffer Beams same as Inside Frames, with the addition of being lined to sample panel, and finished same as clothing.

Brake Pipes to have two coats of approved rubber varnish.

The Paint and Varnish to be obtained from Messrs. Docker Bros., or approved makers.

Sample Panels will be provided, and the greatest care must be taken that all the Engines are painted strictly in accordance therewith, and of the same shades throughout.

JOHN G. ROBINSON

Chief Mechanical Engineer.

GORTON,
January, 1903.

Plate 10.3   GCR Class 9K, No. 29
No. 29 is standing at the north end of the Down platform at Leicester Central looking a little scruffy but the lines of an attractive locomotive remain. Note that the tank side has been cleaned to reveal the company's name, but a passenger engine in this state at this period is unusual. No. 29 was allocated to Annesley at the time of the photograph, 7.5 pm, 6th July 1910.   *W. Bradshaw*

This painting scheme could be described as one applied to secondary passenger engines. It is important to remember that because the 9L locomotives had wider tanks and bunkers, the lining was added to those parts in separate panels. Apart from this the linings were identical.

The boiler and firebox were lined with the white/black/white stripes. At the point where the boiler and smoke-box met only one white line was applied. When 9L engine No. 1120 was new, however, the double white and black was added around that part. The remaining examples of Class 9L may have also received this additional line before being repainted later to conform with the 9Ks. On both classes the front spectacle plate was edged with black and this had a white line against it. The rear spectacle plate on the 9Ks was plain, which strongly suggests that it was black, but this was not the case with the 9L engines. They had green rear plates and these had a black border with the usual white line. Both classes had a black edge around the tank sides and fronts, bunker sides and rear. Separating the edge from the green was one white line, then the white, black and white bands were applied inside a narrow green panel. It has been mentioned that the decoration on the cab and bunker sides differed on these classes. The black border was painted around, then a white line, but this had to be added in separate panels on the 9Ls. The bunker rear of those locomotives was of a totally different shape and this meant that all the linings followed the outline. It is probable that the tank tops on both classes were black but pictures showing this are unknown. If this was the case there may have been a white line separating the black and green. The bases of domes on both classes were lined with the double white and black centre bands.

The framing under the smoke-box, valance frames below the footplate and step plates, equalising pipes and buffer guides were painted crimson, with a black border and a white line. It is this feature which may be used to describe the livery as 'secondary passenger', as normally an express locomotive would have received a red line on these parts. Buffer beams also had a black edge and a white line, but later views indicate that the top of the beam was left plain. There are few pictures of 9Ls to help with this matter. On the front beam on both classes the running number was applied in the usual style: 'No. – draw hook – xxx'. Previous MS&LR practice was continued with regard to the numbering at the rear. The beam was lined as normal, but the running number was placed centrally on the bunker rear, about halfway up the panel.

Lining on the wheels of a 9K engine was usually as instructed and sometimes this included around the tyres which were painted black. When new, the first 9L, No. 1120, had polished wheel tyres but generally wheels on both classes were similarly lined. This consisted of a white line around the axle end or wheel tyre. Mainframes on all engines appear to have been unlined but, later, guard irons on some 9Ks may have been crimson and lined with red or vermilion. Photographs are not available of 9L locomotives which show this feature but when new No. 1120 had brightly polished guard irons.

The standard size of coat-of-arms appears to have been applied to engines of both classes, but the slightly smaller type was employed on certain members of Class 9K. There are not many pictures of the other class to study and this means it is impossible to reach a conclusion on this matter. Some of the 9Ks received the 4½ inches tall letters of 'Great Central' from new and this may also apply to the later class. The characters on buffer beams were probably 6 inches tall when the engines were new but the smaller variety was in use later. The single white line around the numerals on the cab side plate appear to have been added to both classes at some period. The painting on all engines seems to have changed very little but one alteration is worthy of note. A rear view of No. 1061 shows the running number in the centre of the bunker, but the abbreviated form of number, 'No.', has been omitted.

In the years immediately before the First World War, W. Bradshaw photographed the 9Ks that worked in the Leicester area. It is a little surprising to note a picture of No. 29 in a shabby state, as generally passenger locomotives were kept in good condition. These classes gave sterling service to the L&NER and later BR. Indeed, when replacements were necessary, both classes of locomotive, by this time C13 and C14, were still the crew's first preference.

ABOVE: Plate 10.4   GCR Class 9L, No. 1120
The photographer was in attendance for the first visit to Neasden shed of a new 9L 4-4-2T. The occasion was 1st June 1907 and at least three pictures were taken of this, the prototype engine, No. 1120. These locomotives and the very similar 9Ks were always painted in what is best described as a secondary passenger livery. Notice the white lining around the smoke-box framing, the valances, steps and the equaliser pipes, which were all painted crimson. On a tender express engine this lining would normally be red. The MR signal box at Neasden Junction is on the left.
Locomotive Publishing Co.

ABOVE: Plate 10.5   GCR Class 9L, No. 1127
A very similar photograph of No. 1127, also at Neasden. The livery is nearly the same as on No. 1120, but the wheel tyres are black and smaller letters form the company's name. This picture is not easy to date, but it was certainly recorded after 1912.   *L.G.R.P. 8219*

Plate 10.6   GCR Class 9L, No. 1121
This view has been selected as it shows the decoration on the bunker rear. The characters on the tank side and on the bunker are all of the 4½ inches tall variety. Unfortunately, the white lining on the spectacle plate is not clear but this does show on other photographs. The train is an Up stopping passenger on the GW/GC Joint line, near Ruislip and Ickenham. It is composed of three 50-foot London suburban vehicles and an 8-compartment clerestory Third.   *Real Photographs T7966*

CHAPTER 11
CLASSES 8B, 8D, 8E AND 8J 4-4-2S

Ken Grainger

Class 8B, the L&NER's Class C4, ultimately totalled twenty-seven locomotives and was introduced in four batches. Nos 192 and 194 were delivered by Beyer, Peacock & Company in December 1903 and were built for comparison with the two, otherwise similar, 8C 4-6-0s, Nos 195 and 196.

There was a requirement to determine which type was the more suitable for the traffic department's express passenger work so comparative trials were undertaken. Held in early 1904, these showed that there was little to choose between either the 4 or 6-coupled designs. Indeed, both classes recorded excellent performances. Nevertheless, further examples of the 4-4-2s were ordered, whereas Class 8C was not multiplied.

Beyer, Peacock & Co. supplied five more 8Bs, Nos 263–267, in July 1904. A deeper firebox was provided and the boiler tubing was fine-tuned, but they were outwardly similar to their prototypes. Their tenders, like those of Nos 192 and 194, had coal rails, but those of subsequent engines had coal guard plating to the same profile. There is, however, ample photographic evidence of tenders being readily exchanged between locomotives.

The third batch of twelve, Nos 1083–1094, was built by the North British Locomotive Company, half being delivered in each of October and November 1905.

The remaining eight were unhurriedly produced during 1906 by Gorton, as follows: No. 260 in February, No. 261 in March, No. 262 in April, No. 358 in May, Nos 360 and 362 in June, No. 361 in July and No. 363 in August.

Classes 8D and 8E each comprised two three-cylinder compounds. Their detail variations were insufficient for the L&NER to differentiate between them, even by 'part' numbers, and all became Class C5. They were built at Gorton as follows: No. 258 in December 1905, No. 259 in February 1906, and Nos 364 and 365 in December 1906.

When new they were nameless but by June 1909 all had received names. No. 258 became *The Rt. Hon. Viscount Cross G.C.B. G.C.S.I.* in June 1909, No. 259 was named *King Edward VII* in November 1906, No. 364 became *Lady Henderson* in March 1907 and in October of that year No. 365 was named *Sir William Pollitt*. The name on No. 364 was changed to *Lady Faringdon* in 1917 when Lady Henderson's husband, the GCR chairman, was elevated to the peerage.

The solitary member of Class 8J was a rebuild of 8B No. 1090, as a three-cylinder simple with Walschaert's valve gear. She ran thus until, on the eve of grouping, reverting to a Class 8B in September 1922. The 8J configuration required removal of the running plate footsteps between the coupled wheels, which were replaced at the front end, immediately behind the buffer beam. On reversion to an 8B, the substitute front end footsteps were removed, but No. 1090 retained her individuality by never regaining the mid-length footsteps.

The 'Atlantics' were always, and universally, known as the 'Jersey Lilies'. This has been generally accepted as a tribute to their undoubted beauty, likening them to the celebrated Edwardian beauty and music-hall star Lillie Langtry. In later years O.S. Nock quite emphatically refuted this origin, insisting the nickname arose rather from the locomotives' then unprecedented size and that the 'Jersey Lily' after whom they were known was the sarcastic euphemism for an excessively fat woman landlord at a public house local to Gorton. As something of a romantic, the author prefers the former explanation!

GREY LIVERY

The first two 8Bs, Nos 192 and 194, were delivered to the GCR painted grey, being finished in full green livery by Gorton when

Plate 11.1   GCR Class 8B, No. 192
The engine has been in service for six months in this view of No. 192 at Neasden on 4th June 1904. Notice polished wheel tyres, polished brass covers to the rear axle box and dampers and white-lined splasher sides. The photographer may have been Harold Hopwood.   *LCGB Ken Nunn Collection, H1127*

everything proved to be satisfactory. No. 192 was photographed at least twice whilst in grey. A broad, left hand side view is available in the Pouteau list as G.C.-33. Another picture, probably taken on the same occasion, was published in *The Railway Magazine*, vol. XIV, p. 61. No. 266 was also recorded in the livery when new, probably at Beyer, Peacock's works. No. 1083 was illustrated in grey in the *G.C.R.J.*, vol. I, p. 262, of May 1906.

Another example which received the photographer's attention several times was No. 361. It was superheated in March 1912 and an excellent view was taken by the official photographer at Gorton. The Leicester photographer, William Bradshaw, photographed the engine at Abbey Lane on 25th May 1912. The engine is in grey and the view is on page 16 of *William Bradshaw: Leicester Railway Cameraman*, by John Hurst and Mike Kinder. *The Railway and Travel Monthly* for March 1914, p. 211, included a picture of a grey No. 361 working a Marylebone–Sheffield train.

Some of the compound 'Jersey Lilies' were also noted and photographed carrying grey paint and Nos 258 and 259 are known to have worked trains so finished. The former locomotive hauled a train to London Marylebone for an official inspection by the board, which was reported by the *G.C.R.J.* (vol. I, p. 162, January 1906) with the comment '*it is at present painted lead colour*'. Indeed, the pair spent several weeks, when new, working various classes of train. The same journal (vol. 2, p. 19, July 1906) noted that, although No. 259 remained in lead colour, No. 258 was now in full green passenger livery. No. 259 was photographed near Northwood, possibly by R. Welby King, painted grey and hauling the celebrated 3.25 pm Down express. This must have been taken around the summer of 1906 as the engine is not named. The finish of the locomotive appears to be very plain with little to relieve the grey. A copy of this will be found in *Locomotives Illustrated*, No. 145, p. 18, and is also in the Pouteau list as G.C.-99. No. 364 of Class 8E was also the subject of the photographer and this is particularly interesting, as it shows the

nameplate set on top of the splasher. The picture is a three-quarter right-hand view and may be studied on p. 98 of David Jackson's biography of Robinson, *A Lifetime's Work*.

The 8J convert was photographed on three occasions, at least, in grey livery. The *G.C.R.J.* included two different views in vol. IV, March 1909, p. 195, and in vol. V, July 1909, when another picture formed the frontispiece, which the official photographer has recorded in a right-hand view. The first *G.C.R.J.* reference also comments that No. 1090 worked its first passenger train on 2nd February 1909. This means that the engine ran in grey until sometime in late April or May, as the same issue of the journal on p. 269, states that the locomotive is '*now in the Paint Shop and is being painted the standard green and lake adopted for passenger engines on this line*'.

BLACK OR GREEN LIVERY?

As a general rule of thumb, the GCR policy was to finish locomotives intended exclusively for passenger traffic in the green livery; but any engine, however prestigious, which spent any proportion at all of its time working goods trains, wore the lined black scheme. Surprisingly then, the original specification issued to Beyer, Peacock & Co. for Nos 192 and 194 stipulated black paint, substantiating the idea that the GCR was, at that time, toying with the adoption of black for all of its locomotives. Notes made by Allan Brown from Beyer, Peacock's records indicate other breaks with convention. These changes included the positions of the builder's plates which were to be on the leading splashers, and the number plates on the driving-wheel splashers beneath the nameplates. Note that it was originally intended that No. 192 be named *King Edward VII* and No. 194 *Queen Alexandra*. None of the above had occurred, however, when, on 25th November 1903, the stipulations regarding black livery, builders and number plates were all crossed

Plate 11.2   GCR Class 8B, No. 194
No. 194, the second 'Jersey Lily', is waiting with an Up train at Woodford in this photograph. The green sides to the splashers are indicative of an early date of about 1905. Note that the lining on the tender rear matches that on the side, and the tender number plate which appears to be No. 192.   *J. Quick collection*

Plate 11.3 GCR Class 8B, No. 264
No. 264 is brand new and probably on trials in this photograph at Fairfield. Note green splasher sides and the 6 inches tall buffer beam characters which appear to be shaded with one shade of blue. The buffer bodies are decorated with a black edge and a white line. The use of white seems not to have lasted very long before it was replaced with red.

J.R. Morton collection

out. The builders and number plates were now to be positioned *'nr. smoke box and house side'* respectively and that the engines were to be painted green. 'House side' was the GCR term for cab side.

There were two basic varieties of the green livery, as applied to the 8Bs, which may be described as 'green splashers' and 'crimson splashers'. The first named was initially applied to the first two batches, Nos 192, 194 and 263–267. The crimson splasher scheme was introduced from new with the North British batch and the later Gorton engines, and the earlier locomotives were subsequently changed. The 8D and 8E compounds were finished in a variant of the crimson splasher livery.

GREEN SPLASHERS

Robinson's first express passenger locomotive, the 11B, had – in common with his predecessor's 4-4-0s – combined the cab side sheets and the rear splasher. It was on the 11Bs built by Vulcan Foundry and Sharp, Stewart that black edging to the cab and splasher circumference (inside the brass beading) with a thin white line became established. It is important to remember that this statement is only correct after the Sharp engines had lost their original paint scheme. The 8Bs continued the basic express passenger livery, viz.: Brunswick green for the wheels and above the footplate, with the exception of the black smoke-box, running plate and cab roof. The raised framing beneath the smoke-box, like the running plate valance, footsteps' backplate, cylinders and outside framing to

the trailing axle and tender, were crimson, separated from the black edging by vermilion lining.

CRIMSON LAKE SPLASHERS

The crimson lake splasher livery was introduced with the North British batch of October and November 1905. This has been questioned on the basis of a paint specification dated April 1905 continuing to stipulate green splashers. It has to be presumed that there must have been a change in the specification before delivery, as no photographic evidence has come to light of any North British-built 8B with green splashers. The *G.C.R.J.*, vol. I, No. 7 of January 1906, comments:

The last of the 12 locos of the standard simple Atlantic type has been delivered by the North British Locomotive Co. … There are one or two slight alterations from Engine 267, the splashers are painted red.

The livery change involved the splasher sides being painted crimson lake, with vermilion lining to the same pattern as had been the white lining on green splashers. The livery and lining was otherwise unchanged, including the splasher tops which remained green. Vermilion lining on crimson lake does not typically show up well on contemporary photographs but it can be picked out on the photograph of No. 262 in *Locomotives of the G.C.R*, vol. 1, p. 81, by Eddie Johnson.

PAINTING

Boiler to receive two coats of oxide of iron before being lagged, one whilst hot.

Clothing Plates, two coats of lead colour inside.

Splashers, Cab, Clothing, and Wheels to receive two coats of lead colour, filled up with white lead mixed with gold size, rubbed down, followed up with two other coats lead colour, sand-papered, after which two coats Brunswick green in oil.

Outside Frames, Main Frame above platform near Smoke-box, Sand-boxes, Buffers, and Footstep Plates same as Splashers, &c., except two coats crimson lake in oil instead of green.

Outside Frames, Wheels, Sand-boxes, Buffers, Footstep Plates, Splashers, Cab, and Clothing to receive one coat under varnish, picked out with black and lined afterwards to receive one more coat under varnish and two coats best finishing body varnish. To be flatted down with pumice stone and horse hair between each coat.

Numbers in gold leaf, shaded with blue, to be placed on Buffer Beam, after first coat of varnish.

Company's Coat of Arms (Transfers of which will be supplied) to be placed on each Leading and Driving Splasher.

A brass Number-plate, fixed on Cab Sides, to be painted black between numbers, and with one-eighth white line, half-inch within the raised edge.

Inside of Main Frames, Frame Stay, and Slide-bar Brackets to have two coats lead colour, filled up with white lead mixed with gold size, rubbed down, one coat flesh colour, sand-papered, two coats of vermilion, and three coats hard-drying body varnish.

Outside of Main Frames, Bogie, and Guard Bars to receive two coats lead colour, filled up, rubbed down, one coat of ivory black, and one coat ivory black mixed with varnish, and one coat hard-drying body varnish.

Bodies of Straight Axles to receive one coat white lead and one coat varnish.

Ends of Axles black, lined with white, and varnished.

Smoke-box, Bogie, back of Fire-box, Platforms, Brake Hangers, etc., one coat black and one coat Japan.

Chimney to have two coats lead colour, filled up with white lead, mixed with gold size, rubbed down, and one coat black and one Japan.

Inside Cab, one coat lead colour, filled up, rubbed down, sand-papered, two coats stone colour (to sample), one coat under varnish, and one coat finishing body varnish. To be lined as per sample panel.

Two days to intervene between each of the last three coats of varnish.

Buffer Beams same as Inside Frames, with the addition of being lined to sample panel, and finished same as Clothing.

Brake Pipes to have two coats of approved rubber varnish.

The Paint and Varnish to be obtained from Messrs. Docker Brothers or approved makers.

Sample Panels will be provided, and the greatest care must be taken that all the Engines are painted strictly in accordance therewith, and of the same shades throughout.

Plate 11.4   GCR Class 8B, No. 265
When Sam Fay became general manager GCR locomotives and trains ran far and wide. No. 265 was photographed on Plymouth Laira GWR shed after working an excursion which originated from Manchester, the locomotive taking the train forward from Leicester. Passengers were offered five, eight, ten or fifteen days in the west for £1 7s 0d, returning by ordinary trains. The engine is in as-built condition but of much greater interest is the tender – the livery of which does not match that of the locomotive. The tender may be from an 11B 4-4-0 and appears to have yellow lines alongside black borders, with brown valances and frames. The photograph is dated Good Friday 21st April 1905.
J. Quick collection

PAINTING

Tank Sides, End and Protector Plate to receive two coats lead colour, filled up with white lead mixed with gold size, rubbed down, followed by two other coats lead colour, sand-papered, after which two coats Brunswick green in oil. Transfers of Coat of Arms to be fixed, which will be supplied, and lining to be done same as sample panels, afterwards to receive one coat under varnish and two coats best finishing body varnish. Main Frames, Outside Frames, Axle-box lids, Foot-steps, and Buffers to receive two coats lead colour, filled up with white lead mixed with gold size, rubbed down, followed by two other coats of lead colour, sand-papered, after which two coats crimson lake.

Tank Sides, End, Protector Plate, Main Frames, Outside Frames, Axle-box Lids, Footsteps, and Buffers to receive one coat under varnish, picked out with black, and then lined, afterwards to receive one more coat of under varnish and two coats best finishing body varnish.

Company's name, with letters in gold leaf, to be placed on each side of Tank, to sample.

Buffer Beams, similar to Engine.

Inside Tanks and Well, Outside top of Tank, and Coal Space to have two coats red lead, finished with black.

Tool Box and Sand Boxes two coats lead colour, finished black, and varnished.

Inside of Frames two coats lead colour, finished in oil black.

Axles, same as Engine.

Brake Work and Intermediate Buffers to receive one coat lead colour, one coat oil black, and varnished.

Brake Pipes to have two coats of approved rubber varnish.

The Paint and Varnish to be obtained from Messrs. Docker Bros. or approved makers.

JNO. G. ROBINSON,

Chief Mechanical Engineer.

GORTON,
    APRIL, 1905.

THE COMPOUNDS' LIVERY

All four engines of classes 8D and 8E had crimson splashers when new. Their livery differed from that described above only in splasher treatment. In addition to that around the circumference of the splashers, the compounds also had a brass beading along the bottom of each splasher, flush with the running plate. A literal 'gilding of the lily' which arguably went a bit too far. They also carried their nameplates around the upper edge of the rear driving wheel splasher.

The nameplates of at least one compound, 8E No. 364 *Lady Henderson*, were briefly mounted above the splasher. Class 8F 4-6-0 No. 1097 had been similarly treated only a few months earlier, but obviously neither found approval and it is believed the repositioning of the nameplates around the splasher sides preceded introduction into traffic. One can speculate that had the nameplate over the splasher been adopted, there would have been no change from the 8B livery.

The 8J conversion of No. 1090 did not entail any change from the crimson lake splasher livery but necessitated the displacement of the builder's plates from the otherwise universal Atlantic's position – on the framing below the smoke-box. In its 8J form, No. 1090 had shallow casings extending above the running plate either side of the smoke-box, which necessitated removal of the builder's plates. A photograph of No. 1090 carrying builder's plates during this period has not been found but coloured illustrations of green and crimson painted splashers may be studied elsewhere in this work.

Returning to the specifications issued by the company: that for the two engines, Nos 192 and 194, has not been located, but one dated April 1905 does exist and this is reproduced in full. It was described very well by J.N. Maskelyne in the *Model Railway News*,

May 1952, p. 100. The first section deals with the locomotive. The instructions regarding the painting of the tender appeared in the later pages of the specification.

Page 6 of the specification included requests for official photographs and other information as follows:

Upon the fifth Engine being delivered, the Contractor is to provide the Company's Chief Mechanical Engineer with three dozen large mounted Platinotype Photographs of the Engines and Tenders, exactly as finished, also twelve enlarged Platinotype Photographs, not less than 42¾ inches by 26 inches, and suitably framed; and two complete lists of all Materials used in their construction, including the names of the Firms from whom purchased. Each list to be suitably and conveniently bound together. The cost of all the above to be included in the amount of the Tender.

In accordance with the usual practice, certain parts were to be left bright and polished. These were the smoke-box door centre washer, ring and handle, wheel, hinges and brackets, coupling hooks and shackles, ends of cylinders, coupling, connecting and reversing rods, whistles, all hand rails and pillars, safety valves, buffer heads, raised surfaces on maker's and number plates, and all brass beadings. The covers on spring dampers on trailing wheels and lids on axle boxes on tender and trailing wheels were all polished brass.

Before the lining that decorated these locomotives is described, we must refer again to the words of J.N. Maskelyne, which were published in the May 1952 copy of *Model Railway News*, p. 100. Mr Maskelyne states that a vermilion line was painted in the middle of the black border which was applied around the cab side. This seems most unlikely for two reasons: first, photographs of the 8Bs do not show a line of any sort in the centre of this black edge and second,

Plate 11.5   GCR Class 8B, No. 361   No. 361 is passing Abbey Lane signal cabin, just north of Leicester, with a fairly lengthy Down express on 25th May 1912. The locomotive and tender are painted grey but, nevertheless, it carries the full gamut of lining, coats-of-arms etc. Locomotive record cards suggest that this engine ran for several months in grey livery.   *W. Bradshaw*

a red line in that position would not form a separation from the green, which was its purpose in the first instance. The next doubtful piece of information is '*The splasher covers were always painted green with black edging and white lining with rounded corners*'. At least three of the North British-built engines appear to have had plain painted splasher tops. The writer also notes that '*The buffer sockets were maroon without lining*' and that the buffer beam numbers were shaded black. Although the film in use at that time would not record red lining well, it is more than likely that buffer sockets were lined – a black edge with a vermilion line. The notes are specific to engine No. 267 but blue, of a light tone, shaded the buffer beam numerals when it was new. In the livery described by Mr Maskelyne the standard numerals with different shades of blue would have been applied. Finally, reference is made to a maroon background to the cab number plate, a vermilion line within the raised edge and a single black/white stripe around the plate itself. None of this may be substantiated from photographs but there is much accurate information in this article, as well as one of J.N. Maskelyne's drawings.

As already noted elsewhere, photographs provide the main source of data regarding lining and from which the following notes were compiled.

Boiler bands were black, edged white and the wheels were lined white between the boss and the black axle end. White lining was also around the wheel centre boss and the circumference between the wheel and tyre. Like the tender tank sides and rear, the cab side sheets had an inset black-edged white panel, with radiused corners, repeating the style introduced on Nos 969, 970 and 971 of Pollitt's singles and which would feature on all future express passenger types. The panel followed the side sheet contours except that, unlike those of their successors, the Atlantic's cabside panel ignored the side sheet's forward curve to the bottom front. The black bordering to the cab was separated from the green by a narrow red line, understood to be the same shade of vermilion as lined out the crimson lake. This again set the standard for succeeding express passenger types, though passenger tanks normally featured a white edge to the black border together with inset panels. Unlike the inset panels, the bordering featured squared corners but, as with the inset panel, the cabside bordering ignored the forward curve onto the running plate.

This left a fillet of black, a feature which does not show up well on photographs but is clearly discernible in the rear three-quarter view of No. 1092 on page 96 of David Jackson's biography of Robinson. The Atlantic's cab edging mirrored that on the tender tank and on the coal guard plating where appropriate, but coal rails were black. The green finished cab front and splasher tops also had a black border but separated from the green by narrow white lining; thus, other than on the tender coal guards and flares, the red lining was applied only where black bordering surrounded an inset panel. The cab-front border passed either side of the brass-framed spectacles, which were otherwise unlined.

The tender tank sides carried the 6 inches tall version of 'Great Central'. In addition to that on the tank sides, the 8Bs displayed the coat-of-arms on each splasher. The 8D and 8Es, before being named, would have also carried them on each splasher. However, on the compound classes, the coat-of-arms occupied the leading splasher only, with the monogram set underneath the nameplate. Nos 258 and 259 were photographed in this condition.

It is inevitable that, with twenty-seven examples of Class 8B and four of classes 8D and 8E, over the period of their work for the GCR, differences in liveries occurred. The locomotive and tender buffer beams on all the 'Jersey Lilies' appear to have been lined white and edged black all around when new. Before long, the lining at the top of the beam began to be discontinued. The numerals on buffer beams seem to have been 6 inches tall when the engines were new but the smaller variety was being used after only a few years. One or two views of 8E No. 365 indicate that, at one period, numerals were not applied to the front beam. Lining on buffer guides is rarely recorded satisfactorily on the film emulsions of the day but it is almost certain that the guides were lined and this, normally, would be a vermilion line against a black edge. However, it is known that when engines Nos 264 and 267 were new they carried a white line on guides; this suggests that all locomotives of that batch were similarly finished. These engines' buffer beam characters were unusual as they appear to have been blocked out with one shade of light blue.

Cylinders always seem to have been lined with black borders around the parallel section, next to the polished ends. A vermilion line then separated the crimson from the border. All locomotives

ABOVE: Plate 11.6   GCR Class 8B, No. 1085
No. 1085 was a North British Locomotive Co. product and here is standing in the south bay at Leicester Central, probably ready to take over an Up express. There are three features of interest: the splasher tops appear to be unlined and the coat-of-arms has been placed over the centre tender axle box resulting in an imbalance of the words 'Great Central'; finally, the tender rear carries the number plate 1087.   *J. Quick collection*

BELOW: Plate 11.7   GCR Class 8B, No. 263
Waiting in one of the bay platforms at Leicester station is No. 263 which is ready to take an express forward. The engine is in a well maintained state and was photographed in later GCR days. Splasher sides are now crimson and carry the small sets of coats-of-arms. The standard version has been applied to the tender side, between the 4½ inches tall letters of 'Great Central'. Note also that the cylinder tail-rods have been removed.
                                    R.K. Blencowe collection, F.H. Gillford

ABOVE: Plate 11.8   GCR Class 8B, No. 361

This engine, No. 361, was the penultimate-built member of Class 8B, being completed at Gorton in July 1906. In this view, which is at Leicester shed, the locomotive is in its last few months of GCR ownership. A large coat-of-arms has been placed on the tender, between the large characters of the company's name, but the splashers are decorated with the smaller device. The full lining has been applied, even the base of the dome has two white lines with black between. Henry Salmon recorded this view c. 1922.

L.G.R.P. 1626

BELOW: Plate 11.9   GCR Class 8D, No. 258

Neasden shed about 1910 and compound 'Atlantic', No. 258 of Class 8D, looks in immaculate condition. This is only to be expected as the 'Jersey Lilies' were at that time the premier passenger engines on the GCR. This locomotive ran nameless for the first few years, before it took the name of the company's senior director *The Rt. Hon. Viscount Cross G.C.B. G.C.S.I.* This is a superb view of a very handsome engine.

Locomotive Publishing Co.

appear to have had the double white lining on wheels, but later this looks to have been modified to the simpler style. The 8J, No. 1090, appears to have only carried the simple lining on wheels. Outsides of mainframes appear not to have been lined at any period but some photographs show polished steel guard bars. Valance framing, steps etc., were always crimson, edged black and lined vermilion, and this also applied to the frames below the smoke-box.

Boilers on the 'Atlantics' were always lined in the usual manner, domes also received the same white/black/white bands, which were applied to the base. Some of the lined areas of these engines are shown in chapter 4 and these include the rather complex decoration on splasher sides. Tops of splashers were usually lined white with a black border but a few photographs show plain painted tops. These may have been black, or possibly crimson, and locomotives Nos 1085, 1086 and 1087 are examples of this. The beading which formed the join between the firebox, spectacle plate and footplate had a black centre with white edges but the inner white line was later omitted.

A final point of interest concerns the finish of the tender protector plate which was required to be green. It was fixed on the top of the tool box and had beading irons fastened to the curved upper edge. It has not been possible to confirm if the plate was actually painted green, as it is impossible to detect any lining on photographs. If it was it would have been lined in a similar way to the tenders of 11Bs, Nos 1013–1042, when new. It is plausible that if green was applied then the lining would have been vermilion alongside a black border. Another possibility is that the stipulation for green, along with green splashers, was rescinded before painting began.

The 6-inch transfers of 'Great Central' were used when the locomotives were new but some later received the smaller type. Similarly, the standard size of coat-of-arms gave way to the smaller version on some engines. *The Locomotive News and Railway Notes*, vol. X, 10th October 1921, published a letter from 'Valour'. This correspondent contributed notes of GCR engines and stated in his letter: *'4-4-2 No. 362 has been through shops, but is not superheated; she had a new boiler last time. She has been painted, and has small coat-of-arms on splasher and tank sides'*. The white lines painted inside number plates were later discontinued.

The monogram on the compound No. 258 was not applied when it was new and this may have been the case with its sister, No. 259. Later, towards grouping, it was not used at all on these engines. The history of this adornment on the 8Es is not clear, as all photographs of Nos 364 and 365 show the monogram had been applied. When the importance of the 'Jersey Lilies' to the company is considered, it is surprising that only two pictures are known which show additional distinctive decorative symbols. No. 361 carried a small sword-shaped mark near the top of the smoke-box in a central position at one period and No. 258 was similarly marked.

Some observations made by Percy Banyard about 1920 require recording at this stage. When 8B No. 264 was stationed at York its regular driver was Arthur King and it seems that Driver King could have almost anything that he wanted. The locomotive was reallocated to Leicester and arrived there not only with an exceptional paintwork finish, *'as smooth as glass'*, said Percy, but the tender front, cupboards and lockers were painted crimson lake, completed with a black border and vermilion lining! Percy also noted No. 267 finished in a shade of green that was darker than usual. This would have been during the later part of the engine's GCR service.

The 'Jersey Lilies' were always considered as top link passenger engines. Very many photographs show that they were maintained in the best condition and the pride taken by the staff is obvious. Of all the classes introduced by Robinson, the 'Atlantics' alone injected the company with a massive dose of confidence and just when it was required. The chairman and directors, Sam Fay and Robinson, must have been absolutely delighted with the engines. Apart from their excellence on the road, contemporary enthusiasts and the general public were captivated by them. At times they worked special excursion trains to places as far afield as Plymouth. They carried the GCR's trademarks of locomotives, carriages and liveries to destinations where they had never been seen before.

Under L&NER ownership they continued to work fast trains. Indeed, it was not until the 1930s when new 4-6-0s went to the former GCR section that the C4s and C5s moved to less demanding work. The last C5, No. 2897 *Lady Faringdon*, just failed to become a BR engine, but twenty of Class C4 did and worked out their time on the former GNR and GCR lines in Lincolnshire.

Plate 11.10   GCR Class 8D, No. 258
No. 258 is passing the power station at Neasden with the celebrated 'Sheffield Special'. This train left London Marylebone at 3.15 pm (the time varied a little over the years) and ran non-stop to Sheffield Victoria. It was always one of the fastest trains out of London, slipping a vehicle at Leicester Central and this is visible as the last carriage of the train. There appears to be a small sword-shaped mark on the smoke-box door. This view dates from about 1912.   *Real Photographs 65293*

Above: Plate 11.11   GCR Class 8E, No. 365

Sir William Pollitt, No. 365 of Class 8E is on Neasden shed and in splendid condition. These locomotives, their performance on the road, their magnificent livery and their elegance provided the GCR with a public image for which many railway companies would have yearned.   *J. Quick collection*

Below: Plate 11.12   GCR Class 8J, No. 1090

The solitary 8J engine, No. 1090, is standing on Gorton shed in this view. The locomotive is finished in the usual green and crimson, but the letters on the tender side are of the smaller type. This picture is difficult to date but No. 1090 was rebuilt from Class 8B to 8J in December 1908 and then altered again to become an 8B in September 1922.   *J. Quick collection*

CHAPTER 12
CLASS 8C 4-6-0

The Class 8C engines were built to compare with the two 8B 4-4-2s, Nos 192 and 194, the circumstances of which have already been noted in chapter 11. They formed the second of four very similar classes of the 4-6-0 wheel arrangement that Robinson introduced during the early part of his tenure at Gorton. Only two examples were built, Beyer, Peacock & Company delivering No. 195 in December 1903 and No. 196 soon after, in January 1904.

GREY LIVERY

Engine No. 195 was photographed in grey when it was new. Copies of this were published in *The Engineer*, May 1904, p. 469 and in *The Railway Magazine*, vol. XIV, 1904, p. 379. The same locomotive was recorded again in the special livery, probably by the official photographer of the GCR, and rather later in its life. The subject is coupled to a 4,000 gallon tender and has had the original tapered buffer guides replaced. The picture was probably taken soon after it had received a superheated boiler in August 1912. Although a photograph or written reference has not been established, it seems inconceivable that these engines did not work trains whilst painted grey.

GREEN OR BLACK LIVERY?

Were Nos 195 and 196 green or black? This question has puzzled students of GCR locomotives for many years. There are several references which suggest that green was their livery. C. Langley Aldrich, in his booklet *The Robinson Locomotives of the G.C.R.*, p. 13, comments '*For the first few years of their G.C. life they were painted in the passenger green livery, but were later painted in the black livery with red and white lining*'. George Dow in volume 3 of his work, *Great Central*, tends to agree with this view and Guy Hemingway noted '*but 195/196 almost certainly green*'. The authors of '*L.N.E.R. 4-6-0s*' are of the opinion that No. 195 was green and its classmate black. These are perfectly reasonable conclusions to make. Because they were built to compare with the 8Bs, their 6 feet 9 inches diameter driving wheels were obviously meant for working fast trains. The problem with all the above statements, however, is that there are no accompanying references with which to substantiate the claims. W.A. Tuplin in *Great Central Steam*, p. 62, seems quite sure that the pair were painted black but, once again, he does not provide a reference.

The only surviving specification which concerns Class 8C does not contain painting information. It is simply a secondary document which was supplied to Beyer, Peacock & Company as much of the technical data required by the contractor was already available in the original specification to build the two 8Bs, Nos 192 and 194. Indeed, this is the first sentence: '*To be exactly the same as 2 Engines No. 9034, June 13th/03*' (No. 9034 was the order number); then a list of exceptions followed which concerned the additional driving wheels, coupling rods etc. Ken Grainger has already recorded the fact that originally the two 8Bs were to be painted black and this suggests that the two 8Cs were also to be similarly finished. Ken also comments that later the request to paint the 8Bs black was cancelled. It is possible, then, that the GCR did not change the painting instructions for the 8Cs and that they were both black when new. We shall probably never know the answer to this problem, but any change of mind on Gorton's part could have been conveyed to the builder very quickly.

The specification contains other interesting information. The centre driving wheel tyres were to have thin flanges, but immediately

Plate 12.1   GCR Class 8C, No. 196
This view of No. 196 is one of at least three taken on what was probably the first visit to London of an 8C 4-6-0. The engine was allocated to Neasden shed on 26th March 1904, which may be an approximate date for this photograph. Note that the monogram is not in favour, but the black livery, polished guard irons, wheel tyres, beadings etc., make this an extremely attractive locomotive.
F. Moore 2903

below this is stated *'ditto splasher to have a brass beading round it, instead of Engine nameplate'*, but this has been crossed out and dated 25th November 1903. This means that both engines were to carry names, or, more likely, it was a residual matter from the 8B specification. Once again we may never discover the truth but the 8Cs were not named. Other items of interest are that one engine was to be weighed and one to be photographed with its tender. The photograph of No. 195 in grey to which reference has already been made is probably the product of the latter request. Finally, the GCR wanted both engines to be delivered as quickly as possible following the two 8Bs already ordered and that Nos 195 and 196 should be steamed in November 1903. The last directive was not fulfilled.

Only one authentic reference to the early livery of these locomotives is known and that is regarding No. 196. The Rev. W.J. Scott was a regular contributor to *The Railway Magazine*. In the January 1905 issue he reported a particularly fast run between Nottingham Victoria and London Marylebone and was rather surprised that the train was hauled by a black engine. In the item '1904 – A Great Railway Year', he looked at the developments on the GCR and on p. 23 he commented:

With the 3.30 p.m. up (11.25 a.m. Manchester Central) the load was only four coaches, hauled by an engine wearing 'goods' livery – she is painted black – but capable of the fastest passenger work, the six-coupled No. 196.

The only other source of definite livery information is the photographs taken by various individuals but, unfortunately, there are not many. For example, No. 195 appears not to have been photographed when new. The earliest dated view of this locomotive seems to be Bradshaw's on page 12 of John Hurst and Mike Kinder's book, which was taken in March 1911. The angle of the viewpoint precludes a judgement on the livery but, when Gorton shopping dates are considered, together with the slightly better picture on page 5 of the same work, No. 195 on page 12 was probably black. The same engine was also recorded on a Down train at Leicester about 1921, and that picture portrays a black locomotive.

The position with No. 196 is somewhat better, because the company's photographer seems to have been waiting for the engine on what may have been its first visit to Neasden shed. At least three pictures were taken on this occasion, which may have been during the spring of 1904. This locomotive was allocated to Neasden from late March of that year until the autumn of 1905. There are other early photographs of the engine, one with the National Railway Museum, the other part of the Roger Carpenter collection; more were taken later in the engine's GCR life but the common factor is that all known views of No. 196 show a black engine.

At this stage it is probably safe to conclude that all known photographs of both locomotives in GCR condition indicate that they were painted black; that No. 196 was black throughout its GCR career and that No. 195 was always black from c. 1910 to grouping. However, it is possible that both engines began life in green but were repainted black after a very short period.

If a reader requires details of the green livery that *may* have been applied, the paint scheme for the first two 8Bs, Nos 192 and 194, should be consulted. The black livery of the 'Fish engines' was probably used to finish Nos 195 and 196, and chapter 9, which deals with Class 8, furnishes all necessary information.

Both locomotives were delivered to Gorton painted grey. After

Plate 12.2   GCR Class 8C, No. 196
No. 196 again but photographed later, c. 1921, when 'Iracier' axle boxes had been fitted to the tender, but not on the centre axle on this side, at least. The coat-of-arms appears only on the driving splasher side but monograms are visible on the other splashers. This picture, which is on Neasden shed, also shows a Sacré 2-4-0T of Class 12AT, believed to be No. 449B. If this is the case the photograph may be dated to between late August and October 1921.

R. K. Blencowe

Plate 12.3   GCR Class 8C, No. 195
An illustration of either 8C in green livery is unknown. This is No. 195 in black paint and looking very smart indeed. The engine is standing at the north
end of Leicester Central with a Down express, possibly an excursion. Polished buffer heads, smoke-box fittings, etc., all enhance the finish. Notice the
reflections on the underside of the boiler and the three hinges and smoke-box frame ends have all been well cleaned. The date of this view is not known
but possibly c. 1920.
The Gordon Coltas photographic trust

they had been proved to be satisfactory, the final paint was applied
at Gorton, possibly during January 1904.

Lining details were very similar to those for the Class 8 4-6-0s and
a splasher side for an 8C with a monogram is illustrated elsewhere
in this work. The base of the dome was lined with the red/white,
black centre, white/red stripes when the engines were new but the
lack of suitable photographs prevents a decisive conclusion on this
point later in the engines' lives. For the same reason it is impossible
to say if the double white and red lines at the junction of the boiler
and smoke-box were retained in later years. The frames below the
smoke-box were lined with one red line. Buffer beams were finished
in the usual manner, also the buffer guides. The openings of the
guides received a narrower version of the boiler lining. Cylinders
carried the customary decoration for a black locomotive and the
wheels were finished with fine red and white lines around the cranks
and axle ends.

The tender lining matched that on the engine. The curved flares
received the red/white lines, but outside frames had one red line.
When the upper coal plates were fitted, one red line was applied
just inside the edge. The 6 inches tall transfers of the company's
name seem to have always been used. When new, the buffer beam
numerals were 6 inches tall and they were probably shaded black.
Later, however, the smaller characters were in use, which by that
time were shaded with blue. The upper lining on buffer beams was
later omitted and the lining on buffer openings was also modified,
certainly on No. 196. Generally, however, the livery of lined black
appears to have changed very little.

When they were new, the standard size of coat-of-arms was applied
to the tender sides and to the centre splasher, the other splashers
being lined only. Towards the end of the GCR the tender which was
fitted to No. 196 did not carry a coat-of-arms. The monogram was
probably added to their decoration at about the same time as this
feature was first used on the compound 4-4-2s. The earliest views
do not show the monogram applied. This suggests that from about
1906/07 both engines carried four monograms, which were placed
on the leading and trailing splasher sides, possibly until grouping.
There are no photographs available to indicate if a special mark
was applied to either engine, but some views show that both Nos
195 and 196 appear to have received some additional attention
from the staff. The end section of the framing below the smoke-box
and three hinges just below front of same seem to have been highly
polished. In a letter to the author, Percy Banyard made a revealing
comment *'195 and 196 kept in immaculately clean condition, brass
and steelwork polished, cab fittings looked like a jeweller's shop'!*

The 8C 4-6-0s were used on some of the company's most important
trains, both goods and passenger. Some of their performances have
been described in various journals but the late evening Down mail
out of Marylebone is one of the best examples. In 1923 they became
Class B1 on the L&NER when, ironically, they were repainted in
the famous apple green livery. When Edward Thompson's new
4-6-0s entered service they took the B1 classification, whereupon
the former GCR 4-6-0s, by now 5195 and 5196, became Class B18.
Both locomotives were withdrawn in the last month of the L&NER,
December 1947.

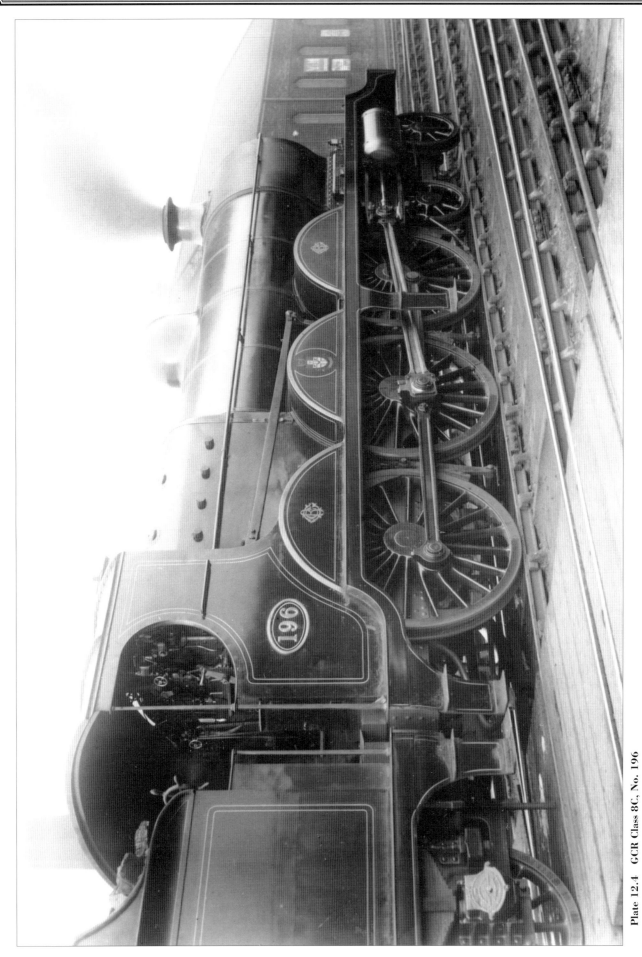

Plate 12.4   GCR Class 8C, No. 196
This is a well-known photograph having been published before but it illustrates well the black lined livery, monograms etc., that were carried by these engines. No. 196 was recorded at the east end of platform 3 at Guide Bridge. It must be a late photograph, c. 1921, as the tender has 'Tracier' axle boxes.

R. K. Blencowe 29875

CHAPTER 13

STEAM RAILCARS

The requirement to reduce the costs of operating certain lines led many British railway companies to search for alternative ways of providing services. The GCR became part of the movement towards greater economy with the construction of three different types of railcar. Three steam railcars were built during 1904 and 1905. In the following year three steam railmotors were introduced and later, probably in 1912, a petrol-electric car was purchased.

A steam railcar as built by the GCR was a self-propelled vehicle that had driving controls at both ends. By contrast, the railmotors were of the 'push-pull' type of passenger train. Robinson rebuilt certain members of the 2-4-0Ts of Class 12AT as Class 12AM; these were coupled to 12-wheel saloon carriages built specifically for use with these locomotives and worked on lines which did not generate sufficient traffic to justify a conventional train.

The steam railcar falls into two classifications, a passenger carriage and a steam locomotive and this would describe the GCR design very well. Approximately one fifth of the carriage carried the steam boiler, coal etc.; most of the remaining part of the body was devoted to passenger accommodation, with a driver's compartment at each end of the vehicle. These cars occasionally hauled a 6-wheel coach, or, at times, one or two goods vehicles so, consequently, their livery has been included in this survey of Robinson's locomotive liveries.

The first two steam railcars were built at Gorton in 1904 to Robinson's design. They were numbered in the passenger carriage series as Nos 1 and 2. *The Locomotive Magazine* of 15th October 1904, p. 180, contains a line drawing of this type. A third car was completed, also at Gorton, in 1905. This carried No. 3, but was a different design from the earlier pair. David Jackson's book on page 72 has an outline diagram of No. 3 and a photograph of No. 1. They were attractive, self-contained vehicles which had compartments for First and Third class passengers and one for luggage – but toilet facilities were not provided, presumably because of the relatively short distances covered by the cars.

INTERIOR LIVERY

These notes refer to cars Nos 1 and 2. The finish of the driving, motor and luggage compartments is not known but it may have been varnished wood. The longitudinal spring seats in the premier class were covered with green cloth. The ceiling was decorated with Lincrusta-Walton, picked out with gold, and the compartments finished with walnut and sycamore. Third class areas had teakwood and pitch pine panels with match boarding. The seats, which were reversible, were covered with rattan. Car No. 3 was probably similarly decorated internally. An article in the *G.C.R.J.*, vol. I, p. 223, refers to only one change regarding the interior of No. 3 and that is that the First class smoking compartment was upholstered with buffalo hide.

EXTERIOR LIVERY

At the time of the introduction of the railcars, GCR carriages were being painted in a two-tone livery, which was essentially cream and brown. This livery was stipulated in a form of tender document issued from Gorton in July 1902. The company was about to place large orders for both clerestory and conventional roof passenger vehicles and it is believed that the railcars were painted to

Plate 13.1   Steam railcar No. 1
Steam railcar No. 1 is standing at the Lincolnshire outpost of the GCR, Barton. These totally self-contained vehicles carried the company's passenger carriage livery of dark brown, with cream upper panels. The car looks quite new and may be in its first year of service.   *J. Quick collection*

PAINTING

The whole of the exterior of the body and underframe must first receive two coats of white lead paint, four coats of filling-up, and one coat of staining; to be stopped with white lead stopper, and afterwards rubbed down with pumice stone and water. The top quarter panels, waist panels, and upright panels then to receive one coat of cream-colour paint. The clerestory sides, bottom quarter panels, end panels, and underframe then to receive one coat of lead colour, to be also stopped, and faced with pumice stone and water. The upper portion of the main body of the carriage from waist to cornice then to receive three coats of cream paint. The ends, bottom panels, and headstocks afterwards to receive one coat of lead colour and two coats of brown paint. The exterior of the underframe soles to receive two coats of black. All facias and mouldings to be picked out with two coats of brown paint round the cream panels and door and quarter light reveals. The whole then to receive one coat of hard drying varnish, which must be flattened down with pumice stone and water. The body then to be gilded, lined, pencil varnished, and lettered as directed. The headstock to be picked out black and lined yellow. The whole then to receive another coat of hard drying varnish, and three coats of finishing body varnish. The panels to be painted to match exactly the sample panels, which will be furnished by the Company.

The Lincrusta in roofs to receive two coats of good white lead paint and one coat of flake white, bound with varnish, and to be left an egg-shell gloss. Quarters and backs to be tinted light cream. The Lincrusta to be picked out in deep gold in the first class compartments, and in colour in the third class compartments according to instructions. The Lincrusta dado in corridors to receive two coats of sienna red and one coat of hard varnish. Underneath seats to receive one coat of stone-colour paint, to be well puttied, and then to receive a second coat of stone-colour paint.

The underframes, bogies, springs, couplings, and all ironwork must first be scraped clear of rust (this will be strictly enforced), and receive one coat of lead colour before being used; afterwards they must receive a second coat of lead colour, and one coat of black for underneath ironwork, and one coat of black japan on buffers, couplings, &c. The bogies, throughout, then to receive two more coats of lead-colour paint, and the insides one coat of oil black paint. The outside of bogies and springs to then receive two coats of black paint and three coats of body varnish.

The brake compartment, inside, to receive one coat of white paint, to be well puttied up; the roof to be finished with two coats of white paint. The sides and ends to receive two coats of light green paint (to sample), and finished with one coat of hard varnish.

The lettering, numbering, and arms to be placed as directed.

All lead paints to contain not less than 10 ounces of blue lead to the pound.

The paints and varnishes to be from approved makers.

In the painting of the carriages throughout, it must be strictly understood that not more than one coat of paint per day is to be applied, which must be quite dry before receiving another coat, and one day at least must be allowed between each coat of finishing varnish.

J. G. ROBINSON,
CHIEF MECHANICAL ENGINEER

Gorton Works,
July 11th, 1902.

this specification, although certain sections are inapplicable to the cars. Guy Hemingway made a copy of the original document and this is reproduced above.

This specification requires a little further comment. The coats-of-arms were placed in four positions on the lower panels of each side of the body. They were of the standard height, but on a photograph of either No. 1 or 2 taken at East Halton, c. 1912, the vehicle appears not to carry the company's device. When new the wheel tyres were painted white, but later this seems to have been discontinued. The lining, which was gold, was probably about ¼ inch wide. The characters which formed the running numbers and lettering were 3 inches tall. They were gold and shaded with black, to the right and below. One point of debate is the buffer beams which may have been painted vermilion; they were certainly lined, but photographs do not assist with this theory. One view of No. 2, however, does show the main area of the beam to be of a slightly different tone from that of the brown of the body.

Only two pictures are available in the later period of their service which help with the livery. They may be of the same vehicle, either No. 1 or 2, and both were taken in the Grimsby/Goxhill areas. One at East Halton was published in David Jackson's book on page 74.

The other is on page 101 of the booklet *Immingham and the Great Central Legacy*, which was compiled by B. Mummery and I. Butler. The picture was recorded at Pyewipe, Grimsby and also taken about 1912. These views show a slight change in painting policy. The panels above the driver's window and the long, narrow panel below are of a light colour, which is probably cream. It is not known if the cars were later finished in a teak-coloured paint, which would have been in accordance with the company's painting policy of older passenger vehicles at that time.

Although many railway companies operated steam railcars, generally they met with indifferent success. The reasons for this on the GCR are unclear but their use by the time of the First World War seems to have been severely restricted. The minutes of the Locomotive & Wagon Committee of 7th January 1921, recorded that it had been decided to convert the cars into 'trailers'. *The Locomotive News and Railway Notes*, of 21st December 1921, noted that cars Nos 1 and 3 had been seen at Nottingham and No. 2 at New Holland where they were, presumably, in store. The steam engines were rebuilt as pumps, but the bodies remained in traffic running as ordinary trailer carriages until withdrawal from service during the 1950s.

Plate 13.2   Steam railcar No. 2
Some lining detail is revealed in this view of No. 2. Note that the buffer beam received some intricate decoration. The steps are extended, but the location is unknown. The Walschaerts' valve gear was a novelty on the GCR at the time, c. 1905.   *J. Quick collection*

Plate 13.3   Steam railcar No. 1 or No. 2
This car is waiting at Grimsby Pyewipe Road whilst working on the Grimsby District line, c. 1909. The panels above and below the driver's window have been repainted with what appears to be cream.   *J. Quick collection*

ABOVE: Plate 14.1   GCR Class 5A, No. 60
This photograph of No. 60 may be the earliest taken on panchromatic film of a GCR locomotive. The engine is brand-new and carries the smaller coat-of-arms and the smaller version of the company's title (*top*). The red lines are clearly visible outside of the adjacent white lines and notice the double red and white bands on the parallel section of the buffer bodies (*right*), in place of on the collars. The date of this picture is the summer of 1906.   *J. Quick collection*

BELOW: Plate 14.2   GCR Class 5A, No. 538
No. 538 is on the former Wrexham, Mold & Connah's Quay Railway shed at Rhosddu, Wrexham, probably fairly early in the engine's career. This engine spent from early 1907 to late 1909 at this shed. It is lined and finished as No. 60, but notice the buffer body lining is now on the collar (*left*) and that the chimney is one of Robinson's alternative designs.   *F. Moore 2745*

CHAPTER 14
CLASS 5A 0-6-0T

Brian Wainwright

For the purposes of shunting at Grimsby docks the company owned a number of small tank locomotives. When replacements were required Robinson introduced the Class 5A. They were, essentially, a larger, improved version of Pollitt's Class 5 saddle tank engine. Ideal for work in restricted areas, they worked not only at Grimsby but at various other locations, notably Immingham, New Holland, Wrexham, Staveley and Liverpool. Nos 60 and 61 originally had condensing gear, the only GCR engines so fitted. A further unusual, but necessary, detail was that they all carried a bell for warning purposes.

There was a total of seven engines built, all by the company at Gorton. Nos 60, 61, 89, 157, 321 and 538 were completed during the second half of 1906. One further example, No. 277, was turned out in June 1914.

GREY LIVERY

Only one picture of a grey engine is known. This is an official photograph, probably taken when No. 157 was new. It is finished in a middle shade of grey and is devoid of any relief except for the number and maker's plates and the words 'Great Central'. The characters forming the company's title are plain white, or possibly very light grey, and appear to be about 6 inches tall.

BLACK LIVERY

A painting specification for the class does not appear to have survived, nor has any written record been found. The introduction of the class was noted, with illustrations, in the *G.C.R.J.*, vol. II, p. 215, but there is no mention of livery. The only definite source of information regarding painting is the very small number of GCR period photographs.

The traffic livery of the 5A engines was always black in GCR days. Two official views of No. 60 were taken on panchromatic film. The red part of the lining has recorded satisfactorily and this greatly helps the student of locomotive liveries. Considering the fact that some of these locomotives spent much of their lives away from the public eye, the lining scheme that they carried was quite elaborate. It is possible that Nos 60 and 61 were finished in this manner as they were intended for use as station pilots at Liverpool Central. Very few additional photographs are known. One of No. 538 at Wrexham is helpful, but this shows the same basic livery as on No. 60. The other views are not useful for a variety of reasons and consequently only an incomplete account may be made of the painting of these locomotives.

They would have received the standard preparatory work before painting and it is likely that the final coat was *'ivory black'*. The lining consisted of red and white, but it was a little unusual and therefore demands as full a description as possible. The boiler was lined with the red/white/black-centre/white/red stripes. The two photographs of No. 60, upon which the main part of this account is being based, only show this lining at the junction of the boiler and the smoke-box; this is because the side tanks shield the boiler top from

view. The base of the dome is not visible either but it is likely that the same stripes were applied to the dome and to the other boiler bands. The sand boxes, tank fronts and spectacle plate had the single red and white bands, the red always being on the outside. The tank, cab and bunker sides received the double white lines which had a wider red band on the outside of the outer white line. This formed a rather complicated shape around the bunker side and number plate. It is more than likely that the bunker rear was similarly finished but photographs which show this are unknown. The buffer beams, which were almost certainly vermilion, had a black border and white line around the bottom edge and the ends. The black buffer guides had the single red/white lines applied to the square base but, near the openings on the parallel section, the decoration appears to be unique. It consisted of two white lines, perhaps 1 inch apart, with a vermilion centre. The ends of the beams, which were a 'sandwich' of timber and iron, were finished with a complete rectangle formed of a red and white stripe. The cylinders, valance framing and steps had single red and white lines but the wheels were not embellished.

Insides of mainframes were, in all likelihood, vermilion; the outsides were black and this included the guard irons. The livery of the cab interior is unknown but it may have been stone colour with a dark coloured border. Visible on the broadside picture of No. 60 is some light coloured lining which is painted against a border and may be white or yellow. Buffer heads, smoke-box hinge, wheel centre etc., all handrails, lubricator cups and pipework, coupling and connecting rods and slide bars, warning bell, main portion of condenser pipes, tank ventilators, whistle and raised areas of maker's and number plates were all polished metal. The safety valves appear to be painted black and, unusually, so were the ends of the cylinders.

A white line was applied around the inside of the number plate. It is probable that the running number was placed on the bunker rear, about halfway up in the centre. However, a photograph showing either the rear of the bunker or the front buffer beam has not come to notice. The numerals on the front beam may have been of the 6 inches tall type when the locomotives were new, but the smaller characters would have later replaced them. The letters of the company's title were the 4½ inches tall type and the small coat-of-arms was placed on the tank side, between the words 'Great' and 'Central'.

It is unfortunate that, due to a shortage of photographs and other information, further details cannot be added to the above. Indeed, the last example to be built, No. 277, may not have carried any lining. It entered traffic quite late in the GCR era and at that time small economies were being made. It is not surprising then that pictures taken later in their career indicate that some lining was being omitted, the coat-of-arms was not being applied etc. A view of No. 61 taken quite late shows the 'Great Central' spaced over a greater than usual length of the tank side.

These little shunting engines served their owners well. As Class J63 on the L&NER and BR, they were not withdrawn from service until diesel shunters took over their duties in the late 1950s.

Plate 15.1 GCR Class 8F, No. 1095
The engine is new in this picture at Neasden c. 1906. The photograph is one of only two known which depict an 8F in the original Brunswick green and crimson. They must have been a splendid sight when new, looking very much like a 'Jersey Lily', but perhaps the lined black scheme suited them rather better. St. Mary's church is in the background.

J. Quick collection

CHAPTER 15
CLASS 8F 4-6-0

Robinson's policy of modernising the locomotive stock of the company continued for several years. An important element of this was the construction of four classes of 4-6-0 tender engines. The first two types, classes 8 and 8C, were already in traffic and the ten examples of Class 8F soon followed. Shortly before their delivery began the *G.C.R.J.* (vol. II, p. 19) reported: '*Ten of these will be a most useful class of engine suitable for fish and perishable goods trains, and when necessary can be used for heavy excursion traffic*'. They were all built by Beyer, Peacock & Company, carried Nos 1095–1104 and were completed in June and July 1906.

This period of GCR history is one of a very enterprising company; a railway that was constantly striving to increase and improve both its services and public image. In its quest the company enjoyed considerable success, which must have been a highly satisfying situation for the board and particularly for the general manager, Sam Fay. It was Fay who was the author of many of the improvements but of paramount importance in the company's plans was the building of the docks at Immingham, a small village close to the River Humber and a few miles north-west of Grimsby. The 12th July 1906 was the day chosen for the ceremony of the cutting of the first sod which was to be carried out by the chairman's wife, Lady Henderson. The train which took directors, officials and guests from Marylebone to Immingham was hauled by brand new 8F No. 1097. The journey may have been the engine's first long-distance outing and to commemorate the occasion No. 1097 received the name *Immingham*. Perhaps it was highly appropriate that six years later,

on 22nd July 1912, when the docks were opened by their majesties the King and Queen, Sam Fay was knighted in No. 2 transit shed.

GREY LIVERY

One member of the class was painted grey, No. 1097. It was photographed several times and the results are of much interest to the historian.

Two pictures of No. 1097 were taken, presumably at Beyer, Peacock's works: a left broadside and a left three-quarter view, both of which show the engine, although grey, lined in the green passenger engine style. The monogram is carried on the leading and trailing splashers, with the standard size coat-of-arms on the centre splasher. The photographs were published at the time, the broadside picture in the *G.C.R.J.*, vol. III, p. 50, and the other in the Locomotive Publishing Co. series as No. 2311. The significant point of interest in both views is that the locomotive is not named.

Another photograph was taken on the same occasion, judging by the position of the driving wheel cranks. The subject is in an identical condition but carries an *Immingham* nameplate. The

Plate 15.2   GCR Class 8F, No. 1097
No. 1097 photographed in the special grey finish and nameless. Another view, which appears to have been taken on the same occasion, shows the engine named *Immingham*, with the nameplate set above the top of the splasher side. The work required to prepare and paint No. 1097 must have been considerable. Note that the curved coal plate on the tender front is lined (*top*).
Locomotive Publishing Co. 2311

Painting.

Boiler to receive two coats of Oxide of Iron before being lagged, one whilst hot.

Clothing Plates, two coats of lead colour inside.

Splashers, Cab, Clothing, and Wheels, to receive two coats of lead colour, filled up with white lead, mixed with gold size, rubbed down, followed up with two other coats lead colour, sand papered, after which two coats Brunswick green in oil.

Outside frames, Main frame above platform near Smokebox, Sandboxes, Buffers and Footstep plates, same as Splashers, &c., except two coats Crimson lake in oil, instead of green.

Outside frames, Wheels, Sandboxes, Buffers, Footstep plates, Splashers, Cab, & Clothing, to receive one coat under varnish, picked out with black & lined, afterwards to receive one more coat under varnish & two coats best finishing body varnish.

To be flatted down with pumice stone & horse hair between each coat.

Numbers in gold leaf, shaded with blue, to be placed on Buffer Beam, after first coat of varnish.

[The next paragraph of the document, which refers to the coats-of-arms, is crossed out and dated 23rd March 1906.]

Company's Coat of Arms (Transfers of which will be supplied) to be placed on each Leading and Driving Splasher.

A Brass Number plate, fixed on Cab sides, to be painted black between numbers and with one eighth white line, half-inch within the raised edge.

Inside of Main Frames, Frame stay, & Slide bar Brackets to have two coats lead colour, filled up with white lead mixed with gold size, rubbed down, one coat flesh colour, sand papered, two coats of vermillion (sic.), and three coats hard drying body varnish.

Outside of Main Frames, Bogie and Guard Bars to receive two coats lead colour, filled up, rubbed down, one coat of ivory black and one coat of ivory black mixed with varnish, and one coat hard drying body varnish.

Bodies of straight axles to receive one coat white lead and one coat varnish.

Ends of Axles, black, lined with white & varnished.

Smokebox, Bogie, back of Firebox, Platforms, Brake hangers, etc. one coat black and one coat Japan.

Chimney to have two coats lead colour, filled up with white lead, mixed with gold size, rubbed down, and one coat black and one Japan.

Inside cab, one coat lead colour, filled up, rubbed down, sand papered, two coats, stone colour (to sample), one coat under varnish, and one coat finishing body varnish.

To be lined as per sample panel.

Two days to intervene between each of the last three coats of varnish.

Buffer Beams same as Inside Frames, with the addition of being lined to sample panel, and varnished same as clothing.

Brake pipes to have two coats of approved rubber varnish.

The Paint and Varnish to be obtained from Messrs Docker Bros.

Sample panels will be provided, and the greatest care must be taken that all Engines are painted strictly in accordance therewith, and of the same shades throughout.

[An addendum dated 23rd March 1906 appears at the end of the specification. This gives the altered instructions for the positions of the coats-of-arms.]

The Company's Coat of Arms (Transfers of which will be supplied) to be placed on the Driving Splasher, & the Company's initials in the form of a Monogram on the Leading & Trailing splashers. When ready for painting, the foreman painter to go across to the Great Central Works to see one of the 9035 Engines (similar class to 9458) lettered this way.

plate is, however, set above the top curve of the splasher, rather reminiscent of the plate fitted to compound 'Atlantic', No. 364 when that locomotive was recorded in grey. Upon closer inspection the nameplate appears to be only resting on the splasher top. It has been suggested that the nameplate is the result of an artist retouching the photograph and, if this is correct, the artist has made a first rate job of it. Another suggestion is that the nameplate is not the genuine article, as it appears to be too big. It is also possible that the plate was 'added' photographically. Nevertheless, all later pictures of No. 1097 confirm that a nameplate was fitted in the customary position, that is, with the top edge of the plate in line with that of the splasher. This exercise tends to support the suggestion that the decision to name an 8F *Immingham* was probably made well before the day of the ceremony and No. 1097 was carrying nameplates at that event. Another conclusion that may safely be made is that, assuming the engine worked the special in green livery, it must have been repainted very quickly indeed after the photographic session. The photograph was published in *Yeadon's Register of L.N.E.R. Locomotives*, vol. 22, p. 65.

GREEN LIVERY

All ten locomotives were initially painted in the company's standard express passenger livery of Brunswick green and crimson lake. Fortunately a hand-written specification exists and this is reproduced above. The reference to 9035 is the order number for the two 8C locomotives, but 9458 referred to the 8F engines. The request that Beyer, Peacock's foreman painter should visit Gorton is an indication of how closely the two companies cooperated in their everyday work.

Certain parts of the document deserve additional comment. First, the main specification is dated 16th January 1906. Tender painting requirements are not included but the contractor may have been asked to use those issued when the 8Bs, Nos 192 and 194, were ordered. Delivery was to commence by 13th April 1906 and continue at the rate of five per month until completed and this was *'under penalty'*. Presumably a penalty, or penalties, were enforced as the first engine, No. 1095, was not released until early June, more than seven weeks late. It was also required that an engine and tender were to be weighed and photographed. The tyres of wheels were to be polished on their outside faces and safety valves were to be left bright. The smoke-box door centre washer, ring, handle and wheel, hinge and brackets were to be polished, also the draw hooks and shackles. Buffer rams were to be turned all over but the brass beadings, reversing rod, handrails etc., are not mentioned.

Although these locomotives were green for only a short period they were still kept in immaculate condition. Information regarding lining and other decorations will be found in the chapter which deals with the Class 8B engines built by the North British Locomotive Co. It is not surprising that only two photographs of green 8Fs are known. No. 1095 was the subject of an unknown photographer when it stood at Neasden locomotive shed and this picture is part of the Lens of Sutton collection. The other view is in the F. Moore series, as No. 2312, and shows No. 1103, also at Neasden. This picture may be studied on p. 90 of David Jackson's biography of Robinson. Both photographs must have been recorded between June 1906 and September 1909.

When they were green the 8Fs received the usual lining but there are a few features to note. Buffer beams were lined all around with white. Buffer guides had white lining on the base and on the opening. This was, of course, similar to the 8Bs, Nos 263–267, when they were new. All wheels were also lined with white around the bosses and the axle ends, the whole making a most attractive sight. *Railway Archive*, No. 3, p. 76, has a smoke-box view of No. 1099. This is an early photograph and the subject is probably painted green. The buffer beam characters are 6 inches tall and the buffer guides are lined with white. The numerals appear to have a variation in their shading. It seems to consist of light blue with darker blue, or possibly black, on the underside which is outlined with white.

The Great Central Railway Journal, vol. VII, illustrated page 157 with a photograph of a working model of No. 1097. It was made to a scale of 1½ inches to one foot by Messrs Bassett-Lowke Ltd, for a Monsieur Adrien Froment of Geneva. Monsieur Froment, who was a great enthusiast, owned several fine model locomotives. The journal commented:

> *During his last visit to England he wished to have a 'Pièce de Résistance', and after visiting all the leading English Railway Companies' termini he selected the G.C.R. 'Immingham' as being the best locomotive for appearance in England today.*

The model was the second Class 8F made by Bassett-Lowke and is of interest because, apart from being painted in the green and crimson lake livery, it carries the nameplate set above the top curve of the splasher, similar to the view of the engine when it was photographed in grey.

BLACK LIVERY

Soon after their introduction to traffic, a decision was taken that black was a more suitable livery. Although the engines worked express and heavy excursion trains, their main employment was on the fast, vacuum braked goods services and this may be why the change was made. The engines were repainted over a period of about a year. The magazine *Railway Notes*, of January 1909, p. 44, reported: *'The 6'6" 4-6-0 engines are being painted black and one of these, No. 1097 "Immingham", is stationed at Grimsby'*. Much more information was published in the company's journal (*G.C.R.J.*, vol. IV, p. 51):

> *No. 1103, one of another type of 6-w.c.* [wheels coupled] *mixed traffic engines of a series of six* (sic.)*, numbered 1095–1104 and built by Messrs. Beyer, Peacock, in 1906, and received from the makers painted green, has now appeared in traffic painted black. It has been found that black is a more suitable colour for engines of that class. No. 1101 is the only other of that batch painted in a similar way so far, but as each one goes into the Shops it will be treated the same.*

Plate 15.3   GCR Class 8F, No. 1100
William Bradshaw recorded this member of the class, No. 1100, on Leicester shed on 4th May 1910. The engine is painted black, has the standard size of coat-of-arms on the tender and driving splasher, with a monogram on both leading and trailing splashers. It was a very attractive turnout. Notice a 5-pointed white star near the base of the smoke-box. The main lines are behind the locomotive, in the distance.   *W. Bradshaw*

Page 96 of the same volume added more detail: '*No. 1104 of the same build as 1103, explained last month, has just been through the Gorton Shops, and has just been painted in a similar way to 1103, that is black*'. Page 141 noted that No. 1097 would shortly be turned out in black. Later, on page 195 a picture of a black No. 1097 appeared. The last *G.C.R.J.* reference is on page 269 of volume IV:

Engine 1096 is again in traffic painted black and 1102 will shortly be running also, it being now in the Paint Shop. This completes all the engines of the 'Immingham' class which were green when put in traffic.

The table which follows has been compiled using information which has already been given and dates extracted from Allan Brown's locomotive record cards. The dates in the black livery column refer to those given by the *G.C.R.J.* Those in the Gorton works column are from record cards and may well have been when the engines were repainted black. Note that the dates for engine No. 1101 seem to disagree. This could be because the locomotive was repainted black on its previous works visit, which was on 7th December 1907.

By the summer of 1909, therefore, all the 8F engines were running in black and this scheme, with a few modifications, remained in use until grouping. In the absence of a specification for the class in black, that and other notes for the 'Fish' engines of Class 8, should be consulted. These will furnish sufficient information to study Class 8F, but it is inevitable that differences occurred and thus require additional comment.

The boiler, firebox, valance frames, splasher tops, spectacle plate, dome and cylinders were all lined in the usual manner but the

Locomotive	New, Green Livery	Black Livery	Ex. Gorton Works
1095	6 / 6 /1906		12/ 7 /1909
1096	7 / 6 /1906	6 /1909	4 / 4 /1909
1097	21/ 6 /1906	3 /1909	31/10/1908
1098	19/ 6 /1906		28/11/1908
1099	23/ 6 /1906		28/11/1908
1100	26/ 6 /1906		5 / 9 /1908
1101	29/ 6 /1906	9 /1908	6 / 2 /1909
1102	30/ 6 /1906	7 /1909	24/ 4 /1909
1103	3 / 7 /1906	9 /1908	4 / 7 /1908
1104	3 / 7 /1906	11/1908	8 / 8 /1908

frames below the smoke-box appear not to have been so finished. The splasher sides were decorated with the red/white lining, usually accompanied by either a coat-of-arms or a monogram and a summary of this is given in the table opposite. The buffer beams appear never to have been lined immediately below the footplate and the numerals applied thereto seem to have always been of the smaller type. Buffer guides were lined, in most cases with the double red/white bands. Sometimes, however, the opening was lined but on other locomotives the lining was added to the parallel section of the guide. One or two photographs show the simple lining of one red/white stripe around axle ends but, later, lining on wheels was discontinued. Mainframes were probably plain black but certain views show that on some engines the guard irons were polished steel. A white line was usually applied around the numerals on number plates and a picture of No. 1102, taken c. 1920, shows a power classification of '3' below the running number.

Plate 15.4   GCR Class 8F, No. 1097
No. 1097 in black livery on Gorton shed. The nameplate is fitted with the top edge in line with that of the splasher. The coat-of-arms and monogram have exchanged places due to the space taken by the nameplate. This is not easy to date, possibly c. 1912.   *J. Quick collection*

SPLASHER DECORATION AS SHOWN IN PHOTOGRAPHS

LOCOMOTIVE	LEADING	DRIVING	TRAILING	DATE	REFERENCE
1095	monogram	coat-of-arms	monogram	19/4/1913	LCGB H1159
	monogram	small coat-of-arms	monogram	c. 1920?	Locos.Illus. 49
	monogram	small coat-of-arms	monogram	c. 1920?	Lens of Sutton
	monogram	small coat-of-arms	monogram	c. 1915	Imm. & GC Legacy
1096	–	small coat-of-arms	–	c. 1920?	Real W7155
	–	small coat-of-arms	–	c. 1920?	S.Rhodes
	monogram	small coat-of-arms	monogram	c. 1922	LGRP 16228
	–	small coat-of-arms	–	?	Loc. GC Vol. 1
	–	small coat-of-arms	–	?	BlencoweWD1297
1097	coat-of-arms	monogram	coat-of-arms	1911	GCRS B207
	coat-of-arms	monogram	coat-of-arms	22/8/1912	Blencowe,Gillford
	coat-of-arms	monogram	coat-of-arms	?	Real W1114
	small coat-of-arms	monogram	small coat-of-arms	c. 1920	LGRP 16225
	small coat-of-arms	monogram	small coat-of-arms	?	Real W3916
	coat-of-arms	monogram	coat-of-arms	?	JQ collection
	small coat-of-arms	monogram	small coat-of-arms	c. 1920	JQ collection
	coat-of-arms	monogram	coat-of-arms	?	Blencowe37515
1098	monogram	small coat-of-arms	monogram	>6/1922	LGRP 16223
	monogram	coat-of-arms	monogram	?	JQ collection
	monogram	small coat-of-arms	monogram	>6/1922	W.Bradshaw84
1099	monogram	coat-of-arms	monogram	c. 1910	Real 65302
	monogram	coat-of-arms	monogram	?	JQ collection
1100	monogram	coat-of-arms	monogram	4/5/1910	W.Bradshaw
	monogram	coat-of-arms	monogram	?	JQ collection
	monogram	coat-of-arms	monogram	c. 1912	LCGB 499
	monogram	coat-of-arms	monogram	?	Real W1115
	monogram	coat-of-arms	monogram	?	Imm.&GCLegacy
1102	monogram	coat-of-arms	monogram	?	Real W7156
	monogram	small coat-of-arms	monogram	c. 1920	JQ collection
1103	monogram	coat-of-arms	monogram	1912	Kelland 2406
	monogram	coat-of-arms	monogram	?	Real W7158
	monogram	small coat-of-arms	monogram	c. 1920	LGRP 16253
1104	–	coat-of-arms	–	c. 1912?	A.F. Shoults
	monogram	small coat-of-arms	monogram	1922	G.C.Album

Tenders were lined to match that on the engine. The curved flares carried the single red/white lines but the upper coal plate and main frames received one red line. The standard size coat-of-arms and the company's name were applied during the early period of black livery. Later, however, the smaller coat-of-arms was used but only on the splasher sides; the tender tank sides always displaying the normal type. Three photographs are available which exhibit a mark on the smoke-box. William Bradshaw recorded No. 1100 at Leicester shed in May, and also in June, 1910. The later photograph may be seen as number 21 on page 19 of the H.M.R.S. publication on Bradshaw's work. The locomotive carries a large 5-pointed white star at the base of the smoke-box. Another picture of the same engine, possibly taken by Henry Salmon, shows that the star had been removed and a small sword shaped symbol is visible in the centre of the upper part of the smoke-box door. Finally, a photograph of No. 1103 in the Real Photographs list, reference W.7158, records no less than three symbols. At the top centre of the smoke-box door is a white cross, then about 6 inches below the cross is a white oval mark. The third character, which is the shape of a teardrop, is approximately 6 inches below that.

The majority of photographs taken in later GCR days all suggest that these locomotives were kept in an excellent condition. Certain components, however, which were formerly polished, appear to have been painted black. These were the reversing rod, handrails and smoke-box door fittings. The 8Fs, or 'Imminghams' as they were known, regularly worked some of the company's most prestigious services. As Class B4 on the L&NER their work was much the same, but the end came for them in the first years of BR. Appropriately enough, the last one in traffic was No. 1482, which was originally No. 1097 *Immingham*. As late as July 1949 this engine took a twelve-carriage express from Leicester to Banbury. It was to be the last occasion a former GCR 4-6-0 worked an express over the London extension. Withdrawal occurred in November 1950. In another reversal of GCR painting policy, the L&NER used apple green paint to finish Class B4; indeed, No. 1482 was withdrawn in that livery.

The list which follows has been prepared from a study of photographs of 8Fs taken throughout the period of the black livery. This should clarify the situation regarding the decoration applied to splasher sides. Photographic references, where known, are given but many dates are not known and, surprisingly, a picture of No. 1101 at any period has not been located.

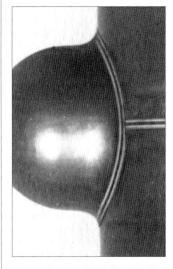

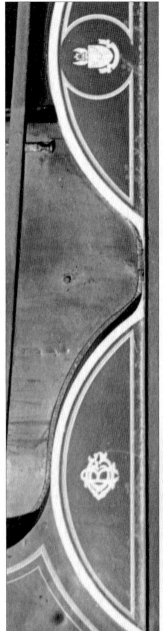

Plate 15.5   GCR Class 8F, No. 1102
No. 1102 photographed in black livery and on panchromatic film. The red outer bands and lines are visible as a middle-grey and even the double red/white stripe around the base of the dome is very clear. The number plate has a white line within the raised edge and a small serif '3' beneath the numerals, which was the power classification of an 8F 4-6-0. The location is unknown but may be in the Manchester area.
J. Quick collection

CHAPTER 16
CLASS 8G 4-6-0

The 8G class of locomotives was the last of four generally similar classes of 4-6-0 to be introduced by Robinson. They were numbered 1105–1114 and were built by Beyer, Peacock & Company during September and October 1906. The company's house magazine, the *G.C.R.J.*, vol. V, p. 208, carried an illustration of No. 1113 and the comments:

Of these engines Nos. 1105, 1106, 1107, 1108, 1109, and 1110 are stationed at Gorton, whilst Nos. 1111, 1112, and 1113 are stationed at Lincoln. They work chiefly on the fish traffic from Grimsby to Manchester, and the G.E. goods from Lincoln and beyond to the West. They are also working on the London goods service, and in the summer months are frequently called upon to work the heavy excursion traffic to Grimsby and Cleethorpes.

GREY LIVERY

Only one view of an 8G in grey is known. It is of No. 1113 and was probably an official photograph. It was published in *The Railway Magazine*, June 1912, vol. XXX, p. 476, and in at least two other publications.

BLACK LIVERY

The 8G engines' traffic livery was lined black. *The Locomotive Magazine*, October 1906, vol. 12, p. 163, noted 'The "Fish engines", nos. 1105-6 are painted black'. However, Ernest Carter's

Britain's Railway Liveries, p. 35, gives some erroneous, yet intriguing, details:

Goods locomotives (4-6-0 Robinson, No. 1113) were painted black, boiler bands being twin red lines. The cab was lined in red, with a fine white line within. Splashers were brass-beaded, with a red line within the beading. Engine valances were outlined with red, the lining continuous round the steps. Cylinders were black, with red and white lining fore and aft. Tender-underframes and steps were continuously lined out in red, whilst the axle-box tie-rods and spring buckles were also lined round. The buffer socket-plates were lined out in red. The engine number appeared in raised figures on a raised brass plate, both figures and oval being polished; the background being black.

Whoever collected the above data failed to record the double white lines on boiler bands; the second, inner white line on the cab; the white line inside the red on splasher sides and on the valance framing, etc. Perhaps engine No. 1113 was finished as described but this seems doubtful as it would be contrary to all previous GCR practice and there are no known photographs of an 8G, or any other black locomotive, so finished. An incomplete understanding of the behaviour of orthochromatic photographic material is the likely reason for this doubtful information.

A hand-written painting specification has survived and this is reproduced here. The schedule is dated 8th March 1906. There was a requirement for a locomotive and tender to be weighed and

Plate 16.1   GCR Class 8G, No. 1108
In this view No. 1108 is finished in the lined black scheme. Notice that the locomotive's wheels are lined, a standard size of coat-of-arms on both tender and driving splasher sides and how the lining on the spectacle plate ends just above the splashers. Other noteworthy features are the polished guard bars and the break in the red/white stripe on the valance, above the left-hand end of the cylinder. The buffer beam appears unlined but has a light coloured band on the near edge; this possibly unique decoration may have been a light shade of grey or blue.
R. Blencowe 24558

Painting

Boiler to receive two coats of Oxide of Iron before being lagged and one whilst hot. Clothing plates, two coats of lead colour inside. Splashers, Cab, Clothing, Wheels, Outside frames, Sandboxes, Footsteps and Buffers to receive two coats of lead colour, filled up with white lead, mixed with gold size, then coat of staining, (vegetable black, turpentine & gold size,) rubbed down, followed by another dark lead colour, sand papered, after which, one coat of ivory black paint, then coat of ivory black and varnish mixed. Lining to be done same as sample panels, afterwards to receive one coat under varnish and two coats best finishing body varnish. To be flatted down with pumice powder & horsehair between each coat. To be numbered on Buffer beam to sample after first coat of varnish. Company's Coat of Arms, (Transfers of which will be supplied) to be placed on each Driving Splasher.
A Brass Number plate, fixed on Cab side, to be painted black between the numbers, and with one eighth white line half inch within raised edge.
Inside of Main frames, Frame stays, and slide bar brackets, to have two coats lead colour, filled up with White lead mixed with gold size, rubbed down, one coat flesh colour, sand papered, one coat of quick drying vermillion (sic.), then two coats of vermillion mixed with varnish.
Outside of Main Frames, Bogie and Guard bars to receive two coats of lead colour, filled up, rubbed down, one coat of Ivory Black, and one coat of Ivory Black mixed with varnish, and one coat of hard drying body varnish.
Bodies of Straight axles to receive one coat of White lead and one coat varnish.
Ends of Axles to be lined, otherwise same as Wheels and varnished.
Smokebox, Back of Firebox, Platforms, Brake hangers, &, One coat of Black and one coat of Japan.
Chimney to have two coats lead colour, filled up with white lead, mixed with gold size, rubbed down, & one coat Black & one Japan.
Inside Cab, one coat lead colour, filled up, rubbed down, sand papered, two coats stone colour (to sample,) one coat under varnish, and one coat finishing body varnish.
To be lined as per sample panel.
Two days to intervene between each of the last three coats of varnish.
Buffer beams same as Inside frames, with the addition of being lined to sample panel, and varnished same as clothing.
Brake pipes to have two coats of approved rubber varnish.

The paint and varnish <u>to be obtained from Messrs Docker Bros.</u>

Sample panels will be provided and the greatest care must be taken that all Engines are painted strictly in accordance therewith, and of the same shades throughout.

---

photographed and this may be the provenance of the official view of No. 1113 mentioned earlier. It was customary for various parts to be left polished. Components specified are: safety valves, 'Pillars to be polished'; smoke-box, 'Smokebox door centre washer, ring, handle & wheel, hinge & brackets, to be finished bright and polished'; draw gear, 'Draw hooks and shackles to be finished bright and polished' and buffers, 'Buffer rams to be turned all over outside'. Unusually, there is no mention of cylinder ends, beadings and handrails, although these were normally bright metal.

The lining on these engines was the usual red/white scheme. The cab sides, boiler, base of dome, firebox, tender sides and end all received the double white and red decoration. The splasher sides were lined with one red/white stripe, the tops also, but later, on some engines, this was omitted. The spectacle plate was lined, the single red/white lines extending to just above the footplate; on some locomotives, however, possibly when they were new, it ended at the same level as the number plate. Buffer beams were lined as usual, at first all round the beam but before long the upper line was not being applied. Buffer guides were also lined; the square base receiving the single red/white lines and at least two examples, Nos 1108 and 1113, had the twin red/white lining on the openings. A Bradshaw photograph of No. 1114, taken on 13th August 1910, shows that the engine's buffer sockets, or guides, may have had some additional lining around the base. A picture of No. 1109 at Nottingham Victoria shows another variation of decoration on guides, the lining being applied to the parallel section only. The buffer beam on No. 1108 appears not to have received any lining at all at one period; however, the edge of the beam seems to have been painted a light colour, perhaps light grey or blue – this deviation from the normal may have been unique on GCR locomotives.

The valance framing and cylinders were always finished with the single red/white lines but the wheels were only lined around cranks and bosses when new. Mainframes were probably plain black, guard irons also, but No. 1108 had polished irons at one period. Photographs do not show red lining on frames below the smoke-box, on the tender frames or on the upper coal plate – but this lining was probably applied to the tender frames and coal plates. The curved flares received the single red/white stripe.

The letters forming the company's name appear to have been of the standard height of 6 inches but in later years some examples received the smaller type. The situation regarding the coat-of-arms was very similar; the full size version was applied when new but later the smaller type replaced them, usually on the driving wheel splasher sides. Few photographs are available to assist with the size of buffer beam numerals but the 6 inches tall characters were probably employed when new. The smaller figures were certainly in use later. A photograph of No. 6110 carrying a new number plate but otherwise in GCR livery, shows a beam devoid of numbers and lining. This view must have been recorded in very early L&NER days, as the engine was renumbered in May 1924. The white line within the number plate's raised edge was not always added and the 8Gs appear not to have ever carried a monogram. At least one engine, No. 1114, had a decorative mark on the smoke-box door; this is visible in the view of the locomotive at Leicester Central on an army special, which was published in the H.M.R.S. book of William Bradshaw's photographs.

These engines were always kept in good condition by the GCR staff. Several photographs were taken in the early post-grouping era showing them reclassified as B9 but in GCR paint and exhibiting clearly visible linings, coats-of-arms, lettering etc. The last examples were removed from service in the second year of their British Railways' ownership.

Plate 16.2   GCR Class 8G, No. 1111
Standing outside Manchester London Road station is No. 1111. The engine looks very smart and the presence of what may be a 6-wheel Third class carriage in the later livery suggests a date in the later period of the GCR. Another piece of evidence supporting the notion of a late date is the small coat-of-arms on the driving splasher.   *J. Quick collection*

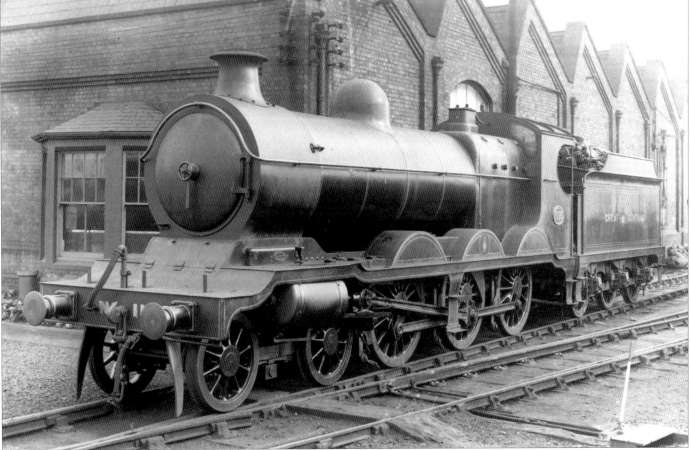

Plate 16.3   GCR Class 8G, No. 1113
This is a fine portrait of the penultimate 8G, No. 1113. The engine is standing on the south side of Leicester shed at an unknown date, possibly c. 1921. Henry Salmon may have been the cameraman.   *L.G.R.P. 16257*

ABOVE AND BELOW: Plates 17.1and 17.2   GCR Class 8H, No. 1171
No. 1171 has a 'Not to be Moved' plate on the left lampiron which indicates that it may be receiving some maintenance. These photographs were taken on 15th July 1922, at Mexborough shed. The photographer(s) was probably a member of the Lancashire branch of the Stephenson Locomotive Society which visited the shed on that day. The locomotive had re-entered traffic after overhaul at Gorton precisely one year before these views were recorded.

J. Quick collection

CHAPTER 17
CLASS 8H 0-8-4T

The GCR moved enormous tonnages of coal. Much of this emanated from the South Yorkshire coalfield and by the early years of the twentieth century the situation regarding the movement of coal was giving cause for serious concern. There were so many coal trains that part of the profit was being lost because of the problems working them. The solution proposed by the company was to build a large marshalling concentration yard at Wath which, very conveniently, was more or less in the centre of the coalfield. The board accepted Logan & Hemingway's tender for the construction of the yard in October 1905 and, little more than two years later, the yard was fully operational.

In order to move very heavy trains up the yard's hump gradient, Robinson designed a massive tank locomotive with the, then unique, wheel arrangement of 0-8-4. The 8H tanks had a three cylinder drive with steam reversing gear. Considering the endless shunting movements, the power reverser must have been appreciated by the footplate men. Four examples were built, all by Beyer, Peacock & Company. Nos 1170 and 1171 were completed on the last day of 1907 and Nos 1172 and 1173 were ready by the end of January 1908.

GREY LIVERY

There are photographs of two members of Class 8H painted in the special grey livery. An excellent side view of No. 1171 has been published more than once, George Dow's *Great Central Recalled* illustrates this on page 38. The engine is fully lined in white and grey, the wheels are lined and it carries a coat-of-arms. Engine No. 1173 was photographed in grey from at least three positions: a broadside view was issued by the Locomotive Publishing Company; the *G.C.R.J.*, vol. III, p. 207, included a two-thirds right-hand side picture, and volume 3 of Dow's *Great Central*, p. 135, has a three-quarters side illustration. The locomotive is lined out in the same basic style as No. 1171 but a dark grey border has been added around the bunker and tank side. The upper areas of the cab are similarly painted but the wheels are not lined as elaborately as No. 1171. It is not known if other members of Class 8H were grey but it is unlikely that any ran at Wath so finished.

BLACK LIVERY

All four locomotives were painted black in GCR service and, fortunately, a specification for this exists and is reproduced here.

The specification also gives details of certain components which were to be left unpainted. These were the smoke-box door centre washer, ring, handle and brackets, draw hooks and shackles. All were to be polished bright. The buffer heads were to be turned and polished.

Painting.

Boiler to receive 2 Coats of Oxide of Iron before being lagged, one whilst hot.

Clothing plates 2 Coats of Lead colour inside.

Splashers, Cab, Clothing, Wheels, Outside frames, Sandboxes, Footsteps & Buffers to receive 2 coats Lead colour filled up with White lead mixed with Gold size, then coat of Staining, (Vegatable [sic.] black, turpentine & Gold size,) rubbed down, followed by another dark lead colour, sandpapered, after which, one coat ivory black paint, then coat of ivory black & varnish mixed.

Lining to be done same as sample panels, afterwards to receive one coat under varnish & 2 coats best finishing body varnish. To be flatted down with pumice powder & horse hair between each coat.

To be numbered on Buffer beam, to sample, after first coat of varnish.

Company's Coat of Arms (transfers of which will be supplied) to be placed on side tanks, also words 'Great Central'.

A Brass number plate fixed on Coal bunker to be painted black between numbers & and with one eighth white line, half inch within the raised edge.

Inside of Main frames, Frame stay & Slidebar brackets, to have 2 coats lead colour, filled up with White lead mixed with Gold size, rubbed down, one coat flesh colour, sandpapered, One coat quick drying Vermillion (sic.), then 2 coats of vermillion mixed with varnish.

Outside of Main frames, Bogie, & Guard bars, to receive 2 coats of lead colour, filled up, rubbed down, one coat ivory black, and one coat ivory black mixed with varnish, & one coat hard drying body varnish.

Webs of Crank Axle & Body of straight axles One coat of White lead and one coat of varnish.

Ends of Axles to be lined, otherwise same as Wheels, and varnished.

Smokebox, Back of Firebox, Platforms, Brake hangers, &. One coat Black and One coat Japan.

Chimney to have 2 coats Lead colour, filled with White lead mixed with Gold size, rubbed down, & One coat Black & one coat Japan.

Inside Cab One coat Lead colour, filled up, rubbed down, sandpapered, 2 coats Stone colour (to sample), One coat under varnish & one coat finishing body varnish. To be lined to sample panel.

Two days to intervene between each of the last 3 coats of varnish.

Buffer beams same as inside frames, with the addition of being lined to sample panel, and varnished same as clothing.

Brake pipes to have 2 Coats of approved rubber varnish.

The Paint & Varnish to be obtained from Messrs Docker Bros. or approved makers.

Sample Panels will be provided, and the greatest care must be taken that all the Engines are painted strictly in accordance therewith, and of the same shades throughout.

It must be understood that not many photographs of the 8H engines in GCR condition are known. This is without doubt due to the nature and location of their work, but this shortage makes it impossible to check certain details. The few pictures that are extant indicate that soon after, and probably during, the First World War they carried the black livery, the company's title and coat-of-arms but that they were not fully lined. A suitable photograph of an 8H in the early part of its career is not available but it is most unlikely that, when new, they were not finished in the usual decorative style.

The following general notes have been collected from a series of excellent photographs of one locomotive, No. 1171. Most of the pictures were recorded at Mexborough shed on 15th July 1922. The Lancashire branch of the Stephenson Locomotive Society visited the shed on that day and it was probably then that No. 1171 was photographed. Two further views are to hand, one taken at Gorton, but all show an engine in the same general state; a very presentable locomotive which must be an indication of the regard staff had for them. Things were very different only a few years before when they were probably in poor external condition and a view of No. 1172 taken in November 1919 confirms this.

The boiler, tank and bunker sides carried lining but, although it was probably the customary red/white lines, the photographs are not of sufficient quality to be sure. The tank fronts and valance frames were lined but the same comments apply. The footsteps, front buffer beam and buffer guides, sandboxes, spectacle plate and cylinders are all unlined. The buffer beam appears to be devoid of any numerals and parts that were normally clean and polished appear not to have received any attention. This all tends to suggest an engine which has worked hard through a difficult period, when the usual standards have to some extent slipped, although it should be remembered that the engines spent very little time on shed. None of the photographs show the bunker rear. It is, therefore, impossible to determine if it and the buffer beam were lined and if the running number was applied to the back of the bunker. It is probable that, when they were new, lining was added in the areas mentioned and that the number was placed in the usual position. The two illustrations in Eddie Johnson's *Locomotives of the G.C.R.*, on pages 102 and 103 of volume 1, show No. 1171 in the state described.

The 8H engines eventually became Class S1 on the L&NER, but they were often known as 'Wath Daisies'. They worked throughout the GCR and L&NER periods, being joined by two more built in 1932. They were all, however, replaced by diesel locomotives in the 1950s. Sadly, the yard at Wath and all its associated traffic has long since vanished.

Plate 17.3   GCR Class 8H, No. 1172
The photographer has recorded the number of this engine which is fortunate because it would be impossible to do so from the photograph. Indeed, it exhibits just how bad the external condition of many goods and shunting types became during and just after the First World War. The view is dated 3rd November 1919 and was taken at Wath. The locomotive had not visited Gorton for overhaul for nearly two years. It appears to be coupled to a single bolster wagon but the main traffic at Wath was always coal.   *LCGB Ken Nunn collection 2420*

CHAPTER 18
CLASS 9N 4-6-2T

The suburban passenger traffic out of London Marylebone had, over the few years after its opening, grown significantly. The completion of the Great Western/Great Central Joint line in 1906 soon began to provide additional revenue but Sam Fay realised the advantages of accelerating these stopping passenger trains. To assist with this Robinson provided a new design of large tank locomotive with the wheel arrangement of 4-6-2. At first they hauled trains consisting mainly of the standard 50 feet long 'London suburban' stock but these carriages began to move away when Robinson's larger, and heavier, 60-foot vehicles entered service.

The GCR built a total of twenty-one engines, all at Gorton:

- Nos 165, 166, 167, 168, 169, 170, 23, 24, 447 and 448 were completed between March and August 1911.
- Another six locomotives, Nos 449, 450, 451, 452, 128 and 129, followed between October 1912 and the end of that year.
- The final five left Gorton between June and October 1917; they were numbered 371, 372, 373, 374 and 411.

Further examples were ordered but were built by the L&NER during the first half of 1923. Later, when more were required, thirteen engines were completed in 1925 and 1926. This gave the new company a total of forty-four locomotives which were now classified as A5.

GREY LIVERY

The prototype engine, No. 165, was photographed at least twice when painted grey. The *G.C.R.J.*, vol. VI, p. 277, contained a three-quarters left-hand view and a broadside postcard, No. 4063, is part of the F. Moore series. It is likely that both photographs were taken on the same occasion. In view of the obvious interest in No. 165, the engine must have worked trains whilst painted grey. Another locomotive of the same batch was also photographed in grey. *The Railway Magazine*, vol. XXX, p. 478, has a left broadside picture of No. 447. The first example of the second batch of the 1912 build, No. 449, was finished in grey, but apparently not recorded photographically. Nevertheless, the *G.C.R.J.*, vol. VIII, p. 158, included notes regarding No. 449, '*She is at present undergoing her trials, and may be seen working local trains painted lead colour*'. F. Moore was also responsible for another left side postcard, of No. 167, in grey. This photograph, No. 6727, shows an oil tank in the bunker and 'Reliostop' gear indicating that the picture was recorded during the coal strikes of 1921.

GREEN LIVERY

Engine No. 165 did not remain in grey for a long period. The *G.C.R.J.*, vol. VII, p. 8, reported '*no. 165 has now been painted standard green*'. A subsequent issue of the same volume, on page 137, informed readers of additional members of the class:

Nos. 166, 167, 169, 170 and 447 of the last order of 4-6-2 passenger engines have now all been painted in the standard green and are working the services of suburban trains in the London district.

It is unfortunate that an official painting document for the class does not appear to exist. The following information, therefore, has been assembled using only photographs as evidence.

The boiler, firebox, rear and front spectacles, cab, tank fronts and sides, bunker rear and sides were painted Brunswick green. The frames below the smoke-box, valance framing, steps, equaliser

Plate 18.1 GCR Class 9N, No. 452
In this slightly blurred photograph No. 452 is running over Ruislip water troughs on the GW/GC Joint line, about 1914. This illustrates well the bunker rear lining and the position of the running number. Note that the spectacle plate is painted green, has a black border and a white line.   *J. Quick collection*

pipes and buffer guides were finished with crimson lake. The cab roof, smoke-box, coal rails and tops of platforms were black. The tops of the side tanks were probably also black. Buffer beams were vermilion and the cab interior was, in all likelihood, very pale yellow. The wheels were green, outsides of mainframes were probably black, the insides vermilion. Guard irons appear to have been painted on some engines and this may have been black or crimson. The buffer

heads, lubricators, coupling hooks and shackles, whistle, fittings to the smoke-box door, hand rails etc. were usually polished bright.

The boiler and firebox were lined with twin white lines which had a black band between them. At the point where the smoke-box and boiler met, only one white line was applied. The tank fronts and sides, cab, bunker sides and rear and both spectacle plates had a black border with a white line which formed a separation from the

ABOVE: Plate 18.2   GCR Class 9N, No. 372
A fine view of No. 372 on Neasden shed and photographed very late in the GCR period. The red lines on the framing are reasonably clear and are just discernible on the parallel section of the buffers. The engine is in a very clean condition but this was generally the case with these locomotives. The important suburban passenger traffic on the Met/GC and GW/GC Joint lines was successfully worked for many years by Robinson's tank locomotives of classes 9K, 9L and latterly by Class 9N.   *J. Quick collection*

BELOW: Plate 18.3   GCR Class 9N, No. 168
No. 168 looks quite new in this view at Neasden shed. Apart from the vermilion lines, which are difficult to see, the other linings are clearly visible. The presence of the 9L, No. 1131, at the rear, suggests a date of about 1912. This 4-4-2T moved away from the London area in the spring of 1915.
                                                                                                                                                Locomotive Publishing Co. 4674

green. The tank sides, cab, bunker sides and rear also had an inset panel of lining. This consisted of two white lines with a black centre. The base of the dome was usually decorated with white/black/white stripes.

The framing below the smoke-box, valance frames, footsteps and equaliser pipes all received a black border and this had a red or vermilion line alongside. The cab interior probably had a black edge with a red line. Buffer beams were finished with a white line against a black border but all photographs show that the top of the beam was not decorated. Many views do not assist with the lining on buffer guides but there is little doubt that they did receive lining and that it would have been the customary vermilion line and black edge; this was added to the square section and to the opening, although one view shows the red line on the parallel part of the guide. During the GCR period wheels were normally lined and this was made up of one white line which separated the black of the tyre from the green of the centre and then a double white line arrangement which had a green centre. This encircled the boss, the axle ends being black. On the driving wheels the double white lines were applied around the cranks, with one line passing around the axle end.

The company's title, formed of 6 inches tall transfers, always seems to have been used. During the early period of the engines' service the standard size of coat-of-arms was also in use but later the smaller version was beginning to be employed. The running number was not placed on the rear buffer beam but on the bunker rear. Some late photographs suggest that the 'No.' was no longer being applied. The small numerals, about 4½ inches tall, were used on the front beam. The single white line inside the edge of the number plate seems never to have been added.

ENGINE NO. 165

All engines of Class 9N would have been painted and lined as described during most or all of their GCR service. Photographs, however, reveal much interesting detail at times, and an anomaly regarding No. 165, the first example, has come to notice. It was certainly green when first painted but it received a vermilion line alongside the black border on the tank fronts and sides, bunker sides and rear, cab sides and spectacle plates, in place of the customary white line. From being new to, at least, the spring of 1913, the engine was running in the express passenger livery but later, perhaps after April 1915, it was repainted to match the other members of the class. This apparently singular treatment was in all probability because No. 165 was the prototype locomotive. A photograph in the L.C.G.B. collection, No. 1039, exemplifies the special finish of No. 165. *Locomotives Illustrated*, no. 98, p. 11, has a fine view which also shows this but it is not known if other class members were similarly painted.

ENGINE NO. 128

Another most interesting irregularity noted on a photograph of No. 128 must be discussed. The postcard is part of the F. Moore series, no. 2189, and it shows a black engine. It was taken at Neasden shed and was published in *Robinson Locomotives* by Brian Haresnape and Peter Rowledge, on p. 69. There is a useful reference to this livery in *The Railway and Travel Monthly*, January 1919, p. 64, '*G.C.R. 4-6-2T no. 128 is again in London district having returned from Gorton painted black, with a red and white lining after style of mixed traffic 4-6-0s*'. Percy Banyard noted in a letter to the author concerning black livery: '*Just prior to grouping, 4-6-2T no. 128 received this colour scheme, I thought it looked quite good*'. The first reference is of particular interest as it is in agreement with the shopping records of the engine. It left Gorton after overhaul on 28th September 1918. Its next works visit was on 3rd July 1920, leaving on 22nd October of that year. The engine's

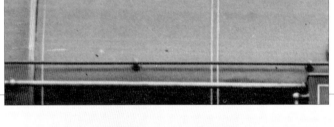

Plate 18.4   GCR Class 9N, No. 24
No. 24 is standing outside Manchester London Road during 1921. It was altered to burn oil fuel in the May of that year, the equipment being removed in October. The wheels are quite elaborately decorated with white lines and black, and a small coat-of-arms on the tank side. Hardly noticeable, however, are the red lines on frames, step plates etc. (*right*). Note the single white line where the boiler and smokebox meet (*top*).
J. Quick collection

Plate 18.5   GCR Class 9N, No. 128
No. 128 is at Neasden shed about 1919. Although the locomotive is painted black, the livery was not the usual scheme but that described below. Percy Banyard noted this engine in black, which may have been a unique finish for a GCR locomotive. The detail images show (*left to right*) the number plate with white line, the red and white stripes on the tank, the boiler barrel and the front framing.
F. Moore 2189

last repair under the GCR was from 21st January to 9th May 1922. Other views of No. 128 painted green, taken in June 1914 and just before grouping, confirm that the locomotive must have been black between September 1918 and either October 1920 or May 1922.

The description of the unusual, possibly unique, black livery that was applied to No. 128 which follows has been deduced from photograph 2189, the only picture known. The picture was recorded using orthochromatic film and is perfectly focussed, exposed and processed. As a consequence it is just possible to see the red lines with close study. The locomotive is painted black and is lined with red and white. The boiler and firebox carry double white lines but it is not possible to see any red lines due to the angle of the photograph. However, it is unlikely that red lines were not applied alongside the white. The framing below the smoke-box was black and lined with one white line. Next to this, on the outside, was a slightly wider red band and on the inside was another red band which may have been marginally less in width. The valance frames appear to be lined in the same style but the three lines, red/white/red, were continuously painted along the frame. The footstep plates were lined separately. The tank fronts and the front spectacle plate appear to have the same lining. The cab, tank and bunker sides and, presumably, the bunker rear carry double white lines. On the outside of the outer line is a wider red band, but on the inside of same is a narrower red stripe. A similar narrow red band is also visible on the inside of the inner white line. The number plate has a white line within the edge. The wheels appear unlined but they may have had red lining. The only other lined area is the front buffer beam and this is the usual black border with a white line, but this has not been applied

along the top beneath the platform. The buffer guides are lined with red and white on the square base and near the opening. The tank side carries the standard size of coat-of-arms and transfers of the company's name.

SPECIAL MARKS

Only one view which shows a special mark on a 9N has been identified. A photograph of No. 447, taken outside Marylebone on 25th September 1915, clearly shows a heart-shaped symbol on the smoke-box door. The reference for this is L.C.G.B. 2058. Another, slightly earlier, picture of this locomotive records it leaving Marylebone on a passenger train and, remarkably, the mark is not present. There is no reason to doubt the photographer's records which means that the mark must have been added between the 11th and the 25th of September 1915. The reference for the earlier view is L.C.G.B. 2056.

The 9N locomotives were very highly regarded by the staff. Many photographs were taken and very few are of engines in poor external condition. They were fitted with water pick-up gear and were capable of, and on occasions did work, fast passenger trains. Their domination of the London suburban services for many years is ample testimony to their excellence but in their later years of L&NER service the A5s were more widely distributed. The first withdrawal of a GCR-built engine occurred in December 1942 but the next one was not removed from traffic until 1957. The remaining locomotives were quickly withdrawn thereafter, the last examples in November 1960.

CHAPTER 19
CLASS 8K 2-8-0

It has already been mentioned, as part of the 8F 4-6-0 class chapter, that the first work on the dock at Immingham began in July 1906. The docks were formally opened by the king six years later with all the publicity that the GCR could muster. Every conceivable cargo was moved through the docks but the facilities for the export of coal were very extensive. The company also invested heavily in associated works. In anticipation of a substantial increase in traffic, a new heavy mineral engine was introduced.

The 8K was based on Robinson's earlier 8A 0-8-0 tender engine. The first one, No. 966, appeared in September 1911 and there was a total of 126 running before the First World War. As a consequence of that conflict a more powerful locomotive was required for service abroad and the 8K was selected as being a suitable type. Between 1917 and 1919, 521 engines were built for the Ministry of Munitions by a wide variety of contractors. Later, at various times between 1919 and August 1921, ninety-three of these war-effort locomotives were on loan to the GCR. Originally the company had agreed to build twenty-five engines at Gorton for the Ministry but, in the event, only six were made and three of these were purchased in April 1919.

The 8Ks were built as follows:

– An order for thirty was placed with Gorton and they were delivered between September 1911 and May 1912. They carried the running numbers 966, 26, 69, 93, 331–335, 102, 133, 155, 346–355, 400 and 402–408.

– Kitson & Company built twenty engines during the summer and autumn of 1912. These were numbered 1183–1202.

– The North British Locomotive Company produced fifty examples between August 1912 and January 1913, with numbers 1203–1252.

– Gorton completed the pre-First World War construction with twenty-six locomotives built between April 1913 and June 1914. They carried running numbers 375–399 and 271.

– The final three engines were built by Gorton for the Ministry of Munitions in the first three months of 1919. Their ROD numbers were 2005–2007 but, on passing into GCR ownership, they were renumbered 1, 5 and 8 respectively.

GREY LIVERY

The first engine, No. 966, was photographed at least twice painted grey when the company's official photographer James W. Wood recorded it brand new. A good left side view is on p. 146 of David Jackson's biography of Robinson. The company's house journal, the *G.C.R.J.*, vol. VII, p. 123, published a three-quarter left side illustration. When No. 353 was altered for fuel experiments it was photographed in a hybrid livery of fully lined black but with grey wheels. This is in the F. Moore collection, No. 2186. The same locomotive was also recorded at about the same time but in the standard black scheme. The third engine of the Kitson batch, No. 1185, was photographed in a very light shade of grey. No.

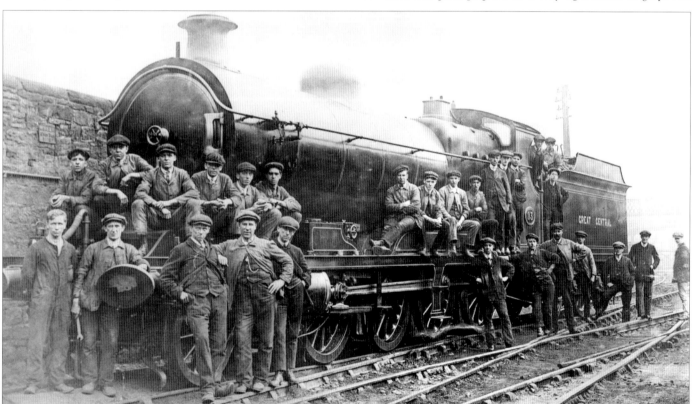

Plate 19.1   GCR Class 8K, No. 93   No. 93 on Barnsley shed about 1912, with twenty-eight members of staff! The interest in the engine is because it was its first visit to Barnsley. There is sufficient visible of No. 93 to see that it is remarkably clean, but does not carry a coat-of-arms. Third from the left on the front of the engine is Ron Silverwood. Ron was a highly respected engineman and spent virtually all his career working from Barnsley depot.

R. Silverwood collection

1209 of the North British contribution was also pictured, at least twice, whilst painted grey. One view is a right-hand broadside and the other has J.G. Robinson standing by the cab. Both pictures are part of the Mitchell Library collection and that with Robinson by the engine was published in *Loco. Profile*, No. 21, p. 195. No. 381 of the second Gorton batch was recorded in grey and this was illustrated on page 136 of Eddie Johnson's *Locomotives of the G.C.R.*, vol. 2.

BLACK LIVERY

The traffic livery used on the 8Ks during the GCR period was always black. The *G.C.R.J.* has three references to this and all of them are in volume VII. On page 216, under 'Locomotive Notes', the following comments appeared: '*nos. 331, 332 of the 2-8-0 mineral engines have now been painted a standard black*'. Page 280 informed readers that No. 966 had had the indicator shelter removed whilst it was being painted and '*nos. 332, 333, 334, 335, 26 and 69 are now painted standard black*'. Finally, page 300 reported that '*385 and 386 have been painted black and are in regular traffic, working in the Sheffield district*'.

A building specification was issued by Gorton in February 1912. This became an agreement between the GCR and the North British Locomotive Company dated 10th May 1912. This document included painting requirements and these are reproduced below. The instructions for painting the tender are on page 29 of the building specification and are reproduced on the facing page.

The GCR required three dozen large mounted platinotype photographs of the first five engines and tenders, also a further dozen of same, framed and not less than 42¾ inches by 26 inches. In accordance with Robinson's usual stipulations, the smoke-box door centre, washer, ring and handle, wheel, hinges and brackets were to be polished. The cylinder ends were to be covered with polished steel casing plates and the coupling rods were to be finished bright, but no mention was made of the connecting rods. In addition all wheel tyres were to be turned and the outside face left bright. All hand rails and pillars on the cab, boiler and tender received the same treatment.

One or two other points require some comment. The first is that the cab interior was to be green and this was something of an innovation in terms of painting policy. The shade of green and the lining colour are unknown; however, given a green area and possibly a black border, a white or red separating line may have been applied. It is plausible that the heraldic symbol was carried by the early locomotives but a picture of an 8K with a coat-of-arms and in service livery has not been located.

The boiler and firebox were lined with the double red/white bands which had a black centre, but only one red/white stripe was painted next to the smoke-box. The spectacle plate, splashers, sandboxes, valance frames, step plates and cylinders also carried the single red/white lines, the red always on the outside. The cab, tender sides

---

PAINTING

Boiler to receive two coats of oxide of iron before being lagged, one whilst hot.

Clothing Plates, two coats of lead colour inside.

Outside Frames, Footsteps, Buffers, Splashers, Cab, Clothing, and Wheels to receive two coats of lead colour, filled up with white lead mixed with gold size, rubbed down, then coat of staining (vegetable black, turpentine, and gold size), rubbed down, then coat of dark lead colour, sand-papered, then one coat of ivory black paint, then one of ivory black and varnish mixed, afterwards to be lined to sample panels, then one coat of under varnish and two of best finishing body varnish. To be flatted down with pumice powder and horsehair between each two coats.

Numbers in gold leaf, shaded with blue, to be placed on Buffer Beam, after first coat of varnish.

A brass Number-plate, fixed on Cab Sides, to be painted black between numbers, and with one-eighth white line, half-inch within the raised edge.

Inside of Main Frames, Frame Stay, and Slide-bar Brackets to have two coats lead colour, filled up with white lead mixed with gold size, rubbed down, one coat flesh colour, sand-papered, one coat of vermilion, and two coats vermilion mixed with hard-drying body varnish.

Outside of Main Frames, Bogie, and Guard Bars to receive two coats lead colour, filled up, rubbed down, one coat ivory black, and one coat ivory black mixed with varnish, and one coat hard-drying body varnish.

Bodies of Straight Axles to receive one coat white lead and one coat varnish.

Ends of Axles black and varnished.

Smoke-box, Bogie, back of Fire-box, Platforms, Brake Hangers, etc., one coat black and one coat Japan.

Chimney to have two coats lead colour, filled up with white lead, mixed with gold size, rubbed down, and one coat black and one Japan.

Inside Cab, one coat lead colour, filled up, rubbed down, sand-papered, two coats green (to sample), one coat under varnish, and one coat finishing body varnish. To be lined as per sample panel.

Two days to intervene between each of the last three coats of varnish.

Buffer Beams same as Inside Frames, with the addition of being lined to sample panel, and finished same as Clothing.

Brake Pipes to have two coats of approved rubber varnish.

The Paint and Varnish to be obtained from Messrs. Docker Brothers or approved makers.

Sample Panels will be provided, and the greatest care must be taken that all the Engines are painted strictly in accordance therewith, and of the same shades throughout.

Plate 19.2   GCR Class 8K, No. 394
Another clean and very presentable 8K, No. 394, on a Down goods at the north end of Nottingham Victoria. The engine is probably new, built at Gorton in April 1914, and this would explain its fine condition – but this was not to last, unfortunately.   *R.K. Blencowe collection, F.H. Gillford*

PAINTING

Main Frames, Outside Frames, Axle-box Lids, Footsteps, Buffers, Tank Sides, End and Protector Plate to receive two coats lead colour, filled up with white lead mixed with gold size, rubbed down, followed by one coat of staining, rubbed down, one coat dark lead colour, sandpapered, one coat ivory black paint, and one coat ivory black and varnish mixed. Transfers of Coat of Arms to be fixed, which will be supplied, and lining to be done same as sample panels, afterwards to receive one coat under varnish and two coats best finishing body varnish.

To be flatted down with pumice powder and horse-hair between coats.

Company's name, with letters in gold leaf, to be placed on each side of Tank, to sample.

Buffer Beams, similar to Engine.

Inside Tanks and Well, Outside top of Tank, and Coal Space to have two coats red lead, finished with black.

Tool Box and Sand Boxes two coats lead colour, finished black, and varnished.

Inside of Frames two coats lead colour, finished in oil black.

Axles, same as Engine.

Brake Work and Intermediate Buffers to receive one coat lead colour, one coat oil black, and varnished.

Brake Pipes to have two coats of approved rubber varnish.

The Paint and Varnish to be obtained from Messrs. Docker Bros. or approved makers.

JNO. G. ROBINSON,

Chief Mechanical Engineer.

GORTON,
   February 1912

Plate 19.3 GCR Class 8K, No. 353

No. 353 was the subject of one of Robinson's fuel trials, this one using pulverised coal. The trials are discussed in more detail in chapter 25. This view shows the engine as altered c. June 1917 and carrying lined black livery but with grey wheels. Note the small '1' below the running number, which was the power classification of an 8K.   *F. Moore 2186*

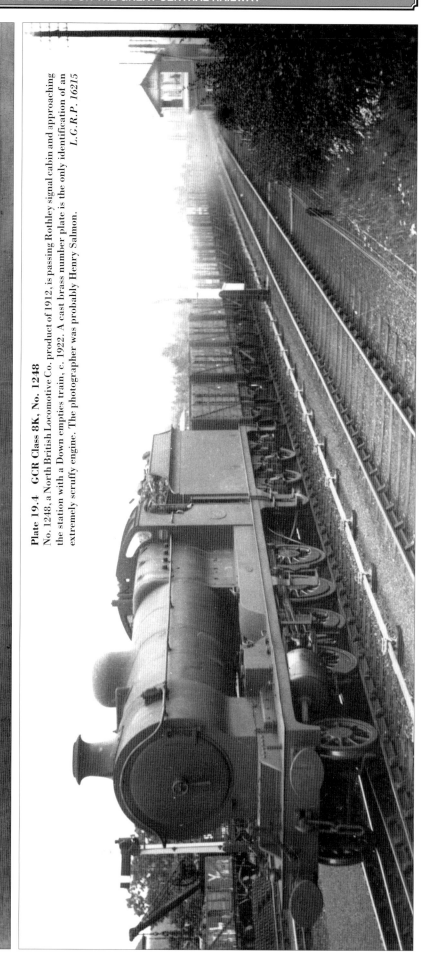

Plate 19.4 GCR Class 8K, No. 1248

No. 1248, a North British Locomotive Co. product of 1912, is passing Rothley signal cabin and approaching the station with a Down empties train, c. 1922. A cast brass number plate is the only identification of an extremely scruffy engine. The photographer was probably Henry Salmon.   *L.G.R.P. 16215*

Plate 19.5   GCR Class 8K, No. 8
This locomotive, No. 8, was built by Gorton for the government in June 1919 as ROD No. 2007. The air reservoir below the cab, the jacks and Westinghouse pump mounting straps on the smoke-box side all betray the engine's provenance. It was purchased by the GCR in 1919 when it may have been repainted lined black. The location is near Ashton Moss junction, about 1921.   *J. Quick collection*

and end received the twin white lines which had a wider red band on the outside of the outer line. Before the First World War, buffer beams were edged black with a white line alongside. Some of the North British batch had lining all around the beam, but generally it was not applied to the top edge. After the war, lining on beams seems to have been omitted completely and photographs also indicate that numerals were not being applied either. The customary red/white lining on buffer guides is visible on early views, but not in the later period. There are remarkably few suitable photographs from which conclusions may be made in certain areas. For example, the lining around the dome, smoke-box frames and wheels are all in doubt.

The decoration on the tender matched that on the locomotive. The curved flares carried the single red/white band and the main frames one red line. Lining is very difficult to detect on the upper coal plate, but this would have consisted of one red line. The transfers of 'Great Central' seem to have always been the standard height but buffer beam numerals were probably always of the smaller variety. The white line around the running number on the cab side plate was certainly added when new and photographs show that some plates also displayed the number '1', which was the power classification of an 8K.

In a letter to the author dated 21st July 1981, Mr E.B. Woodruffe Peacock referred to the painting of the 8K 2-8-0s at the old Lancashire, Derbyshire & East Coast Railway's works at Tuxford. He wrote:

When the G.C. took over at Tuxford there were considerable stocks of locomotive paint for lining out etc., on hand. Thus to save money the directors authorised the use of the basic paint and lining out to continue in L.D.E.C. colours until stocks of paint were used up. Good economy! Hence several consolidations [2-8-0s] and 0-6-0 Gorton engines were so painted at Tuxford.

Photographs of former LD&ECR locomotives painted in what is believed to be this composite livery are known, but none of either the 0-6-0s or the 2-8-0s have been located. The shopping records for the 8Ks are incomplete and this precludes positive identification of the locomotives involved.

The advent of the First World War, with all the attendant problems that it created, seriously affected the condition of steam locomotives generally. An examination of photographs of 8Ks taken in the few years after the armistice shows hard-worked engines; many unkempt and requiring some serious external attention. This is only what would be expected because the movement of wartime traffic was of paramount importance. In the prevailing circumstances it is not surprising that the company's goods engines' paintwork received minimal maintenance.

MINISTRY OF MUNITIONS – PURCHASED ENGINES

The GCR purchased three locomotives from the government during the post-war sale of surplus stock and this has already been noted. They began their new careers in the spring of 1919, probably having done no work at all for their previous owners. At first they carried some, or the remains of some, of their ROD equipment, but all three were lined and finished as the 8Ks were being painted at that time and as described above.

MINISTRY OF MUNITIONS – HIRED ENGINES

Many of the war department 2-8-0s were hired by the GCR. On some engines, at least, a small metal plate lettered 'MM' was fixed below the ROD number and the tender was lettered 'Great Central' with what appear to be the standard height characters. Apart from these small changes the majority probably ran in plain black. However, a particularly interesting note is contained in *The Locomotive News and Railway Notes*, a magazine that was published fortnightly. In the issue for 25th October 1919, as part of a list of ROD 2-8-0s working on the GCR, it commented '2003, 2004 are painted in the standard colours of that line, viz., black with red and white lining'. Records of Nos 2003 and 2004 show that they went to France early in 1919. They must have spent little time there because the company hired them before the date of the report above, finishing them in black lined livery.

In the mid-1920s a number of ROD locomotives were sold to J. & A. Brown of New South Wales, Australia. A handful of these worked into the 1970s and when three were saved from being scrapped their historical significance was recognised. Two were originally ROD Nos 2003 and 2004, both from a batch of six built at Gorton in 1918/19. The third engine was No. 1984, which was built in December 1918 by the North British Locomotive Co. Who would have thought that these three engines would have been preserved 'down under', many years later? Some forty years ago there was a plan to repatriate one of these but nothing came of the notion. It is understood that No. 2004 is under restoration at the time of writing.

When Robinson embarked upon providing his employer with a 2-8-0 heavy goods engine it would never have occurred to him that, over the following years, his basic design would be utilised to supply hundreds more as part of Britain's war effort. No doubt he was confident that the 8K would be successful but unaware that it would later be considered as one of the finest steam locomotives to run in this country. Robinson and the board must have derived extreme satisfaction from their success. The staff gave them the nickname of 'Tinies'; the original 'Tinies', the 0-8-0s of Class 8A, then becoming known as 'Old fashioned ladies', in some areas at least. The ROD engines were equally useful and efficient machines, working abroad in the 1914–1918 war and again, in some cases, twenty-five years later in the Second World War.

The decision to preserve an original 8K as part of the National Collection was highly appropriate; a well deserved tribute to Robinson. No. 102 has been saved and returned to traffic on today's preserved GCR as BR O4, No. 63601. As the engine approached its centenary there were rumours of a repaint into the lined black style used when it was new. Sadly the repaint into GCR livery, of course, didn't happen.

ABOVE: Plate 19.6   GCR Class 8K, No. 405
Standing on Mexborough shed and accompanied by twelve of the shed staff is No. 405. This example looks in good condition which suggests it may be recently ex Gorton works. The date of this picture is unknown but is probably c. 1921. The engine was allocated to Mexborough shed when the GCR became part of the L&NER.   *G.C.R.S. collection D13*

BELOW: Plate 19.7   GCR Class 8K Altd., No. 966
No. 966, the first of Class 8K, was rebuilt to take part in pulverised fuel experiments in September 1921, when this photograph was taken. To all intents and purposes it was an 8M, but one official document classified it as an '8K Altd.' The livery is the usual lined black but the special bogie tender has a vertical panel and this has received a separate rectangle of red/white lines.   *F. Moore 6723*

CHAPTER 20
CLASS 1 4-6-0

The Class 1 4-6-0s marked a remarkable change in direction for GCR express passenger locomotive design. Trains had been increasing in weight and engines were required that had a higher tractive effort. The elegance of Robinson's 4-4-0s and the 'Jersey Lilies' was not transferred to his later classes. The traffic department's needs ended the age of elegant locomotives, both on the GCR and on other lines, which was unfortunate but entirely necessary. The new 4-6-0 brought a new style to the company's express engines, with straight splashers and nameplates and, coupled to the new 60-foot corridor carriages, a massive presence to its trains. They were handsome, superbly finished locomotives, the sight of which gave a suggestion of running fast with heavy trains and their introduction was much anticipated by the railway world in general. The *G.C.R.J.* reported regularly on the first engine's progress through Gorton works, whilst photographs taken during construction appeared in its pages. Clearly, the company considered the newcomer would be a winner, but it is probably fair to say that they were to be disappointed.

The Class 1s were all built at Gorton and were numbered 423–428. No. 423 was completed shortly before Christmas 1912. The remaining five were built during the following year, Nos 424–427 in the spring and No. 428 at Christmas 1913. They were all named, but Nos 424–427 ran nameless until they had been in service for various periods, from four months for No. 424 to two months for No. 427. Sam Fay, the company's general manager, who had been the driving force behind the transformation of the GCR, was knighted on the occasion of the opening of the docks at Immingham. This event occurred only six months before the completion of No. 423, which suggests that the decision to name the prototype *Sir Sam Fay* from new was predetermined. The others carried the names of cities on the system. The last locomotive was named on entering traffic. The list of names is:

423 *Sir Sam Fay*
424 *City of Lincoln*
425 *City of Manchester*
426 *City of Chester*
427 *City of London*
428 *City of Liverpool.*

GREY LIVERY

It is believed that only No. 423 was painted and photographed in grey, as no picture of another locomotive so finished has been identified. The engine was recorded at least six times, probably by the official photographer and, in view of the unprecedented publicity surrounding No. 423, this is hardly surprising. A picture of it painted grey would have been the first sight that many would have of it. Two very similar right broadside views were published, one in *The Railway Magazine*, vol. XXXV, p. 346, the other in *Per Rail*, p. 230. The *G.C.R.J.* contributed with three illustrations, one of which has already been noted. Volume VIII, p. 226, has a fine, right broadside, picture of Robinson, his managers and foremen all arranged in front of No. 423. On page 227 is another, almost identical, photograph but the general workmen have replaced the managers. David Jackson's biography contains a three-quarter right-hand view on page 154 and another, slightly different, one appears in *Per Rail*, p. 16. Photographs of No. 423 were to be found in all the contemporary railway journals, both at home and

abroad, such was the interest in this celebrated locomotive. The GCR regularly placed advertisements in railway magazines and a front smoke-box view in grey livery was soon included in those pages. Under 'Locomotive Notes' in volume VIII, on page 226, the *G.C.R.J.* informed its readers *'The new express passenger engine no. 423 has now been completed, and running her trials on slow passenger trains prior to being painted'*. The same publication later commented that No. 423 worked its first express train on 2nd March 1913; this was the 12.35pm ex Manchester London Road and, by that date, the locomotive would have been repainted in green livery.

GREEN LIVERY AND BLACK LIVERY

Railway historians have tried to interpret why Gorton painted three engines of Class 1 green and the remaining three black. More than one explanation has been offered but, generally, express passenger locomotives were green, and mixed traffic and goods engines black. It is not as straightforward as that statement seems, however, as there are many records of black 4-6-0s working express trains, but rather fewer of green engines on goods trains. The fact remains that engines performed whatever work was required, whenever it was necessary.

The Locomotive Magazine, vol. 19, p. 159, commented, erroneously as it happens,

No. 424 City of Lincoln, *425* City of Manchester, *426* City of Chester *and 427* City of London *(4-6-0 Sir Sam Fay class) have been painted black, unlike 423* Sir Sam Fay *which is standard passenger green.*

Many years later an interesting letter was published in the *Railway Modeller*. In a reply to a correspondent, the February 1960 issue on page 42 contained the following from a reader who had lived in Leicester between 1914 and 1922:

I have no doubt whatsoever from personal recollection that, at this time, nos. 423 Sir Sam Fay, *425* City of Manchester, *428* City of Liverpool *were in green livery and 424* City of Lincoln, *426* City of Chester *and 427* City of London *black.*

The appearance of No. 423 finished in green must have turned many heads. One wonders what comments were made by employees of the North Western at Manchester London Road when the engine stood virtually side by side with that company's locomotives. The letters columns of the *G.C.R.J.* began to bulge with references to 'Sir Sam'. The editor received requests to supply a coloured plate of No. 423 within the pages of the journal and a promise was made to 'Platelayer' to look into the possibility. The May 1913 edition published a photogravure of the engine and another correspondent, whose *nom de plume* was 'Loco', suggested that each station should have a plate of the engine on display.

The house journal continued to supply further details of the painting of the remaining engines. Volume VIII, p. 290, reported *'No. 424, the second of the new 4-6-0 engines being built at the Gorton Shops has been completed and is now being painted black after having run her trials'*. On page 358 appeared *'No. 426 has now been turned out of the shops painted black, and is at present undergoing her trials prior to being placed in regular service'.*

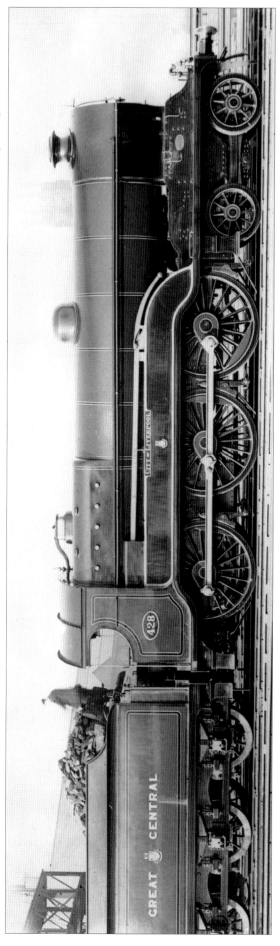

ABOVE: Plate 20.1   GCR Class 1, No. 426

No. 426 *City of Chester* was built as a black engine but in this view, which is at Neasden shed, the engine carries green paint. No. 426 left Gorton as such on 15th June 1921 and this is in accordance with the fitting of a fuel oil tank on the tender.   *J. Quick collection*

BELOW: Plate 20.2   GCR Class 1, No. 428

No. 428 *City of Liverpool* in a lovely broadside view, taken outside Manchester London Road station. The engine appears to be quite new and this would date this photograph to c. 1914. The lining is very clear, particularly around the wheels but note that the bogie frames and those immediately above the bogie are painted crimson, have a black border and a red separating line.   *P.F. Cooke*

Volume IX, p. 2, under 'Locomotive Notes', provided additional news on the Class 1s:

> *The City Class* [note the nickname], *the large 4-6-0 express passenger engines recently built at Gorton are, with the exception of no. 423, being named after the various cities through which the line passes;* 424 *City of Lincoln,* 425 *City of Manchester,* 426 *City of Chester,* 427 *City of London, of these no.* 425 *is being painted green as is the case with no.* 423.

On page 266 it was reported that '*no. 428* City of Liverpool *was out of shops being painted before work*' and p. 300 concluded the introduction of the class with the following '*No. 428* City of Liverpool, *last of the (4-6-0) Sir Sam Fay type has now been completed and is now in traffic painted green, the standard for passenger engines*'.

The first engine was to have attended the International Exhibition at Ghent, Belgium in 1913, carrying its magnificent livery and the unique copper-capped chimney, very much *à la* GWR. *The Railway Magazine* of July 1913 noted that only a series of illustrations of the engine was sent instead, but that these were accompanied by a very large scale model of Immingham Docks. The model was made by Messrs Bassett-Lowke Ltd and measured 26 feet by 15 feet! The same company also supplied models of No. 423 for advertising purposes.

GREEN LIVERY IN DETAIL

Three Class 1s, Nos 423, 425 and 428, were painted in the standard Brunswick green and crimson lake livery when new but an official document which specifies this is unknown. The following is believed to be a reasonably accurate description of the painting scheme.

The boiler and firebox, cabsides, spectacle plate and all wheels were green. The short cover to the reversing rod was also green. The splasher sides, buffer bodies, frames below smoke-box, valance framing below footplate and step plates were crimson. The cab roof, platforms, smoke-box, tops of splashers, footsteps and chimney were black. The chimney on No. 423 had a copper cap when new but this seems to have been removed after a short period. Insides of mainframes were vermilion, the outsides were probably black, but those behind the bogie were certainly crimson. The framing of the bogie above the large springs was crimson and the lower section may also have been that colour. The cab interior was definitely light coloured, as illustrated in the *G.C.R.J.*, vol. VIII, p. 260; this indicates that the usual very pale yellow or stone shade was applied, which had a black border with a thin red separating line.

The tender end and sides were green and this included the flares and upper coal plates. The mainframes, valance frames, footstep plates and buffer bodies were painted crimson. The top and front of the tender, the tops of the running plate and of the footsteps were all black.

The locomotive and tender were lined out in the usual manner. The boiler and firebox were decorated with twin white lines which had a black centre. The base of the dome was similarly painted. The spectacle plate had one white line applied around the plate and set alongside a black edge. Cab sides had a black border and then a red line which separated the black from the main green area. A continuous green border came next, then another continuous stripe which was formed of two white lines with a black centre. The splasher sides and the frames supporting the smoke-box had a black border and this had a red, probably vermilion, line alongside. The valance framing was finished in the same manner but the lining on the framing continued across the tops of the footsteps. The buffer bodies also received a black border with a red line, which was applied on the edge of the square base and at the opening. Buffer

beams were vermilion. They had a black border which had a white line adjacent to it but this did not continue along the top of the beam. Locomotive wheels were lined in white; around the crank and the hub of the bogie wheels. A white line was applied around the axle ends which were black but between the white lines was green. The crimson on the bogie frame and on the framing behind the bogie was lined with one red line which had a black edge.

The tender was lined to match the engine. The end and sides had a narrow black border with the customary red line and inset were double white lines which contained a black centre stripe. The flares and upper coal plates had separate black borders and each had a red line alongside. The small plate supporting the handrail top near the tank front also received red lining inside a black border. The mainframes had a black edge, lined with red. This appeared on the cut-outs and on the spring dampers, as well as around the bottom edges. The buffer bodies and beams were lined as the locomotive.

Adding to the splendid sight of a 'Sam Fay' in full livery, the polished parts were many. These included the smoke-box ring, centre wheel, handle and hinge, buffer heads, the coupling slot on buffer beams, all handrails and beadings, reversing and coupling rods, guard irons, copper cap on No. 423's chimney, safety valve bonnet, whistle, brass spectacles, couplings etc. The wheel tyres of No. 423 were polished when it was new but no photographs of other class members with this feature are known. When new, this engine also had a highly polished fitting in the centre of the bogie frame. When it was undergoing trials the locomotive was fitted with an indicating shelter. The colour of the shelter is unknown, but in all probability it was black, with the small look-outs having brass beadings, as mentioned in *The Railway & Travel Monthly*, May 1914.

The standard size of coat-of-arms appeared on the tender side but the smaller version adorned the splasher sides. This was set inside a double vermilion lining arrangement which had black borders. The coloured illustration in chapter 4 makes this clear. Transfers forming the company's name were the usual type but the smaller characters, which were about 4½ inches tall, were used on buffer beams. The monogram appears to have never been used, nor does the white line within the number plate seem to have been applied. One view is known which shows a distinctive mark. A picture taken c. 1920 on the western side of Woodhead Tunnel shows No. 423 standing by a stop signal with 'Reliostop' equipment on the left of the engine. A small, light-coloured arrowhead-shaped figure is prominent near the top of the smoke-box door.

There is no question that No. 423 was a very special locomotive, as the foregoing has attempted to indicate. There were so many expectations placed upon it: the publication of details before it was completed, the proposed visit to Ghent, the choice of name and the extra special livery. The polished copper cap to the chimney and the wheel tyres – the latter of which really belonged to the past on the GCR – and the other fittings not normally polished all gave the engine an almost unique appeal. Later express passenger types, for example the 11E 4-4-0s, had crimson painted tender fronts, edged black and lined vermilion. It is possible that the tender fitted to No. 423 also carried this special finish, but photographs do not clarify this matter. In the late GCR period, when all these 4-6-0s were running in green livery, their tender fronts may have had crimson paint and been finished as described.

BLACK LIVERY IN DETAIL

The following engines of Class 1 were painted black from new: Nos 424, 426 and 427. Again, and sadly, a painting document has not been located, but the notes which follow have been compiled using photographs and should provide useful information.

The locomotive and tender were painted black, relieved by lining, polished parts, buffer beams etc. The boiler and firebox were lined

Plate 20.3   GCR Class 1, No. 424
No. 424 is standing on the turntable at Manchester Central. The engine is new and in original condition, being painted black and nameless, which dates
the picture to the early part of 1913.   *J. Quick collection*

with the red/white/black-centre/white/red stripes, but where the
boiler met the smoke-box only one red/white band was applied, the
red being nearer the dome. The spectacle plate received a single red/
white stripe around the edge and over the top of the firebox. The
base of the dome was also lined with red and white but photographs
do not show if the double lines were used. The sides of the splashers
were lined similarly, a red/white band with the red always on the
outside. These lines were painted inside the beading around the
nameplate and the coat-of-arms. This is illustrated in colour in
chapter 4. The valance frames were finished in the same style, the
red and white alongside each other and passing over the step plates,
which were separately lined. The frames below the smoke-box
were lined around with a red line only. The cab sides carried twin
white lines which had a black centre. A wider red band was painted
alongside, on the outside of the outer white line. The number
plate had a white line just inside the edge and this surrounded the
numerals. The vermilion buffer beams had a black border around
only three sides and this had a white line adjacent to it. This lining
was not added along the top of the beam. The bodies of the buffers,
which were black, carried red and white lines on the square edge of
the base and near the opening.

Locomotive wheels appear to have been lined with a red line
applied around the inner edge of the tyres. The engine mainframes
were finished with vermilion on the insides but were black on the
outside and in all likelihood were not lined.

The tender lining matched that on the engine. The flares received
one continuous stripe of red/white lines but the upper coal plate had
only a red line which was also painted on the mainframes, around
axle boxes, cut-outs etc.

This very attractive livery was further enhanced by the polished
components. These were: all smoke-box door fittings, buffer heads,
all handrails and beadings, reversing rod and guide, coupling
rods, guard irons, safety valve cover, whistle, spectacle frames,
couplings etc.

The usual size of letters forming the company's title were added to
the tender side which also carried the standard height version of the
coat-of-arms but the smaller type of arms appeared on the splasher
sides. The smaller style of numerals was, in all probability, always
used on buffer beams but the monogram seems never to have been
applied.

GREEN LIVERY ONLY

The Class 1 engines ran in traffic in either green or black for
several years but, before long, a decision to repaint the black
examples in green at their next repair was taken. This may have
been because these locomotives began to work the company's best
expresses out of London Marylebone at about this time. There are
references in the contemporary journals to these changes, but not in
the house magazine, as it had ceased publication.

The Locomotive News and Railway Notes, no. 59, 10th August
1921, noted that '*nos. 426 and 427 now green, but 424 is still black*'.
Another item of interest in the same feature mentioned that all the
Class 1s '*nos. 423–428 are fitted for oil burning*'. A subsequent issue
of the same magazine, 25th June 1922, p. 104, reminded readers that
City of Lincoln, no. 424, was at Gorton for repair. An examination
of the engines' records provides further data. Engine No. 424
must have been repainted green when released from Gorton after

Plate 20.4   GCR Class 1, No. 424
No. 424 again but now named *City of Lincoln*. The engine is in black livery and remained so finished until August 1922, but this photograph must date from the second half of 1921 because of the oil fuel tank. The clerestory roof vehicle behind the tender is one of Parker's former dining cars. The location is Guide Bridge, platform 3, east end.
Real Photographs W3903

overhaul on 13th August 1922, No. 426 was green when it left works on 15th June 1921 and No. 427 was green by 22nd April 1921. These dates are in accordance with dated and undated photographs. In the case of the 'Sir Sams' the common problem of dating photographs is easier, because at that time the engines were being fitted with 'Ross pop' safety valves and oil burning equipment. When oil tanks were added they were probably plain black, but the livery situation of the class may be quickly summarised. Engines Nos 423, 425 and 428 were always painted green in GCR days. Nos 424, 426 and 427 were finished in black when new but towards the end of the pre-grouping period they were repainted green.

There is no doubt at all that the 'Sir Sam Fay' engines were always kept in first class condition regardless of livery and this is not difficult to substantiate. In a letter to the author, Percy Banyard commented '*4-6-0s nos. 424, 426 and 427 (Sir Sam Fay class) when cleaned looked superb, bear in mind Gorton and Grimsby kept them spotless*'. Many photographs add much evidence to Percy's words but two in particular are crucial. Both were taken at Neasden locomotive shed in north London, in more or less the same position. The first is of No. 423 when it was brand new and possibly recorded on the locomotive's first visit to London. It was published on page 9 of *The Robinson Locomotives of the G.C.R. 1900–1923* by C. Langley Aldrich. The other, also of No. 423, is part of the L.C.G.B. collection, ref. 3468, and taken on 5th May 1923. There are approximately ten years between the dates of these

pictures but the condition of the locomotive is virtually the same in both cases. There are, however, small differences in the livery which, in all probability, were due to the difficulties and shortages experienced during, and immediately after, the First World War. There were fewer polished parts, for example wheel tyres on No. 423, guard irons etc. and, perhaps, less lining in certain areas. One photograph, taken by F.H. Gillford of No. 425, shows the engine devoid of buffer beam numerals.

In more recent years some railway historians have not referred to the class in favourable terms. In truth the engines have received a very mixed obituary, some of which may well be deserved – but David Jackson, in his typical style, has leapt to their defence in his biography of Robinson. There are, in fact, some reports of excellent work performed by them, particularly on the most difficult part of the GCR, the Woodhead line. Other pieces of evidence seem to strengthen the likelihood that they were not quite as unsuccessful as some writers would have us believe.

As Class B2, the L&NER used the engines on a wide variety of services. The conditions imposed by the Second World War were such that, at times, they worked passenger trains consisting of as many as fifteen bogie carriages. Shortly after the hostilities ended they were reclassified for the second time, becoming B19 but their days were numbered. The last example, now No. 1492, originally GCR No. 427, just failed to become the property of the newly-formed British Railways, being taken out of traffic in November 1947.

Plate 21.1   GCR Class 1A, No. 441
This photograph was taken on Neasden shed, c. 1915. It is possible to see the red lines on the original print of No. 441. Perhaps the excellent lighting has contributed to the reproduction of the same.   *L.G.R.P. 14470*

Plate 21.2   GCR Class 1A, No. 445
No. 445 is standing on Gorton shed in this view. This is not easy to date, but the engine may be new. The red lining is visible on the original print.   *Real Photographs W4881*

CHAPTER 21

CLASS 1A 4-6-0

Another type of tender engine with the 4-6-0 wheel arrangement soon followed those of Class 1. The Class 1As were, indeed, junior versions of the 'Sir Sams'. Their driving wheels were rather smaller than those of Class 1 and this meant that they were destined to spend much of their time on a speciality of the GCR – fast, fully fitted, goods trains. They were often used on passenger trains as well but, because of their primary occupation, they qualified for the lined black livery. The class took the nickname of 'Glenalmonds' after the first example, No. 4.

In total eleven engines were built, the first one, No. 4, appearing only six months after No. 423 of Class 1. A year later, in July 1914, No. 439 was the first of a batch of eight, numbered 439–446. Two more completed the class; they were No. 279, new in December 1914, and No. 280 which was finished in January 1915. They were all built at Gorton.

The *G.C.R.J.* was always including details of the company's locomotive stock and in volume IX, September 1913, p. 74, under 'Locomotive News', published a picture of No. 4, which was an official view by James W. Wood. The engine is painted grey and the illustration is accompanied by the comments *'This engine is built for conveying heavy loads of general goods traffic'* and *'This engine is now in traffic undergoing her trials and is painted black picked out in red'*. The February 1914 issue of the same journal, on page 244, offered further information: *'An order for 10 4-6-0 mixed traffic engines of the "Glenalmond" type is being put in hand at the Gorton Works at the present time. The numbers will be 279, 280 and 439–446 ... the first of these engines will be called "Sutton*

Nelthorpe".' Four members of the class carried names. No. 4 was named *Glenalmond* when new. Glenalmond House was the Scottish home of Sir Alexander Henderson, the GCR chairman. No. 439 was fitted with plates bearing the name of *Sutton Nelthorpe* who was a Lincolnshire director of the company. Nos 279 and 446 were named in 1915: the former became *Earl Kitchener of Khartoum*, the other No. 446 *Earl Roberts of Kandahar*; both were, of course, famous soldiers. A novel feature of the nameplates on all four locomotives was that they were fixed along the top edge of the splasher.

GREY LIVERY

Apart from the view of No. 4 painted grey, which has already been mentioned, at least two other pictures exist of that engine painted grey. The April 1914 edition of the *G.C.R.J.*, vol. IX, p. 300, included a three-quarter view of No. 4 and *Great Central Steam* by W.A. Tuplin, p. 29, has a two thirds illustration of the engine. Presumably all three photographs were recorded on the same occasion by James W. Wood. On page 129 of the 10th July 1922 issue of *The Locomotive News and Railway Contractor* was published a view of No. 446 painted grey.

BLACK LIVERY

The traffic livery of these locomotives was always black during the GCR period. A specification for this has not been found, but the following notes have been assembled from a study of photographs of the engines.

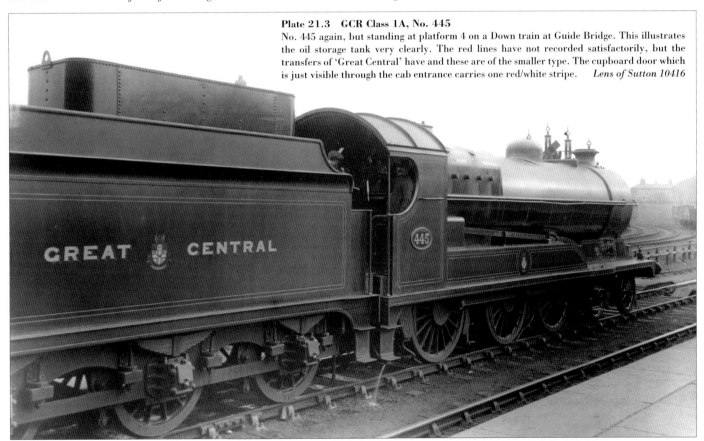

Plate 21.3   GCR Class 1A, No. 445
No. 445 again, but standing at platform 4 on a Down train at Guide Bridge. This illustrates the oil storage tank very clearly. The red lines have not recorded satisfactorily, but the transfers of 'Great Central' have and these are of the smaller type. The cupboard door which is just visible through the cab entrance carries one red/white stripe.   *Lens of Sutton 10416*

The locomotive, tender and all wheels were black. Buffer beams were vermilion and the cab interior probably stone colour. The firebox and boiler carried the usual double red/white stripes with a black centre. The base of the dome was, in all probability, similarly finished, but photographs are not of sufficiently good quality to be sure. The top feed, when this was fitted, may also have been lined and the spectacle plate certainly received one red/white band of lining.

The cab sides were lined with two white lines which had a black centre. A wider red band was painted on the outside of the outer white line. The splasher sides also had this arrangement of decoration but near the centre it formed an incomplete circle, into the middle of which was placed the standard size coat-of-arms. The splasher tops appear to have been plain black. The valance frames and those below the smoke-box had a red/white stripe and the lining on the former continued over the tops of the footsteps which were similarly, but separately, lined. The red/white lining beneath the smoke-box was unusual, as normally this consisted of only a red line on certain types of black engines. The buffer beams were edged black and lined white, but only on three edges as it was not applied along the top. The buffer guides also had red/white lining, around the square base and the opening. The cab interior in all likelihood had a black border with a red separating line alongside it. The small locker doors on the locomotive by the cab entrance were black with one continuous red/white band.

Insides of the locomotive mainframes were vermilion, the outsides black and probably unlined. Some engines had polished guard irons, but generally these appear to have been plain black. Locomotive wheels probably had a red line around the tyres, but photographs are not clear on this. A white line which surrounded the numbers on the cast number plate seems to have been applied.

The tender sides and end were finished as the cab sides: two white lines with a red stripe on the outside. The curved flares carried one red/white continuous line, whereas the upper coal plate received only a continuous red line. One red line was also applied around the axle boxes, cut-outs etc, on the mainframes. When a fuel tank was fitted to the tenders of these locomotives it was almost certainly plain black.

The standard size of coat-of-arms was normally placed on both tender tank and splasher sides. The 6 inches tall transfers of the company's name were also in general use, but the small numerals of about 4½ inches in height were applied to buffer beams. At least one locomotive, No. 444, ran without identification on the engine buffer beam.

The locomotives had the customary highly polished components, particularly when they were new. All handrails, spectacle frames, safety valves and casings, whistle, lubricators, smoke-box fittings and all buffer heads were normally kept clean.

One or two members, at least, of Class 1A had a mark applied to the smoke-box door. No. 279 had a small sword-shaped symbol on the upper part of the door. During 1916 *The Railway Magazine* carried a series of advertisements for D. Napier and Son Ltd, manufacturers of business vehicles, and included in one of these was a smoke-box view of a 1A, the number of which is unknown but it was possibly No. 446. The smoke-box door has no less than four marks on the central upper part. Three are placed symmetrically, with the fourth attached to, but above, the one in the centre. All four marks are diamond shaped.

Most photographs of these engines indicate that, generally, they were kept in excellent condition. One or two show that they had suffered somewhat in later years and this was, without doubt, because of the First World War. As Class B8 on the L&NER they continued to perform useful work until, after another world conflict, they were withdrawn, becoming extinct in the spring of 1949.

Plate 21.4   GCR Class 1A, No. 279
No. 279 *Earl Kitchener of Khartoum* is waiting at the west end of Guide Bridge's platform 4 with a Down stopping train. The tender oil tank dates this picture to between May and October 1921. The engine is in a splendid condition and linings are clearly visible. The buffer beam has the small characters and is not lined along the top. The single red/white band around the framing below the smoke-box is unusual, as generally this consisted of only one red line. The smoke-box door has a small decoration in the form of a sword-shaped symbol.
Real Photographs W3907

CHAPTER 22
CLASS 11E 4-4-0

The 11E locomotives were intended for express passenger work and were virtually a four-coupled version of the Class 1 4-6-0. They, and the very similar 11F 4-4-0s, were exceptional engines. They quickly showed that they were capable of working the best GCR trains, both to time and with economy. They have been referred to as the best inside cylinder 4-4-0s in Britain.

The *G.C.R.J.* announced the forthcoming engines in April 1913 (vol. VIII, p. 290) as part of 'Locomotive News'. The magazine commented *'There are at the present time being built in the Gorton Shops a further order of 2-8-0 engines ... also some 4-4-0 express passenger engines with 6' 9" coupled wheels'*. The October 1913 edition, p. 102, had much more information, nearly all technical, and this included an outline drawing (see page 112).

Ten examples of the class were built, all at Gorton. They appeared in the unusually short period, at least by GCR standards, between August 1913 and the end of the year. They were all named from new, taking the names of members of the GCR board, hence their nickname of 'Directors'. They carried the following names and numbers:

429 *Sir Alexander Henderson*
430 *Purdon Viccars*
431 *Edwin A. Beazley*
432 *Sir Edward Fraser*
433 *Walter Burgh Gair*
434 *The Earl of Kerry*
435 *Sir Clement Royds*
436 *Sir Berkeley Sheffield*
437 *Charles Stuart-Wortley*
438 *Worsley-Taylor*.

There were some changes in names in later years. The older 11B 4-4-0, No. 1014, lost its name of *Sir Alexander* when No. 429 appeared. When the first of the 9P 4-6-0s was built in 1917, that engine took the name of the newly elevated GCR chairman, Lord Faringdon, and No. 429 was then renamed *Sir Douglas Haig*. When that gentleman became Earl Haig, No. 429 was renamed for the second time, becoming *Prince Henry*. The other engine which had a change of name was No. 437. Charles Stuart-Wortley was created Baron Stuart of Wortley in 1916 and No. 437 became *Prince George*.

GREY LIVERY

There are at least four photographs of No. 429 painted grey which were taken by the company photographer. A three-quarter left-hand view was made with the coupling rod splasher removed and a three-quarter right side picture was published in the *Model Engineer* of 25th April 1962, on p. 524, also with the splasher removed. A broadside photograph, with the engine in the same condition but facing left, was included on p. 97 of *Robinson Locomotives* by Haresnape and Rowledge. Another broadside illustration appeared in *The Railway Magazine* (vol. XXXV, p. 346) but in this one the locomotive faces to the right and the splasher has been fitted. During the GCR period both classes of 'Directors', 11E and 11F, ran with coupling rod splashers, but they were subsequently removed by the L&NER. No. 433 was another locomotive photographed in grey in a three-quarter left facing picture. A fine illustration of the cab interior of No. 437 was published in the *G.C.R.J.*, vol. XII, November 1916, p. 92; this appears to have been taken when No. 437 was painted grey. Finally, No. 438 was also grey when it was recorded photographically and a copy of this left-hand view is also on p. 97 of *Robinson Locomotives*.

Plate 22.1 GCR Class 11E, No. 430
No. 430 *Purdon Viccars* is at Neasden shed about 1914. The lighting and cleanliness of the subject have assisted with the reproduction of the lining. There is a small circular symbol on the smoke-box door, possibly a cleaner's mark.

J. Quick collection

Plate 22.2   GCR Class 11E, No. 434

This is an excellent view of No. 434 *The Earl of Kerry* at Neasden shed, taken on 27th June 1914. The 'Directors' of Class 11E were highly capable express locomotives and worked some of the company's most important trains.   *LCGB Ken Nunn collection 1790*

GREEN LIVERY

The original 'Directors' of Class 11E were finished in the full green and crimson passenger livery throughout their GCR ownership. The October 1913 copy of the *G.C.R.J.*, p. 102, included the followed notes:

> *The first of these engines which has been turned out of the shops has made a few trial runs, and is at the present time being painted the standard green picked out with black and white lines and with crimson lake under frames.*

An official specification for this livery is not known, which appears to be the case with all Gorton-built locomotives. What follows therefore, is based upon the very many photographs that were taken of these engines.

The boiler, firebox, spectacle plate, cab and splasher sides, wheels and short cover to the reversing rod were Brunswick green. Note that the splasher sides were green, which was unusual. The buffer guides, valance framing, step plates and the frames below the smoke-box were crimson. Smoke-box, tops of splashers, cab roof, wheel tyres and the top of the running plate were black.

The insides of the mainframes were vermilion, the outsides probably plain black. The guard irons were polished steel at times, and painted, possibly plain black, at other periods. Buffer beams were vermilion, the cab interior a very pale yellow. The small locker doors by the cab entrance were certainly dark coloured and this means that they may have been black, green or crimson.

The tender was painted to match the locomotive. The tank sides and end, flares, upper coal plate and wheels were green. The frames, valance frames, step plates and buffer guides were all crimson. In a letter to the author Percy Banyard opined *'The 1913 series of "Directors" looked smart, their tender end cupboards and lockers on the footplate painted crimson and lined out vermilion'*. Percy did not, unfortunately, give a date for his observations which were c. 1920, but it is possible that they were so painted from new.

Linings on engine and tender were the customary black, white and vermilion, as used on many express locomotives. The boiler, firebox, and the base of the dome received the twin white lines which had a black centre, but only one white line was painted around the join of the smoke-box and boiler. The spectacle plate had a black border and this had one white line painted alongside. This decoration, in the majority of pictures, seems to have been applied across the top edge, down each side and then terminated where the splasher side met the platform immediately in front of the cab. The cab sides had a black border, then a red line alongside. A wide green border separated the red line from twin white lines. These had a black centre and the whole arrangement followed the outline of the cab. The green splasher sides had a black border. One white line was applied adjacent to the border and this allowed the nameplates to be set inside the same. Below the nameplate was placed the coat-of-arms which was surrounded by a complete circle of white, then a narrow black annulus, around which was another white circle.

Plate 22.3   GCR Class 11E, No. 430
This photograph has been selected to illustrate the light coloured interior of the cab of No. 430 (*top*). Judging by the interest shown by the onlookers this may be a society visit to Neasden locomotive depot.

J. Quick collection

Outline drawing of the Class 11E locomotives published in the October 1913 edition of *The Great Central Railway Journal*, p. 102. Resized to a scale of 4mm:1ft.

Plate 22.4 GCR Class 11E, No. 432
Standing just outside Manchester London Road, and in superb condition, is *Sir Edward Fraser*, No. 432. The engine must be quite new because of the presence of the former MS&LR 6-wheel Third class carriage, No. 283, behind the tender; this vehicle was one of fifteen GCR carriages which were destroyed in the horrific accident at Quintinshill in May 1915. *Real Photographs W7106*

Plate 22.5   GCR Class 11E, No. 432
Sir Edward Fraser, No. 432, is about to pass below Charwelton station road bridge with a Down excursion. In the distance is bridge No. 491 and beyond are the water troughs from which the crew have filled the tender. The stock is of interest as it is entirely Third class, consisting mainly of 'Barnum' carriages, four saloons and a brake saloon. A strengthener has been provided with a Parker Brake Third which is immediately behind the tender.
L.G.R.P. 16181

Though this circle was incomplete, it joined the main white lining both above and below the coat-of-arms. Curiously, the white line which was often seen around the numbers on the number plate seems not to have been applied on these engines.

The framing below the smoke-box had a continuous black border with a vermilion line alongside. The valance frames were lined rather elaborately with the same colours. The parallel section had the border painted around and this had a red line separating it from the crimson. The coupling rod splashers received the same lining but it was applied separately, meaning that the valance frames and coupling rod splasher panels had a common black edge. The lining along the bottom of the valances was carried across the tops of the step plates, which were similarly, but separately, lined. The buffer beams received a black border with one white line but not along the top of the beam. The buffer guides were lined, which comprised a black edge and a red line around the base and around the opening.

The engines' wheels were lined with white. One line was applied to the inner edge of the tyres, with another painted around the axle ends which were black. A further white line was added to the inner edge of bosses on the bogie wheels which left a green annulus around the centre of the wheels. The cranks were green and they had a white line around the edge.

The green upper coal plate and the curved flares on the tender had separate black borders which had a red line alongside and these made continuous panels. The tank sides and end had a black border and this had a red line adjacent to it. There then followed a green border and the twin white lines as already described for the locomotive. The valance frames' lining was identical to that on the engine and the mainframes also received this decoration around the axle boxes, cut-outs etc. The step plates were similarly finished but lined separately. The lining along the valance bottom was applied over the tops of the steps. The buffer beams and buffer guides were lined as the engine. When the tender front was crimson it would have been edged black and have a red separating line. The inside of the tender top and the wheel tyres were probably plain black. The short vertical plate at the front of the tender which supported the handrail had a black border along the bottom and along the edge nearest the hand rail. Red separating lines were applied alongside the borders.

Many components were polished bright metal. These included all buffer heads, handrails and pillars, smoke-box fittings, lubricators, reversing rod, safety valve cover, whistle and all beadings. The usual size of letters forming the company's title seems to have always been used, likewise the coat-of-arms. Buffer beam characters look to have always been of the small type and at least two locomotives, at some time, carried a mark on the smoke-box: No. 430 had a circular symbol high on the smoke-box door and No. 432 was adorned with a very distinctive six-pointed star in the same position.

The 11E 'Directors' were always seen in excellent condition. Even the difficulties during the First World War appear not to have changed things to a great extent. Percy Banyard's remarks in a letter of 3rd January 1977 confirm this. He noted: *'I cannot recall the 'Directors' and 4 cylinder passenger engines* [Class 9P 4-6-0] *in anything but lovely greens and linings'*. They had a long and useful life working into the British Railways era, the last ones not being withdrawn until the autumn of 1955.

Plate 23.1   GCR Class 1B, No. 276

No. 276 looks very new in this photograph taken at Gorton, in which case the date is April 1915. The black painting scheme has recorded well despite the orthochromatic film which was used. Note the three separately lined panels on tank, cab and bunker sides.

J. Quick collection

CHAPTER 23
CLASS 1B 2-6-4T

This class of tank locomotive was built in order to improve the working of coal traffic which emanated from the north Nottinghamshire coalfield and was conveyed to the docks at Grimsby and Immingham. It is generally accepted that the design contained some elements of the former LD&ECR Class D 0-6-4T which had been built ten years earlier for precisely the same purpose. The GCR took over the LD&ECR on 1st January 1907, the locomotive superintendent of the smaller company, Mr R.A. Thom, then moving to a new position at Gorton. It is believed that Mr Thom had some influence on Robinson's decisions regarding the 1B engines.

The *G.C.R.J.*, August 1914, vol. X, p. 32, announced the intention to construct a new tank engine *'of very large size, to be used for mixed traffic work'*. The October issue, p. 90, published much more information, mainly technical with dimensions, weights etc., and this included a line drawing. The February 1915 copy carried a view of the first engine, No. 272, on the frontispiece. This also had an interesting quote from the *Manchester Guardian* which originated from a review of the technical journal *Engineering* of 1914:

This is one of the handsomest tank engines which have made their appearance anywhere in recent years and fully maintains the reputation of the G.C. for managing to retain some elegance and seemliness in their locomotives in spite of their ever growing bulk within the fixed height and width.

The footplate men obviously had different views as they nicknamed them 'Crabs'! Another humorous name which was given them was 'Zeppelins'. Of all Robinson's designs these engines were surely the least attractive, but steam locomotives were built to work; the era of elegant engines was fast coming to an end.

Two examples were completed during December 1914, Nos 272 and 273. Nos 274–276 quickly followed them in the spring of 1915. The final fifteen locomotives, Nos 336–345 and 366–370 were built between April 1915 and May 1917, Gorton works being responsible for their construction.

GREY LIVERY

The view of No. 272 in the *G.C.R.J.* which has already been noted shows the engine painted grey and has been published many times. It is an interesting picture as a coat-of-arms has been placed on the tank side and normally this was positioned on the cab side of Class 1B engines. No. 342 was also recorded in grey paint. The locomotive is without any decoration except for the number plate and is illustrated on page 19 of Eddie Johnson's work *Locomotives of the G.C.R.*, volume 2.

BLACK LIVERY

The service livery for these engines was emphatically black in GCR ownership, but they did receive the full lining of red and white.

Very few really good photographs of Class 1B engines in GCR days are available for study. This, and the fact that pictures of them were recorded immediately after the end of the First World War,

Plate 23.2   GCR Class 1B, No. 273
Photographed at Gorton, and looking quite presentable, is No. 273. This is not easy to date but this engine spent two periods working from Gorton shed before the grouping.   *Real Photographs W354*

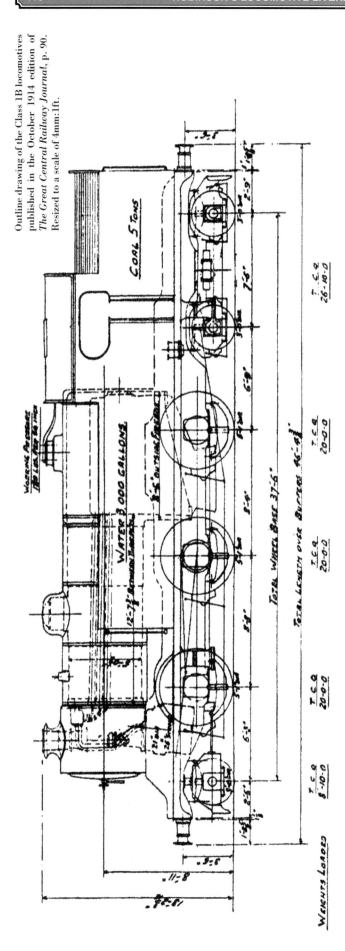

Outline drawing of the Class 1B locomotives published in the October 1914 edition of *The Great Central Railway Journal*, p. 90. Resized to a scale of 4mm:1ft.

contribute to the difficulty of making an accurate record of their livery. During and after the end of the war, many goods engines were not in a good external state. Consequently the notes which follow have been made from a study of the few useful photographs that are available.

The boiler and firebox carried the double red/white stripes which had a black centre. The lining on the front spectacle plate is not easily visible on photographs but it was certainly applied to some, if not all, engines. It consisted of one red/white band and was probably also added to the base of the dome. The sides of the locomotive, the tanks, cab and bunker were decorated with three separate panels. Each panel received twin white lines which had a black centre, but on the outside of the outer white line was a wider red band. The panels on the tank and bunker sides were rectangular but that on the cab side followed the outline of the cab. The tank fronts also received a red/white continuous line and the cab interior was probably stone colour; this would also have had a black border with a red line separating the edge from the lighter coloured area. A photograph showing the bunker rear has not been found but another lining panel was, in all probability, painted there; this would have followed the shape of the rear and matched the lining on bunker sides, etc. The splasher sides, valance frames and step plates all carried the single red/white lines, that on the valances continuing over the steps which were lined separately. The frames below the smoke-box only had a red line. Buffer beams were lined in the usual manner, but the line was not added to the top edge of the beam. Buffer guides also had single red/white lines painted in the customary positions.

The insides of mainframes were vermilion, the outsides were black and, in all likelihood, unlined. A few photographs suggest that the tyres may have been lined with red but it is impossible to make a conclusion on this. Similarly, the sandboxes and water equalising pipes appear to have been plain black.

The usual size of transfer of 'Great Central' and coat-of-arms always seem to have been employed. The coat-of-arms was, according to all photographs, placed in the centre of the lined panel on the cab side. A white line was usually painted inside the raised edge of the number plate. It is not known with certainty if the bunker rear carried the running number in its usual form, that is, 'No. XXX', but it seems highly unlikely that these engines were not finished in accordance with custom. The buffer beam numerals on the few photographs which show them were of the smaller type.

There seem to have been fewer polished parts than on other classes of locomotive. It is likely that only when new were some components regularly cleaned, these being the buffer heads, handrails, smoke-box fittings, spectacle frames, safety valves and casing, and the whistle. The splasher sides had a beading attached to the upper edge but, unusually for a GCR engine, it appears not to have been polished.

The condition of these engines changed during the few years before the L&NER was formed, undoubtedly because of wartime problems. Photographs taken during these years show that the company's name, coats-of-arms and lining are scarcely visible. A typical example of this is a picture of No. 339 at Neasden shed taken on 1st July 1922. The lining, company name and coat-of-arms are almost indiscernible. The frames beneath the smoke-box, buffer beam and buffer bodies are devoid of any decoration and latterly, most members of the class did not carry identification on the buffer beam.

The work for which the 1Bs was intended soon ceased because of the outbreak of war, so they were found alternative duties including some passenger trains. It seems that, although they were perfectly capable of hauling heavy trains, the lack of a tender, and hence some braking power, proved to be a problem at times. Nevertheless they outlived the L&NER, not becoming extinct until the summer of 1955.

CHAPTER 24
CLASS 9P 4-6-0

This class was Robinson's final attempt to introduce to the GCR an engine that was capable of working the heaviest passenger trains over the difficult gradients of the company's system. They were by far the most powerful passenger locomotives on GCR lines, their four cylinders providing an approximate tractive effort of 25,000 lbs. However, although a reasonably satisfactory engine, the locomotive department realised that the 4-4-0s, of classes 11E and 11F, were better. The 4-4-0s could handle heavy trains with equal or better efficiency and with increased economy. The use of a 9P on an express passenger train was really only justified when the trailing load was beyond the abilities of a 'Director' 4-4-0.

Six engines comprised the class. No. 1169 was the first on the road, being new in November 1917. The remaining five were all completed between June and October 1920 and took the running numbers 1164–1168. All six were built at Gorton. They were not all fitted with the same design of cab. Nos 1164, 1166 and 1169 had the early, arc-sided type, whereas the other three examples were provided with their designer's later version which had two side windows.

All six engines carried names from new as follows:

1164 *Earl Beatty*
1165 *Valour*
1166 *Earl Haig*
1167 *Lloyd George*
1168 *Lord Stuart of Wortley*
1169 *Lord Faringdon*.

No. 1169 was named after the chairman; the class was often referred to as the 'Lord Faringdons'. Nos 1164 and 1166 took the names of First World War leaders, of the navy and of the army respectively. No. 1168 was named after a director of the company. The naming of Nos 1169 and 1168 made it necessary to rename certain members of Class 11E, details of which have already been discussed. No. 1167 carried the name of the wartime prime minister. The engine was, however, named *Rt. Hon. David Lloyd George* for a very short period. The locomotive was noted, named thus, in Gorton works in 1920 by the well-known railway photographer, W.H. Whitworth. A reference in the G.C.R.S. archives adds that No. 1167 never left the works so named. *The Locomotive News and Railway Notes*, of 25th November 1920, remarked: '*Two further engines of 1169 class will shortly be running, numbered 1167 and 1168. No. 1167 is named* Right Hon. D. Lloyd George *and 1168* Lord Stuart of Wortley'. David Jackson's *J.G. Robinson – A Lifetime's Work* (p. 204) contains an excellent broadside picture of No. 1167 which has a blank area where the nameplate would normally fit – a glance will make it obvious that the blanked portion is much longer than would be necessary if it was named 'Lloyd George'. It is likely that the engine was photographed in the period between nameplates.

No. 1165 was a most special locomotive on the GCR. *The Locomotive News and Railway Notes*, in its edition of 10th August 1920, commented '*The first of the new 4 cylinder 4-6-0s is 1164* Earl Beatty. *It is understood that one of these engines is to be named* 'Patriot', *similar to the L.N.W.R. memorial engine*'. No. 1165 was certainly the company's memorial engine, but it was named *Valour*. This was in memory of the fallen GCR men and the unique shield-shaped nameplate said it all: '*In memory of GCR employees who gave their lives for their country 1914–1918*'. During the few years to grouping, and for many thereafter, No. 1165 carried wreaths of laurel and poppies to take its place at the Armistice Day ceremony at Sheffield Victoria station.

Plate 24.1   GCR Class 9P, No. 1164
No. 1164 *Earl Beatty* is about to pass beneath bridge No. 354 at Rothley station, with the 12.42 pm Cleethorpes–Leicester express in 1922. The formation of the train is unusual as it would normally have had a string of fish vans attached at the rear. The engine is in the sort of condition that was remembered by Percy Banyard. The photographer was probably Henry Salmon.   *L.G.R.P. 16198*

GREY LIVERY

There are only two engines in this class for which photographs in grey paint are not known – they are Nos 1164 and 1166 but it is possible that they were at one time so finished. The prototype engine, No. 1169, was recorded at least twice in the livery. *Great Central*, vol. 3, p. 329, has a good three-quarter left-hand view and this is also reproduced in *The Railway Magazine*, April 1918, on the frontispiece. The latter illustration is a superb picture with the full background of Gorton, whereas that in George Dow's work is of a smaller format and has the background totally removed, a practice that was not uncommon at that time. Another left broadside picture appeared in *The Railway Magazine*, February 1918, on page 122. No. 1164 may or may not have been painted grey but the next one, No. 1165, was photographed several times in that state. A good left broadside picture of this engine will be found on page 137 of Eddie Johnson's *Locomotives of the G.C.R.*, vol. 2. A really fine, nearly three-quarter left-hand photograph is on page 27 of the same author's work, *Woodhead: Scenes from the Past*, No. 29. The Locomotive Publishing Company offered a postcard which is very similar to this print. Another three-quarter left-hand card was published, possibly by the Van Nette Studio of Stockport. A good photograph of No. 1167 in David Jackson's biography of Robinson has already been noted. Finally, No. 1168 was recorded in grey and forms plate 30 in *Great Central Steam* by W.A. Tuplin.

GREEN LIVERY

As the company's premier express passenger locomotives it is unthinkable that the 9P 4-6-0s were not always kept in the very best of condition. Perhaps Percy Banyard's comments in a letter to the author bear repeating *'I cannot recall seeing "Directors" and 4 cylinder passenger engines [9P class] in anything but lovely greens and linings'*. Painting instructions, if any were actually issued, appear not to exist. Nevertheless, very many photographs were taken in the few years of GCR service and a comprehensive study of these has allowed what is believed to be an accurate record of their livery to be drawn up.

The boiler, firebox, reversing rod cover, cab sides, dome, spectacle plate, all wheels, tender sides and end, flares, upper coal plate and wheels were Brunswick green. The buffer guides, cylinder bodies, framing supporting the slide bars, valance frames, splasher sides, step plates, tender main frames and valances, buffer guides, tender front, cupboards etc., were crimson lake. Chimney, smoke-box, tops of running platforms, all steps and tops of splashers, cab roof and the tender top were black. Buffer beams were painted vermilion and the interior of the cab was probably stone colour.

The insides of the engines' mainframes were vermilion and the outsides almost certainly plain black. The guard irons appear to have been painted, either black or possibly crimson, but this point cannot be clarified as photographs do not show guard bars in any clarity.

A freshly painted 9P was a magnificent sight; all paintwork neatly lined but the final touch was all the highly polished parts. These included all handrails and pillars, buffer heads, couplings, coupling and connecting rods, reversing rod and its support, all smoke-box fittings, whistle, safety valves, all beadings, cylinder ends and all raised surfaces on the maker's name and number plates.

The boiler and firebox carried the usual twin white lines and these had a black centre but only one white line was applied next to the smoke-box. The base of the dome was lined but with only one white line which had a black edge. The spectacle plate had a black border which had a white line alongside, the whole making a continuous band which commenced by the splasher side, then up and just under the cab roof, to the other side of the engine. Those locomotives which had the earlier style of cab (Nos 1164, 1166 and 1169) had a

Plate 24.2   GCR Class 9P, No. 1165
It is Armistice Day 1921 and the company's remembrance locomotive, No. 1165 *Valour*, is standing at platform C of Manchester London Road. Although the engine has been cleaned to perfection and wreaths have been placed around the smoke-box door centre and the nameplate, the gloomy interior of the station adds to the sombre occasion. The driver is Bill Chapman, with his fireman Harry Turner.
B.J. Miller

Plate 24.3   GCR Class 9P, No. 1166
Earl Haig, No. 1166, in magnificent condition at Leicester Central around 1922. The engine was allocated to Gorton at this time and may have just arrived with an Up express.   *Lens of Sutton*

black border which followed the outline of the cab. Alongside this was a red line, then a broad green border and then twin white lines as earlier described. The other three engines, with the side window cabs, received the outer black border which had a red line against it. A broad green border was left before two more white lines were applied, but only on the lower part of the cab and these had a black centre. The splasher tops appear to have been plain black but the crimson sides received a black border just inside the beading, then a red separating line was added. This arrangement passed around the outline just inside the edge, but deviated slightly; first to allow the nameplate to lie within the border and also to pass above the small big-end crankpin splasher, which was probably black. The valance framing, step plates, cylinder sides, framing supporting the crossheads and buffer guides were all crimson and received a black edge which had a red line applied next to it. The step plates below the cab and near the cylinders were lined separately. The buffer beams had a black border with a white separating line but it was painted only along the lower edge and the ends.

Assuming the inside of the cab was the usual stone colour, it would have had a black border with a red line. The small cupboard doors inside the cab, by the entrance, may have been finished green, in which case they would have been similarly finished. Unfortunately, photographs do not show this area well enough to make a firm conclusion on this matter. The locomotive's wheel tyres were black, a white line then separated the tyre from the green centre. On bogie wheels a white line was painted around the boss then, after a wider green annulus, another white line was added around the black axle ends. This scheme was repeated on the driving wheels but the lining around the edge of the boss continued round the cranks.

As a matter of course the tender received the same lining that was applied to the engine. The sides and end carried the identical decoration as the cab sides. The small plate in front of the tank, which supported the vertical handrails, appears to have had a narrow black border along the bottom edge and along the edge which was adjacent to the handrail. Red lines would have been painted on each inner edge. The flares and upper coal plates each had separate black

borders with red lines alongside the inner edge. The mainframes carried the normal style of lining, a black border with a red line. This would have been added around the axle boxes etc., and the same decoration finished the step plates, valance framing and buffer guides. The tender front and cupboards etc., when painted crimson received similar lining. The tender wheel tyres were black but it is unlikely that they were lined.

The usual size of coat-of-arms seems to have been employed but only on the tender sides. Six inches tall characters formed the company's title but the buffer beam numerals were always of the smaller type that were probably standard by this time on the GCR. These engines never carried a monogram and the white line inside the number plate appears not to have been applied. A photograph of a 9P with a distinctive mark has not been located.

The 'Lord Faringdons' did not have many opportunities to demonstrate their capabilities before they became Class B3 on the L&NER. The 11E and 11F 4-4-0s were much more suitable for the majority of trains but, notwithstanding this, the big 4-cylinder 4-6-0s were impressive locomotives, well maintained by the staff and were to be the subject of important trials on the former GNR main line before long. Later, some were rebuilt to improve their fuel consumption and one engine, No. 6166, was completely altered – making it look rather like an Edward Thompson B1 with a GCR tender. The 9Ps were worn out by the late 1940s and were all withdrawn around the time of the formation of British Railways.

Two locomotives of Class 9P deserve some additional comment. The extraordinary relationship between the staff and No. 1165 *Valour* has already been noted. The engine received its last GCR livery in the spring of 1922. It was ex works in August 1923 with the same paintwork merely touched up. The original 1922 finish must have been an extra-special effort on the part of the staff because the locomotive was available to attend the Armistice Day services of 1923 and 1924 in its old livery. Volume 22 of *Yeadon's Register of L.N.E.R. Locomotives* records the engine entering Gorton for overhaul on 15th November 1924 and leaving the works at the end of January 1925 in L&NER apple green. For some time after the demise of the GCR the locomotive was a constant reminder not only of the old company but also of those men who made the ultimate sacrifice.

The other engine that requires further remark is No. 1169 *Lord Faringdon* itself. It was photographed at Gorton in very early L&NER days and it appears to be in GCR livery. This picture has been published in Eddie Johnson's *Locomotives of the G.C.R.*, vol. 2, p. 45. Another, different, view will be found as plate 121 in

the same author's *Manchester suburbs: Scenes from the Past, No. 8*. In the background of this latter picture is part of a tender which is painted in L&NER livery and this suggests a date of 1923/24. Though No. 1169 appears to be painted in GCR colours, the crimson areas look to be painted green. The number plate appears to have a red line around the characters – but was this an attempt to show the engine in an early L&NER livery? We shall probably never know.

Plate 24.4   GCR Class 9P, No. 1169
The first engine of Class 9P, No. 1169 *Lord Faringdon*, is waiting at the western end of platform 4 at Guide Bridge, with a Down express. The lining has recorded very well in the excellent lighting of the subject. Note that the 'No' on the buffer beam appears to be shaded with one shade of light blue, with black on the lower areas of the character.

Real Photographs W1137

Plate 24.5   GCR Class 9P, No. 1165
The memorial engine, *Valour*, is on Neasden shed in this view, c. 1921 and in its customary first class condition. 'Iracier' tender axle boxes were fitted in August 1920. This engine was destined to carry the full green livery until November 1924.

Locomotive Publishing Co.

CHAPTER 25
CLASS 8M 2-8-0

This class was a development of the 8K, the main difference being the larger boiler of the 8Ms. The reason for Robinson's decision to build the large-boilered engines was, of course, all part of the desire for further fuel economy. Fuel trials had commenced on the GCR before the first of the nineteen-strong class of 8Ms was built and, later, certain engines of the class were altered in connection with the experiments. The price and quality of coal during and after the First World War had persuaded Robinson to search for cheaper alternatives. These were coal dust, pulverised coal and a mixture of coal dust and oil – but although some successes were achieved the results were not considered sufficiently advantageous to proceed further. There was one other small difference within Class 8M: the arc-sided cab was fitted to all but the final five examples. Engines Nos 14, 15, 17, 19 and 22 all had the later type of cab which had two side windows.

They were all built at Gorton, Nos 412–415 being completed in the first five months of 1918 and Nos 417–419 quickly followed. There was a period of nearly a year before Nos 10–13 and 420–422 appeared. Then Nos 14, 15 and 17 were built in late 1920 and, finally, in early 1921 Nos 19 and 22 completed the class.

GREY LIVERY

The first engine, No. 412, was illustrated in *Great Central*, vol. 3, p. 329, painted grey. The picture is part of the Locomotive Publishing Company collection as No. 3603. No. 417 is shown on page 137 of Eddie Johnson's second volume of *Locomotives of the G.C.R.*, also in grey. The last engine of the class was photographed at least three times whilst in grey when it was on its running trials. One photograph is in the Real Photographs collection, W7013. Another, the work of P.F. Cooke was published in *Locomotives Illustrated*, no. 112, p. 20. The third is similar and may also have

been Cooke's work. All three views show the locomotive in a light shade of grey, with the slightly darker grey smoke-box, cab roof and number plate relieving the plain appearance of the subject. Curiously, the cylinder ends have been polished.

BLACK LIVERY

The service livery of these locomotives during their GCR days was black. Details of their construction and of their livery etc., were published in an article written by David Jackson which appeared on pages 8–10 of *Great Central Link*, no. 5, April 1995. This journal was produced over a relatively short period of only twenty-eight issues, which is a great pity for there was much contained within its pages to interest the GCR enthusiast. The fact that Jackson has included a painting specification for Gorton-built locomotives is noteworthy, as it is the first to have been found. It appears to be the same as that issued for the 8Ks built by the North British Locomotive Company and is reproduced in chapter 19. Details of the lining and other information will be found in the 8K notes but, as always, there are a few points which require some discussion.

Jackson also mentions that only Nos 14, 15, 17, 19 and 22 – that is, the last five to be built – carried the coat-of-arms. To these must be added No. 420, the tender of which was so decorated when the engine was involved in the fuel experiments. Some locomotives which took part in the trials had a small plate fixed either above, or below, the running number and Nos 966 and 422 are examples with this feature. The former engine was the prototype 8K but was rebuilt with a large boiler becoming the solitary member of Class '8K Altd'. The plates probably gave information regarding the special work in which the engines were involved. During the trials the fuel tanks were, in all probability, plain black, but the bogie tender fitted to No. 966 was lined in the usual style and had additional single red/

Plate 25.1   GCR Class 8M, No. 420
No. 420 was converted to burn 'colloidal' fuel, a mixture of pulverised coal and oil, during January 1920. Seen here with a tender that was not carrying the coat-of-arms, the engine nevertheless looks in an excellent state in this illustration at Guide Bridge.   *Real Photographs W3875*

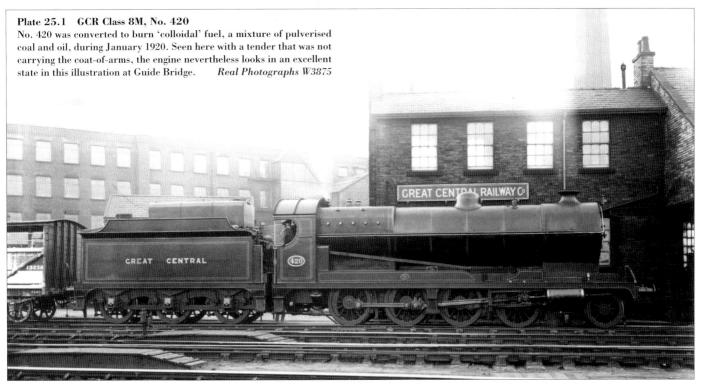

white lining applied to the plate nearest to the cab. The smaller type of buffer beam numerals appear to have been employed, but one or two engines seem to have received an even smaller version, perhaps only 3 inches tall. Some photographs indicate that the upper tender coal plate had a red line inside the beading, but the evidence for any decoration on the dome, or on the tender frames, is uncertain.

Photographs of the 8Ms suggest an improving situation regarding their condition and their livery. Several show engines in a poor external state but many are of examples which are much cleaner and obviously well maintained. A picture of one in the second category was published in *Locomotives Illustrated*, no. 112, p. 20. In this view No. 19 was recorded c. 1923 and the finish is complete with the usual red/white lining throughout and a coat-of-arms on the tender. Even the buffer sockets are decorated but the buffer beam numerals appear to be of the smallest type employed by the GCR and may be about 3 inches tall.

Robinson's notion of fitting a larger boiler to his 8K locomotive was not entirely successful but this and the fuel experiments are examples of his attempts to improve the steam locomotive. Eventually, as L&NER Class O5, they received smaller boilers, becoming additional members of Class O4, the last conversion occurring in January 1943.

ABOVE: Plate 25.2   GCR Class 8M, No. 22
P.F. Cooke was probably responsible for this picture of No. 22 in plain grey paint whilst on trials at Guide Bridge in February 1921.

J. Quick collection

Plate 25.3   GCR Class 8M, No. 14
No. 14 looks as though it hasn't had a clean for years but some lining may be seen on the sandbox and splasher in this photograph at the east end of Guide Bridge on 26th January 1924.

W.H. Whitworth

CHAPTER 26
CLASS 8N 4-6-0

Although only three examples of this class were built, their origin is of considerable interest. No. 416 was the first on the road and it remained the solitary example for nearly three years. The running number was more or less in the middle of a consecutively numbered batch of the big 2-8-0s of Class 8M, and it was whilst that run of 2-8-0s was under construction that No. 416 appeared. The two classes were virtually the same except, of course, for the wheel arrangement but otherwise all the major components were compatible. The driving wheels on the 4-6-0s were 5 feet 8 inches in diameter and this strongly suggests that they were meant for mixed traffic work.

No. 416 was ex works in July 1918 but the other members of the trio were not completed until the spring of 1921; No. 52 in March and No. 53 in April. All three engines were built at Gorton. The cab on No. 416 was the earlier type but on Nos 52 and 53 the new double window version was fitted.

GREY LIVERY

No. 416 was recorded in grey, probably when new. This has been published in the F. Moore series, ref. 5977. A very good illustration of this is contained in *Yeadon's Register of L.N.E.R. Locomotives*, vol. 22, p. 4 and a coat-of-arms is carried on the tender side. It was also reproduced in *The Railway and Travel Monthly* of June 1919. This showed the same picture of a grey No. 416, but the red component of the lining has been very crudely added thus producing a half and half colour and monochrome illustration. Two views of No. 52 are known. One picture shows only the locomotive but the other is a fine photograph taken at Gorton in May 1921 when the engine was on trial.

BLACK LIVERY

As mixed traffic engines the members of Class 8N received the lined black livery when their trials ended satisfactorily. They were products of Gorton works, which is probably why instructions regarding painting are not known to exist. They carried the same livery as the 8Ms and fortunately there are some excellent photographs from which reasonably comprehensive painting notes may be made.

The engine and tender were painted black relieved by vermilion buffer beams, polished parts, number plates, lettering and lining. The boiler and firebox received the customary double red/white bands which had a black centre, but only one red/white stripe was applied next to the smoke-box. The dome was similarly finished around the base. The cab on No. 416 was lined out with the double white arrangement, which had a wider red band on the outside of the outer white line, following the outline of the cab and making a continuous lined panel. The lining on the cabs of Nos 52 and 53 was rather different, the lower part of the cab received the same decoration as that painted on the cab of No. 416 but around the upper side windows was one continuous red line. On all three

Plate 26.1   GCR Class 8N, No. 416
In lined black paint and standing on Neasden shed is No. 416. The date must be after August 1920 when 'Iracier' tender axle boxes were fitted. Note that a coat-of-arms has not been applied to the tender and that a diamond-shaped cleaner's symbol has been added to the smoke-box door.

J. Quick collection

locomotives the spectacle plate was continuously lined with one red/white stripe, the red being on the outside of the white. The whole passed around the plate, then across the bottom of it, just above the splashers. The splasher sides were adorned with a red/white line, but the tops were plain black. The frames below the smoke-box on No. 416 had one red line but this is not visible on views of the other two engines. The valance frames on the engine also had a red/white band and this passed along the tops of the steps. The step plates received the same lining but this was applied separately. The bodies of the cylinders and of the buffers also had the same lining; that on the former being slightly inwards of the steel straps. On buffer guides it was added along the square base but a slight modification was made at the openings. Here the boiler band style of lining was painted, i.e., red/white/black-centre/white/red. Buffer beams were edged black and lined white but not along the top edge below the running plate.

The colour of the inside of the cab is one of debate. It may have been the usual stone colour, which had a black edge and a red line, but the first engine was built concurrently with locomotives of Class 8M where it has already been noted that engines were probably painted to the earlier 8K specification which asked for green cab interiors. It is possible, then, that No. 416 was similarly finished but until firm evidence is revealed this situation is in doubt.

The insides of engine mainframes were vermilion, the outsides were probably plain black. Driving and bogie wheels on Nos 52 and 53 seem not to have been lined but on No. 416 one red line was painted around the inner edge of the tyres. Guard bars on No. 416 were polished but were painted black on the other engines.

The tender was lined to match the locomotive. The lining on the tank sides and end was the same as that applied to the cab sides and the valance lining was also identical to that on the engine. The curved flares had one red/white stripe, but the upper coal plate received only one red line. The mainframes also carried a red line, mainly around the cut-out sections. No. 416 appears to have had what

may have been a unique lining feature: on the tender front, at the same height and very close to the tank side lining, a single red/white band is visible in certain views; it appears to begin at the corner of the tender, then continue for a few inches to turn down through 90 degrees to terminate above the short plate which supported the handrail. A plausible explanation for this may be because the vertical band of red and white continued to tender footplate level, thereby creating a lined panel. Unfortunately, photographs are not available which confirm this.

A steam locomotive painted in the black scheme described made a very attractive sight, particularly when it was clean. Adding to the spectacle were the polished parts and these included all buffer heads, smoke-box fittings, all handrails, cylinder ends, coupling and connecting rods, spectacle beadings and raised edges to maker's and number plates etc.

The view of No. 416 in grey which has been noted shows the tender with a coat-of-arms but this device seems not to have been employed on any engine in traffic livery. Photographic evidence indicates that the 6 inches tall transfers of the company name were always used. Buffer beam numerals were of the smaller style, about 4½ inches tall, and the single white line around the brass number plate appears to have been universally applied. The monogram was not carried by the Class 8N engines, but No. 416 did have a diamond-shaped symbol on the upper part of the smoke-box.

The 8N locomotives, though small in number, were, by all accounts, very useful machines, working all types of traffic. David Jackson, in his biography of Robinson, relates that they worked the celebrated Aberdeen–Penzance passenger service for a period. This train used the GCR London extension for part of the journey. Other commentators have praised them as successful engines and there can be no doubt that the GCR staff kept them in good condition. On becoming the property of the L&NER they were classified as B6. After more than twenty years of useful service for that company they were all withdrawn from traffic just before the formation of British Railways.

Plate 26.2   GCR Class 8N, No. 52
No. 52 has been completed for only a few weeks in this picture taken at Gorton in May 1921. The locomotive is finished in plain light grey paint and, presumably, undergoing proving trials. The date of the application of lined black is not known. This postcard was sent to J.N. Maskelyne on 26th August 1921.

J. Quick collection

Plate 26.3   GCR Class 8N, No. 53
No. 53 is standing in sidings at Guide Bridge about 1922. This engine, and No. 52, had Robinson's later style of cab which had a red line around the windows, in addition to the customary red/white lining.

J. Quick collection

Plate 27.1 GCR Class 11F, No. 501
No. 501 *Mons* is standing by the coaling stage at Leicester shed. The locomotive is only weeks old and finished in the Brunswick green and crimson livery. Notice the usual size of coat-of-arms on the self-trimming tender with the smaller type beneath the nameplate. The bogie locomotive coal wagon, behind the engine, is also worthy of note.
L.G.R.P. 16274

CHAPTER 27
CLASS 11F 4-4-0

This class was Robinson's last design for an express passenger locomotive. They were considered an improvement upon the earlier 11E class, to which they were very similar. They rapidly moved into the top position as passenger engines, the 11Es then finding other important work. It is generally accepted that the class was one of the finest inside cylinder 4-4-0s to work in the British Isles and there are many records of their work. No. 510 *Princess Mary* was mentioned in the contemporary press, on more than one occasion, as being a particularly good engine. If the First World War had not occurred it is probable that the 11Fs would have been introduced rather earlier but, by the time the last ones were entering service, Robinson was on the point of retirement.

There were eleven engines of Class 11F, all built at Gorton and they were all named from new. Although they were known as 'Directors', or 'Improved Directors', only the first two carried names of members of the board. The others took the names of members of the royal family and events connected with the First World War. They were named in order of building, as follows:

506 *Butler-Henderson*
507 *Gerard Powys Dewhurst*
508 *Prince of Wales*
509 *Prince Albert*
510 *Princess Mary*
501 *Mons*
502 *Zeebrugge*
503 *Somme*
504 *Jutland*
505 *Ypres*
511 *Marne.*

No. 506 was completed late in 1919 and Nos 507–510 quickly followed in the spring of 1920. The second batch of six was built during the autumn and last four months of 1922. Nos 506–510 all carried the full express livery when new – but of the second lot only Nos 501 and 502 were so finished. There are no photographs of the remaining engines, Nos 503–505 and 511, that show GCR livery. These locomotives received a hybrid painting scheme which consisted of the GCR Brunswick green, crimson, lining detail, number plates and even a small coat-of-arms but 'LNER' appeared on the tender side above large numerals which formed the running number. The L.G.R.P. collection includes a very interesting photograph of an 11F piloting an 8B 4-4-2 (reference no. 4948) and which is included in this chapter. The picture was probably taken early in 1923 and shows a lengthy Down express just north of Culworth junction. The 11F appears to be No. 503 and the length of the nameplate tends to support that identification but which, unfortunately, still remains uncertain. The tender is in GCR livery and this poses the question: was No. 503 painted in the livery also? The answer is probably no, because there were some exchanges of tenders around this time and No. 503 received the tender from 9P No. 1167, which happened to be still carrying the old livery.

GREY LIVERY

No. 506 was turned out in this scheme and photographed, a copy of which is available in the Real Photographs collection, ref. 65374. It was published in *Great Central*, vol. 3, p. 332. No. 502 was also recorded in grey livery and a right broadside copy of this will be found in *Great Central Steam*, plate 32.

In a letter to the author, dated 19th April 1975, Percy Banyard

Plate 27.2   GCR Class 11F, No. 506
The first of the class, No. 506 *Butler-Henderson*, on Neasden shed, c. 1920. The standard size of coat-of-arms on the splasher is an indication that this picture was taken before late February 1922, when the engine received its only general repair and repaint under the GCR.   *J. Quick collection*

Plate 27.3   GCR Class 11F, No. 508
Prince of Wales is standing on Gorton shed in this view which was probably recorded between July 1922 and February 1924. This photograph was taken on panchromatic film and, consequently, the red lines are clearly visible. Note the separate panels of lining on the valance and coupling rod splasher.   *Real Photographs W3885*

recalled when No. 506 visited Leicester, almost certainly for the first time. Percy commented *'How well do I remember this engine coming to Leicester early in 1920 still in shop grey, its driver being Jack Howard, official trial trip man at Gorton'*. Percy continued his memories in the G.C.R.S. journal *Forward*, no. 7, of December 1975:

> *A few weeks elapsed before seeing 506 again, but what a beautiful sight it presented when running into Leicester station with a train; it certainly gave me much pleasure to once again step on the footplate, take the shovel and pull coal forward. The G.C.R. green paint and linings together with polished brass and steelwork set 506 off to such an extent numbers of passengers waiting on the station platforms stood to gaze at the new 'Director' class locomotive.*

GREEN LIVERY

The following notes refer only to locomotives Nos 501, 502 and 506–510, as only these engines were finished in GCR livery.

The livery applied to the 11Fs was identical to that carried by the very similar 11E class. This is, of course, not unexpected but one point of interest concerns the coat-of-arms which was placed below the nameplate on the splasher side. Photographs of engines Nos 506–510 show that both large and small versions of the coats-of-arms were employed at different times. Very few pictures are dated but it is likely that, when built, the standard large size was used. All these locomotives made only one visit to Gorton for overhaul before grouping and other views suggest that they all left the works carrying the smaller device. Nos 501 and 502 also received the small heraldic symbol. A really first class photograph of No. 508 makes an interesting study; it shows all the lining detail exceptionally well as a consequence of being recorded on panchromatic film. It is a Real Photographs collection print, ref. W3885, and is reproduced here.

The 'Directors' of Class 11F worked right through the years of the L&NER and well into the period of British Railways. The last ones were not taken out of service until late 1960, an excellent achievement. They became Class D11 on becoming part of the locomotive stock of the L&NER and H.N. Gresley, the chief mechanical engineer of the new company, paid the GCR, and J.G. Robinson in particular, an enormous compliment by ordering further examples for use in Scotland.

No. 506 BUTLER-HENDERSON

This engine ended its first active life on 28th October 1960, having spent much of that year in store. It only worked from late June to the middle of September 1960 before being selected for preservation. It was an appropriate choice as, apart from being the prototype, it was the only remaining example to retain the original arrangement of cylinders with short travel valves. It spent some time at Gorton before work began in 1961 to restore it to near original condition. From the point of view of the livery an extremely good job was made of it but it was more or less inevitable that some errors would ensue. The basic shades of green and crimson are

Painting Specification for Restored Butler-Henderson

The main colour scheme was green and claret, the green being Mid-Brunswick, BS.6-074 with blue added, the claret being Dockerlux Crimson 750 with Sorrel 760 added. The engine is lined Post Office Red with a Signal Red buffer beam.

Details of the colour scheme are as follows:

Boiler clothing	– green – clothing bands black with white edging.
Boiler dome	– green – edged with black – lined white.
Splashers	– green – polished brass frame – edged black – lined white, top of splasher black.
Cab sides	– green – edged black – lined red with black band edged white. Number plate – black background, brass edging with white line inside. Nameplate similar without white line.
Cab front	– green – edged black with white line.
Cab top	– black.
Smoke-box sides, front and fall plate	– black.
Reversing rod	– polished natural.
Foot plating	– black.
Frame below smoke box	– claret – edged black – lined red.
Platform angle and valance [sic] plates	– claret – edged black – lined red.
Buffer beams	– signal red – edged black – lined white – numbers gilt, shaded red and black – drawgear and plate – black.
Buffers	– claret casing lined red – black collar – black buffer heads.
Wheels	– green – rim lined white – bosses green lined white with black axle ends – lined white tyres black.
Frame below platform	– black – rail guards claret – lined red.
Footsteps	– claret – lined red.
Tender tank	– green – edged black with red line – black band edged white – back of tender similar.
Tender coping plate	– green – black edging with red lining.
Tender curved plate beneath coping	– green – black edge – white lining.
Tender frame and angle	– claret – black edging – lined red.
Springs and axleboxes	– claret – lined red.
Tender lettering	– gilt shaded red and crimson.

probably quite accurate but other details are not. The locomotive is reasonably accurately lined but the tender curved flares should be edged black and lined red, not with white. The worst error is the lettering of 'GREAT CENTRAL'. This is too tall and the separation of the two words is too great; the effect is to destroy the balance that the GCR achieved. The numerals applied to the buffer beam appear to be incorrect, the original transfers having a bold, yet quite elegant, look to them, being embellished with shading. The restoration transfers look too small and the impression is spoiled as they are devoid of shading and, consequently, they do not give the beam any character. A black border and white line was painted along the top edge of the beam although originally the lining did not extend to that edge.

An old Gorton painter supplied painting information to the authorities at the time of 506's restoration. The notes were retained by the late Phil Hinchliffe and Bryan Longbone has kindly provided a copy. They are reproduced above.

Butler-Henderson, No. 506, is the only tangible reminder of the express passenger locomotive fleet of the former GCR. It has spent time in various places since restoration: the erstwhile Transport Museum at Clapham, at Loughborough on the present-day GCR, at the National Railway Museum at York and, much more recently, at the Barrow Hill roundhouse near Chesterfield. Whilst at Loughborough it was returned to working order and regularly worked passenger trains into the 1990s, only to be retired for what may be the last time.

Plate 27.4   GCR Class 11F, No. 503
This view shows an 11F piloting an 'Atlantic' on a Down express. The pilot is believed to be No. 503 *Somme* which appears to be in GCR livery. The 'Atlantic' is painted in the very early scheme adopted by the L&NER and this is a guide to the date of this picture. Although coupled to a GCR tender, it is generally accepted that *Somme* never carried GCR livery. The explanation is that No. 503 is coupled to the tender of 9P 4-6-0, No. 1167, which was still carrying the old livery. The location is a little north of Culworth junction and photographed from bridge No. 502.   *L.G.R.P. 4948*

CHAPTER 28
CLASS 9Q 4-6-0

This class of 4-6-0 was Robinson's final design for the company and his ninth plan for an engine with that wheel arrangement. A respectable total of twenty-eight was built by the GCR and this has encouraged some to believe that they were the best of Robinson's 4-6-0s. A 9Q was essentially a smaller, mixed traffic version of a 9P 'Lord Faringdon' type, which used the 4-cylinder layout of that design. They have been referred to as 'Black Pigs', a nickname which, apparently, was never used by the footplate men. However, that name, incorrect or otherwise, does contain some truths. They were black, enormous locomotives and because they worked many heavy trains over difficult gradients, their coal consumption was significant.

The first examples, Nos 72, 73 and 78, were all built at Gorton in the spring and summer of 1921. Vulcan Foundry contributed ten more in the autumn of that year; these carried numbers 36, 37, 38 and 458–464. Gorton continued production with another ten, Nos 465–474, built between August 1921 and the following August. Beyer, Peacock & Company built five engines during the summer of 1922 and they were numbered 31–35. The L&NER built ten locomotives at Gorton in 1923 and 1924, they were numbered 475–482 and 5483/84.

GREY LIVERY

P.F. Cooke photographed No. 72 painted grey whilst it was fitted for burning fuel on the 'Unolco' system. Another picture, reference unknown, shows the engine in grey, in a broadside right-hand view. A particularly interesting record of No. 72 was made by W.H. Whitworth, who photographed it on an Up passenger train at Guide Bridge. It may have been the same as that published in *The Locomotive News and Railway Notes*, no. 59, which was probably dated 15th July 1921. No. 72 was also the subject of the official photographer in a left-facing broadside view. The Lens of Sutton collection contains an excellent photograph of the engine coupled to a goods train. Another unknown cameraman captured a very similar picture and this was complete with footplate staff. Finally, a very good photograph was recorded of No. 72 at Neasden whilst it was grey. All seven pictures must have been taken in the period of 25th May to August 1921, when it carried the special fuel equipment. The aforementioned journal contained a letter from 'Valour' in vol. X, 10th October 1921, p. 50, in which the correspondent commented *'The 4-6-0 4 cylinder goods, no. 72, is still running in grey livery'*. Thus, between late May of 1921 and November 1923, when it received a general overhaul and presumably its new L&NER livery, it must have worked very many trains painted grey, unless it was called into Gorton and repainted GCR black soon after 'Valour' had made his observation.

The next engine was No. 73 and a right-hand broadside illustration of it painted grey is in *Great Central Steam*, plate 31. This is also on page 137 of *Locomotives of the G.C.R.*, vol. 2, by E. Johnson. Several photographs of No. 78 are known. *Locomotives Illustrated*, no. 49, has a good rear view of the engine which appears to be coupled

Plate 28.1 GCR Class 9Q, No. 72
Unfortunately the quality of this photograph is not of the best but it shows a locomotive working a train whilst painted grey. No. 72 has just left platform 3 at Guide Bridge with an Up express. The tender has a tank carrying oil fuel and this dates the picture to the summer of 1921. The photographer may have been W.H. Whitworth.
J. Quick collection

ABOVE: Plate 28.2   GCR Class 9Q, No. 472
No. 472 is standing on Gorton shed, at some time between late 1923 and May 1924. This photograph was taken on orthochromatic film, hence the red portion of the lining has not recorded. It shows the lower boiler mountings that were fitted experimentally in late 1923 to enable the class to conform to the L&NER loading gauge. A further ten engines were built at Gorton by the L&NER and these were fitted, from new, with shorter chimneys, lower domes, modified cabs and altered safety valves and whistle position.
                                                                                                R.K. Blencowe

to an old Sacré tender. An unknown enthusiast also recorded it from the opposite side. The Real collection contains a good left broadside picture, ref. 65212, taken at Neasden; the subject is finished in a middle shade of grey which is relieved only by the maker's and number plates. The H.M.R.S. has further examples: No. 464 was photographed at the Vulcan Foundry works, the reference numbers being AJ703 and AJ710, and there may be other prints in that collection. The Locomotive Publishing Co. has an excellent print, ref. 2193, of No. 464 and this appeared on page 21 of C. Langley Aldrich's *The Locomotives of the G.C.R. 1900–1923*. In a report in the journal *The Locomotive News and Railway Contractor*, vol. XII, 10th May 1922, several 9Qs were noted on Cup Final specials in the London area. Amongst them was No. 468 which was painted *'in shop colour'*. Page 104 of the 25th June 1922 issue of the same journal commented *'No. 468 which worked in grey livery, now painted in standard black livery.'*

BLACK LIVERY

Although some papers which give many technical details of their construction do exist, they do not include painting instructions. This situation is both frustrating and surprising as, presumably, specifications were issued to both the Vulcan Foundry and Beyer,

Peacock & Company. The surviving document may be part of what was sent to the latter works; it consists mainly of lists of drawing numbers and is dated 21st July 1921, but there are a few points of interest. One requirement, which appears to have been added to the first page on 30th November 1921, is that *'Engine and Tender to be Photographed according to instructions'*. Another, dated 11th July 1922, was: *'Each Engine and Tender will be required to run 2000 miles consecutively without showing any defects in material or workmanship'* – most of this is emphasised by being underscored. The solitary reference to painting is contained within the standard procedure regarding the boiler: *'The Boiler to receive one coat of Oxide of Iron whilst hot, and another when cooled down'*.

In the absence of any official specification, photographs are, therefore, the main source of information. One in particular was taken of No. 472 when W.H. Whitworth was at Gorton shed, sometime just before or, possibly, immediately after grouping, and weather conditions were perfect. His camera was loaded with panchromatic film and with perfectly exposed, focussed and processed material, his photograph shows the red bands on the outside of narrower white lines with great clarity. Close study reveals the red/white/black/white/red lining on the boiler, also that on the cylinders and other parts; the reference for this view is Real Photographs W3915. To emphasise the highly significant differences when using

BELOW: Plate 28.3   GCR Class 9Q, No. 472
This is another view of the same engine, taken on the same occasion and from nearly the same position. The photographer has, however, used panchromatic film and the red bands are visible as a middle shade of grey. Looked at closely, the red lines on the cab and tender sides are revealed as being significantly wider than the adjacent white lines and, also, that a continuous red line has been painted around the cab windows. Single red lines are also discernible on the tender upper coal plate, tender mainframes, springs and dampers. Observe also the collar on the near buffer body which has double red/white lines. This is an extremely helpful photograph of a brand-new locomotive.   *Real Photographs W3915*

panchromatic and orthochromatic emulsions on subjects with red areas, the engine was also photographed on the same occasion, from more or less the same position, but using the second grade of film. This picture is part of the R.K. Blencowe collection, but it does not show any portion of the red lining. It is probably true to say that W.H. Whitworth's photograph, Real W3915, has revealed more information regarding the black livery than any other.

Engine and tender were painted black, relieved only by the vermilion buffer beams, the brightly polished parts, the various transfers and the red and white lining. The boiler, firebox and the base of the dome carried the red/white/black/white/red bands. The cab sides received two styles of lining. Around the two side windows was a continuous red line, and the lower part of the cab had two white lines, the outer with a wider red band on its outside edge, which made a continuous panel of lining. The splasher sides, spectacle plate, valances, cylinder sides, step plates and the heavy framing supporting the slide bars all carried the same single red/white stripes, the red part of which was a little wider than the white. The square bases of the buffer guides also had this decoration but the opening of the guide had a narrower variety of the boiler and firebox lining. The buffer beams had a black border, then a white line alongside. The majority of photographs indicate that this was only applied along the sides and bottom of the beam and not along the edge underneath the running plate. At least one exception to this was No. 32, but the practice of lining all around the beam was, by now, unusual on GCR engines. The cab interior may have been stone colour, in which case it would have had a black border with a red line. The wheels appear to have been lined only around the axle ends, light in tone and either white, or more likely red/white, the red on the outside. It is not possible to be absolutely certain on this point because most photographs do not show lining of any sort.

Engine mainframes were vermilion on the insides but were black on the outside, probably unlined. The guard irons or bars appear to have been polished steel.

The lining on the tender matched that on the engine. The sides and end had two white lines with a wider red band painted alongside the outside of the outer white line. The valances, step plates and flares received a single red/white stripe, but the mainframes and upper coal plate only had a red line applied. On the mainframes the red line was applied to the springs, dampers, axle boxes and cut-outs. The buffer guides were decorated on the square bases with a red/white line and the openings were probably similarly finished as those on the locomotive.

The final touches were the polished parts and these included all buffer heads, all handrails, coupling and connecting rods, reversing rod and support, smoke-box fittings, safety valves, whistle, beadings, cylinder front and end and all raised surfaces on maker's and number plates.

The standard size of company name transfers were always used and the smaller characters on the buffer beam also. Another standard feature was the coat-of-arms which was only carried on the tender side. The white line which encircled the numerals on the number plate appears to have been applied throughout. However, the monogram was never employed and no picture showing distinctive symbols has been discovered.

For a short period the 9Qs were the premier mixed traffic locomotives on the GCR and were maintained to an extremely high standard. They became Class B7 on the L&NER and were used on all types of fast traffic. They outlived that company but, with the introduction of many brand-new locomotives, they were withdrawn from service by British Railways between the spring of 1948 and the summer of 1950.

Plate 28.4   GCR Class 9Q, No. 38
The 6-wheeled carriages behind No. 38 indicate that this may be a test train. This picture was taken at Guide Bridge on 20th May 1922. The locomotive has spent a little more than six months in traffic at this time.

Real Photographs W4894

BIBLIOGRAPHY

UNPUBLISHED, PHOTOGRAPH AND MISCELLANEOUS COLLECTIONS

Biltcliffe collection
R.K. Blencowe collection
R. Carpenter collection
The Gordon Coltas photographic trust
Great Central Railway Society collection
Historical Model Railway Society collection
W.H.C. Kelland collection
Lens of Sutton collection
Locomotive and General Railway Photographs collection
LCGB Ken Nunn collection
Locomotive Publishing Company collection
Mitchell Library collection
F. Moore series
E. Pouteau collection
Real Photographs collection
Valentine's series

Great Central Railway – locomotive record cards
Great Central Railway Society archives
Museum of Science and Industry (Manchester). Great Central Railway – locomotive building specifications
National Railway Museum, York
Private correspondence to the author from P.H.V. Banyard and E.B. Woodruffe-Peacock
University of Glasgow. Great Central Railway – locomotive building specifications

JOURNALS / SERIALS

The Engineer
Great Central Link
The Great Central Railway Journal
The Journal of the Great Central Railway Society – Forward
The Locomotive Magazine
The Locomotive News and Railway Contractor
The Locomotive News and Railway Notes
Locomotives and Railways
Locomotives Illustrated
Model Engineer
Model Railway News
Moore's Monthly Magazine
The Railway and Travel Monthly
Railway Archive
The Railway Magazine
Railway Modeller
Railway Notes

All of the above journals are held in the library of the National Railway Museum, York.

BOOKS / MONOGRAPHS

Carter, E.F., *Britain's Railway Liveries: Colours, Crests and Linings*. 2nd edn. Harold Starke. 1963
Clay, J.F. and Cliffe, J., *The L.N.E.R. 4-6-0 Classes*. Ian Allan. 1975
Dow, G., *Great Central Volume 2: Dominion of Watkin 1864–1899*. Locomotive Publishing Co. 1962
Dow, G., *Great Central Volume 3: Fay Sets the Pace 1900–1922*. Locomotive Publishing Co. 1965
Dow, G., *Great Central Album: A Pictorial Supplement to Great Central*. Ian Allan. 1969
Dow, G., *Great Central Recalled*. Bradford Barton. 1978
Evans, M., *Atlantic Era: The British Atlantic Locomotive*. Percival Marshall. 1961
Great Central Railway, *Per Rail: Transportation is the Lifeblood of Commerce*. Knapp Drewitt and Sons. 1913
Haresnape, B. and Rowledge, P., *Robinson Locomotives: A Pictorial History*. Ian Allan. 1982
Heaton, N., *Outlines of Paint Technology*, 3rd edn. Charles Griffin. 1947
Hurst, G.H., *Dictionary of Chemicals and Raw Products Used in the Manufacture of Paints, Colours, Varnishes and Allied Preparations*. Scott Greenwood. 1901
Hurst, J. and Kinder M., *William Bradshaw: Leicester Railway Cameraman 1909–1923*. Historical Model Railway Society. 2002
Jackson, D., *J.G. Robinson: A Lifetime's Work*. Oakwood Press. 1996
Johnson, E.M., *Railways In and Around the Manchester Suburbs. Scenes from the Past No 8*. Foxline. 1989
Johnson, E.M., *Locomotives of the Great Central Railway. Volume 1: 1897–1914*. Irwell Press. 1989
Johnson, E.M., *Locomotives of the Great Central Railway. Volume 2: 1912 to British Railways*. Irwell Press. 1992
Johnson, E.M., *Woodhead: Manchester London Road, Gorton, Guide Bridge, Glossop and the Longdendale Valley. Scenes from the Past No 29 part 1*. Foxline. 1996
Langley, Aldrich C., *The Robinson Locomotives of the Great Central Railway 1900–1923: A Brief Descriptive Illustrated Souvenir of Types*. E.V. Aldrich. 1946
Lyons, A.W., *Grammar of Lettering: A Handbook of Alphabets. Systematically Arranged for the Use of Art Students, Architects, Decorators, Signwriters and all Classes of Craftsmen*. Maclaren and Co. 1908
Mummery, B. and Butler I., *Immingham and the Great Central Legacy*. Tempus. 1999
Reed, B., *ROD 2-8-0s. Loco profile No 21*. Profile Publications. 1972
Sabin, A.H., *The Industrial and Artistic Technology of Paint and Varnish*, 3rd edn. John Wiley; Chapman and Hall. 1927
Tuplin, W.A., *Great Central Steam*. Allen and Unwin. 1967
Yeadon, W.B., *Yeadon's Register of L.N.E.R. Locomotives: Vol. 22 – Class B1 (B18), B2 (B19) and B3 to B9: the Great Central 4-6-0s*. Booklaw / Railbus. 2001

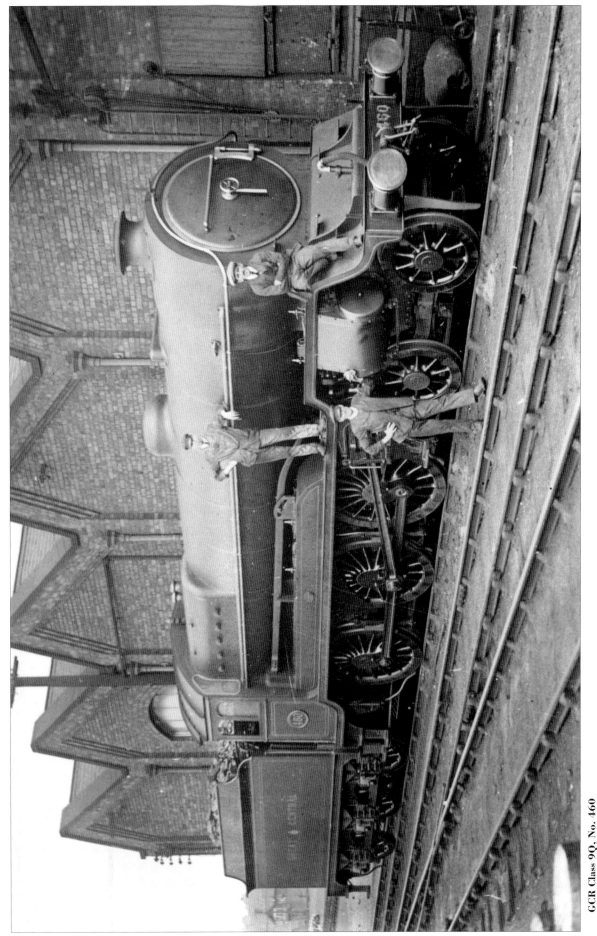

GCR Class 9Q, No. 460
No. 460 is at Leicester shed on 13th August 1922. Fireman Percy Banyard is standing on the locomotive, which was a Vulcan Foundry product of October 1921. Leicester South Goods signal cabin is just visible behind the tender and the cameraman was Henry Salmon.

L.G.R.P. 16256